AF661397

CULTURAL SOCIOLOGY

CULTURAL SOCIOLOGY

Dr. Bindeshwari Pd. Mandal

CENTRUM PRESS
NEW DELHI-110002 (INDIA)

CENTRUM PRESS
H.O.: 4360/4, Ansari Road, Daryaganj,
New Delhi-110002 (India)
Tel: 23278000, 23261597, 23255577, 23286875
B.O.: No. 1015, Ist Main Road, BSK IIIrd Stage,
IIIrd Phase, IIIrd Block, Bangalore-560085 (INDIA)
Tel: 080-41723429
Email: centrumpress@gmail.com
Visit us at: www.centrumpress.com

Cultural Sociology

© Reserved

First Edition, 2011

ISBN 978-93-80921-54-9

PRINTED IN INDIA

Printed at Tarun Offset Printers, Delhi-110053

Contents

Preface

Cultural Sociology is branch of Sociology. It deals with the study of culture both in the broad sense (lifestyles, mentalities, value orientations) and in the more specific sense of referring to cultural fields like the arts, popular music, and organized religion. Culture is approached sociologically as rooted in, emerging from and impacting on social (economic, political) relations and group processes. Moreover, culture is conceived in dynamic terms, and viewed in the context of social changes. The sociology of culture concerns culture—usually understood as sets of cognitive meanings—as it is manifested in society. For Georg Simmel, culture referred to "the cultivation of individuals through the agency of external forms which have been objectified in the course of history". Cultural sociology first emerged in Weimar Germany, where sociologists such as Alfred Weber used the term Kultursoziologie (cultural sociology). Cultural sociology was then "reinvented" in the English speaking world as a product of the "cultural turn" of the 1960s, which ushered in structuralist and so-called "postmodern" approaches to social science. This type of cultural sociology may loosely be regarded as an approach incorporating cultural analysis and critical theory. Cultural sociologists tend to reject scientific methods, instead hermeneutically focusing on words, artifacts and symbols.

"Culture" has since become an important concept across many branches of sociology, including resolutely scientific fields like social stratification and social network analysis. As a result, there has been a recent influx of quantitative sociologists to the field. Thus there is now a growing group of sociologists of culture who are, confusingly, not cultural sociologists. These scholars reject the abstracted postmodern aspects of cultural sociology, and instead look for a theoretical backing in the more scientific vein of social psychology and cognitive science. "Cultural sociology" is one of the largest sections of the American Sociological Association. The British establishment of cultural studies means the latter is often taught as a loosely-distinct discipline in the UK. The sociology of culture grew from the intersection between sociology, as shaped by early theorists like Marx, Durkheim, and Weber, and with the growing discipline of anthropology where researchers pioneered ethnographic strategies for describing and analysing a variety of cultures around the world. Part of the legacy of the early development of the field is still felt in the methods (much of cultural sociological research is qualitative) in the theories (a variety of critical approaches to sociology are central to current research communities) and substantive focus of the field. For instance, relationships between popular culture, political control, and social class were early and lasting concerns in the field. The belief that culture is symbolically coded and can thus be taught from one person to another means that cultures, although bounded, can change. Cultures are both predisposed to change and resistant to it. Resistance can come from habit, religion, and the integration and interdependence of cultural traits. For example, men and women have complementary roles in many cultures. One sex might desire changes that affect the other, as happened in the second half of the 20th century in western cultures (see women's movement), while the other sex may be resistant to that change (possibly in order to maintain a power imbalance in their favour). Cultural change can have many causes, including: the environment, inventions, and contact with other cultures. For example, the end of the last ice age helped lead to the invention of agriculture. Some inventions that affected Western culture in the 20th century were the birth control pill, television, and the Internet.

Several understandings of how cultures change come from anthropology. For instance, in diffusion theory, the form of something moves from one culture to another, but not its meaning. For example, the ankh symbol originated in Egyptian culture but has diffused to numerous cultures. Its original meaning may have been lost, but it is now used by many practitioners of New Age Religion as an arcane symbol of power or life forces. A variant of the diffusion theory, stimulus diffusion, refers to an element of one culture leading to an invention in another. Contact between cultures can also result in acculturation. Acculturation has different meanings, but in this context refers to replacement of the traits of one culture with those of another, such as what happened with many Native American Indians. Related processes on an individual level are assimilation and transculturation, both of which refer to adoption of a different culture by an individual.

It is hoped that his book will not only meet the requirements of students but will also be useful as a guide to the academic professionals.

1

Introduction

Culture consists of the beliefs, behaviours, objects, and other characteristics common to the members of a particular group or society. Through culture, people and groups define themselves, conform to society's shared values, and contribute to society. Thus, culture includes many societal aspects: language, customs, values, norms, mores, rules, tools, technologies, products, organizations, and institutions. This latter term institution refers to clusters of rules and cultural meanings associated with specific social activities. Common institutions are the family, education, religion, work, and health care.

Popularly speaking, being cultured means being well-educated, knowledgeable of the arts, stylish, and well-mannered. High culture—generally pursued by the upper class—refers to classical music, theatre, fine arts, and other sophisticated pursuits. Members of the upper class can pursue high art because they have cultural capital, which means the professional credentials, education, knowledge, and verbal and social skills necessary to attain the "property, power, and prestige" to "get ahead" socially. Low culture, or popular culture—generally pursued by the working and middle classes—refers to sports, movies, television sitcoms and soaps, and rock music. Remember that sociologists define *culture* differently than they do *cultured, high culture, low culture*, and *popular culture*.

Sociologists define society as the people who interact in such a way as to share a common culture. The cultural bond may be ethnic or racial, based on gender, or due to shared beliefs, values, and activities. The term *society* can also have a *geographic* meaning and refer to people who share a common culture in a particular location. For example, people living in arctic climates developed different cultures from those living in desert cultures. In time, a large variety of human cultures arose around the world.

Culture and society are intricately related. A culture consists of the "objects" of a society, whereas a society consists of the people who share a common culture. When the terms *culture* and *society* first acquired their current meanings, most people in the world worked and lived in small groups in the same locale. In today's world of 6 billion people, these terms have lost some of their usefulness because increasing numbers of people interact and share resources globally. Still, people tend to use *culture* and *society* in a more traditional sense: for example, being a part of a "racial culture" within the larger "U.S. society."

Culture and Cultural Sociology

The sociology of culture concerns culture—usually understood as sets of cognitive meanings—as it is manifested in society. For Georg Simmel, culture referred to "the cultivation of individuals through the agency of external forms which have been objectified in the course of history". Whilst early theorists such as Emile Durkheim and Marcel Mauss were influential in cultural anthropology, sociologists of culture are generally distinguished by a concern for modern (rather than ancient or primitive) societies. Cultural sociology may loosely be regarded as an approach incorporating cultural analysis and critical theory. Cultural sociologists tend to reject scientific methods, instead hermeneutically focusing on words, artifacts and symbols. Non-positivist methodology is dominant in the field.

Cultural sociology is a product of the "cultural turn" of the 1960s, which ushered in structuralist and so-called "postmodern" approaches to social science. "Culture" has since become an important concept across many branches of sociology, including resolutely quantitative fields like social stratification and social network analysis. As a result, there has been a recent influx of quantitative sociologists to the field. Thus there is now a growing group of sociologists of culture who are, confusingly, not cultural sociologists. These scholars reject the abstracted postmodern aspects of cultural sociology, and instead look for a theoretical backing in the more scientific vein of social psychology and cognitive science.

Development of Sociology in Culture

Early Researchers and Development of Cultural Sociology

The sociology of culture grew from the intersection between sociology, as shaped by early theorists like Marx, Durkheim, and Weber, and with the growing discipline of anthropology where researchers pioneered ethnographic strategies for describing and analyzing a variety of cultures around the world. Part of the legacy of the early development of the field is still felt in the methods (much of cultural sociological research is qualitative) in the theories (a variety of critical approaches to sociology are central to current research communities) and substantive focus of the field. For instance, relationships between popular culture, political control, and social class were early and lasting concerns in the field.

Karl Marx

As a major contributor to the Conflict Theory, Marx's ideas also dealt with culture. Marx's belief of culture is that the most powerful members of a society are those who live in the ruling class. These members set up the culture of a society in order to provide the best interests to that society. He has also talked about how a society's economic status determines their values and ideologies.

Emile Durkheim

Durkheim had the belief that culture has many relationships to society which include:

- *Logical*-Power over individuals belong to certain cultural categories, and beliefs such as God.
- *Functional*-Certain rites and myths create build social order up more by having people create strong beliefs, the more people who believe in these myths will strengthen social order.

- *Historical*-Culture had its origins in society, and from those experiences came evolution into things such as classification systems.

Max Weber

Weber innovated the idea of a status group as a certain type of subculture. Status groups are based on things such as: race, ethnicity, religion, region, occupation, gender, sexual preference, etc. These groups live a certain lifestyle based on different values and norms. They are a culture within a culture, hence the label subculture. Weber also had the idea that people were motivated by their material and ideal interests, which include things such as preventing one from going to hell. Weber also explains that people use symbols to express their spirituality, and that symbols are used to express the spiritual side of real events, and that ideal interests are derived from symbols.

Georg Simmel

For Simmel, culture refers to 'the cultivation of individuals through the agency of external forms which have been objectified in the course of history'. Simmel presented his analyses within a context of 'form' and 'content'.

Anthropology

Anthropologists lay claim to the establishment of modern uses of the culture concept as defined by Edward Burnett Tylor in the mid-19th century. Some of the 20th century scholars include Malinowski, Radcliffe-Brown, and Mauss.

Bronishaw Malinowski

Malinowski collected data from the Trobriand Islands. Descent groups across the island claim parts of the land, and to back up those claims, they tell myths of how an ancestress started a clan and how the clan descends from that ancestress. Malinowski's observations followed the research of that found by Durkheim.

Alfred Reginald Radcliffe-Brown

Radcliffe-Brown put himself in the culture of the Andaman Islanders. His research showed that group solidification among the islanders is based on music and kinship, and the rituals that involve the use of those activities. In the words of Radcliffe-Brown, "Ritual fortifies Society". Radcliffe-Brown's observations also followed the research of that found by Durkheim.

Marcel Mauss

Marcel Mauss made many comparative studies on religion, magic, law and morality of occidental and non-occidental societies, and developed the concept of total social fact, and argued that the reciprocity is the universal logic of the cultural interaction.

Claude Lévi-Strauss

Lévi-Strauss, based, at the same time, on the sociological and anthropological positivism of Durkheim, Mauss, Malinowski and Radcliffe-Brown, on the economic and sociological marxism, on freudian and Gestalt psychology and on structural linguistics of Saussure and Jakobson, realized great studies on areas myth, kinship, religion, ritual, symbolism, magic, ideology (souvage pensée), knowledge, art and aesthetics, applying the methodological structuralism on his investigations. He searched the universal principals of human thought as a form of explaining social behaviours and structures.

Additional Anthropology

- In an anthropological sense, culture is society based on the values and ideas without influence of the material world (Radcliffe-Brown). "The cultural system is the cognitive and symbolic matrix for the central values system" (Parsons).
- Culture is like the shell of a lobster. Human nature is the organism living inside of that shell. The shell, culture, identifies the organism, or human nature. Culture is what sets human nature apart, and helps direct the life of human nature.

Major Areas of Research in Sociology of Culture

In order to understand the potential applicability of Bourdieu's theories to the study of computer-mediated communication and its virtual environments, it is necessary to first understand the constructs underlying the theories. Bourdieu's model of society and social relations has its roots in Marxist theories of class and conflict. Bourdieu characterizes social relations in the context of what he calls the field, defined as a competitive system of social relations functioning according to its own specific logic or rules. The field is the site of struggle for power between the dominant and subordinate classes. It is within the field that legitimacy—a key aspect defining the dominant class—is conferred or withdrawn.

Bourdieu's theory of practice is practical rather than discusive, embodied as well as cognitive and durable though adaptive. A valid concern that sets the agenda in Bourdieu's theory of practice is how action follows regular statistical patterns without the product of accordance to rules, norms and/ or conscious intention. To explain this concern, Bourdieu explains habitus and field. Habitus explains the mutually penetrating realities of individual subjectivity and societal objectivity after the function of social construction. It is employed to transcend the subjective and objective dichotomy.

Cultural Change

The belief that culture is symbolically coded and can thus be taught from one person to another means that cultures, although bounded, can change. Cultures are both predisposed to change and resistant to it. Resistance can come from habit, religion, and the integration and interdependence of cultural traits. For example, men and women have complementary roles in many cultures. One sex might desire changes that affect the other, as happened in the second half of the 20th century in western cultures, while the other sex may be resistant to that change (possibly in order to maintain a power imbalance in their favor).

Cultural change can have many causes, including: the environment, inventions, and contact with other cultures. For example, the end of the last ice age helped lead to the invention of agriculture. Some inventions that affected Western culture in the 20th century were the birth control pill, television, and the Internet.

Several understandings of how cultures change come from anthropology. For instance, in diffusion theory, the form of something moves from one culture to another, but not its meaning. For example, the ankh symbol originated in Egyptian culture but has diffused to numerous cultures. Its original meaning may have been lost, but it is now used by many practitioners of New Age Religion as an arcane symbol of power or life forces. A variant of the diffusion theory, stimulus diffusion, refers to an element of one culture leading to an invention in another.

Contact between cultures can also result in acculturation. Acculturation has different meanings, but in this context refers to replacement of the traits of one culture with those of another, such as what happened with many Native American Indians. Related processes on an individual level are assimilation and transculturation, both of which refer to adoption of a different culture by an individual.

Griswold outlined another sociological approach to cultural change. Griswold points out that it may seem as though culture comes from individuals – which, for certain elements of cultural change, is true – but there is also the larger, collective, and long-lasting culture that cannot have been the creation of single individuals as it predates and post-dates individual humans and contributors to culture. The author presents a sociological perspective to address this conflict,

Sociology suggests an alternative to both the unsatisfying it has always been that way view at one extreme and the unsociological individual genius view at the other. This alternative posits that culture and cultural works are collective, not individual, creations. We can best understand specific cultural objects... by seeing them not as unique to their creators but as the fruits of collective production, fundamentally social in their genesis. In short, Griswold argues that culture changes through the contextually dependent and socially situated actions of individuals; macro-level culture influences the individual who, in turn, can influence that same culture. The logic is a bit circular, but illustrates how culture can change over time yet remain somewhat constant.

It is, of course, important to recognize here that Griswold is talking about cultural change and not the actual origins of culture (as in, "there was no culture and then, suddenly, there was"). Because Griswold does not explicitly distinguish between the origins of cultural change and the origins of culture, it may appear as though Griswold is arguing here for the origins of culture and situating these origins in society. This is neither accurate nor a clear representation of sociological thought on this issue. Culture, just like society, has existed since the beginning of humanity (humans being social and cultural). Society and culture co-exist because humans have social relations and meanings tied to those relations (e.g. brother, lover, friend). Culture as a super-phenomenon has no real beginning except in the sense that humans (homo sapiens) have a beginning. This, then, makes the question of the origins of culture moot – it has existed as long as we have, and will likely exist as long as we do. Cultural change, on the other hand, is a matter that can be questioned and researched, as Griswold does.

Current Research

Computer-mediated Communication as Culture

Computer-mediated communication is the process of sending messages—primarily, but not limited to text messages—through the direct use by participants of computers and communication networks. By restricting the definition to the direct use of computers in the communication process, you have to get rid of the communication technologies that rely upon computers for switching technology (such as telephony or compressed video), but do not require the users to interact directly with the computer system via a keyboard or similar computer interface. To be mediated by computers in the sense of this project, the communication must be done by participants fully aware of their interaction with the computer technology in the process of creating and delivering messages. Given the current state of computer communications and networks, this limits CMC to primarily text-based messaging, while leaving the possibility of incorporating sound, graphics, and video images as the technology becomes more sophisticated.

Cultural Institutions Studies

Cultural activities are institutionalised; the focus on institutional settings leads to the investigation "of activities in the cultural sector, conceived as historically evolved societal forms of organising the conception, production, distribution, propagation, interpretation, reception, conservation and maintenance of specific cultural goods". Cultural Institutions Studies is therefore a specific approach within the sociology of culture.

Cultural Diversity

Cultural diversity is the variety of human societies or cultures in a specific region, or in the world as a whole. (The term is also sometimes used to refer to multiculturalism within an organization. This article does not currently cover that alternative meaning.) There is a general consensus among mainstream anthropologists that humans first emerged in Africa about two million years ago. Since then they have spread throughout the world, successfully adapting to widely differing conditions and to periodic cataclysmic changes in local and global climate. The many separate societies that emerged around the globe differed markedly from each other, and many of these differences persist to this day.

As well as the more obvious cultural differences that exist between people, such as language, dress and traditions, there are also significant variations in the way societies organize themselves, in their shared conception of morality, and in the ways they interact with their environment.

By analogy with biodiversity, which is thought to be essential to the long-term survival of life on earth, it can be argued that cultural diversity may be vital for the long-term survival of humanity; and that the conservation of indigenous cultures may be as important to humankind as the conservation of species and ecosystems is to life in general. The General Conference of UNESCO took this position in 2001, asserting in Article 1 of the Universal Declaration on Cultural Diversity that *"...cultural diversity is as necessary for humankind as biodiversity is for nature"*

This position is rejected by some people, however, on several grounds. Firstly, like most evolutionary accounts of human nature, the importance of cultural diversity for survival may be an un-testable hypothesis, which can neither be proved nor disproved. Secondly, it can be argued that it is unethical deliberately to conserve "less developed" societies, because this will deny people within those societies the benefits of technological and medical advances enjoyed by those of us in the "developed" world.

In the same way it is unethical to promote poverty in underdeveloped nations as cultural diversity it is also unethical to promote all religious practices simply because they contribute to cultural diversity. Particularly, there are some practices that are recognized by the WHO and UN as unethical: Female Genital Mutilation, Sati (burning the widow on the husbands burial pyre), polygamy, child brides, human sacrifice, etc.

Some individuals, particularly those with strong religious beliefs, maintain that it is in the best interests of individuals and of humanity as a whole that all people adhere to a specific model for society or specific aspects of such a model. For example, evangelical missionary organisations such as the New Tribes Mission actively work to support social changes that some observers would consider detrimental to cultural diversity by seeking out remote tribal societies to convert them to Christianity; and Islamic groups strategically buy up land in Papua New Guinea.

Cultural diversity is tricky to quantify, but a good indication is thought to be a count of the number of languages spoken in a region or in the world as a whole. By this measure, there are signs that we may be going through a period of precipitous decline in the world's cultural diversity. Research carried out in the 1990s by David Crystal (Honorary Professor of Linguistics at the University of Wales, Bangor) suggested that at that time, on average, one language was falling into disuse every two weeks. He calculated that if that rate of language death were to continue, then by the year 2100 more than 90% of the languages currently spoken in the world will have gone extinct.

Overpopulation, immigration and imperialism (of both the militaristic and cultural kind) are reasons that have been suggested to explain any such decline.

Cultural Heritage

The Universal Declaration of UNESCO on Cultural Diversity of 2001 is regarded as a legal instrument recognizing for the first time, cultural diversity as "common heritage of humanity" and considers its safeguarding to be a concrete and ethical imperative inseparable from respect for human dignity.

There is also the Convention for the Safeguarding of the Intangible Cultural Heritage ratified in June 20, 2007 by 78 States which said:

> *"The intangible cultural heritage, transmitted from generation to generation is constantly recreated by communities and groups in response to their environment, their interaction with nature and their history, and gives them a sense of identity and continuity, thus promoting respect for cultural diversity and human creativity."*

Cultural diversity was also promoted by the Montreal Declaration of 2007, and by the European Union. The idea of a global multi-cultural heritage covers several ideas, which are not exclusive.

Defence

The defence of cultural diversity can take several meanings:

- A balance to be achieved: thus, the idea of defence of cultural diversity through the promotion of actions in favor of "cultural minorities" said to be disadvantaged;
- Preservation of "cultural minorities" thought to be endangered;
- In other cases, one speaks of "cultural protection", which refers to the concept of "cultural exception", which is mainly used in France under the title "French exception". This makes the link between the social vision of culture and the vision inherent in its commercialisation. The cultural exception highlights the specificity of cultural products and services, including special recognition by the European Union in its Declaration on Cultural Diversity. In this context, the objective is to defend against what is seen as a "commodification"-considered harmful to a "disadvantaged" culture — supporting its development through grants, promotion operations, etc., also known as "cultural protectionism".

- This defence may also refer to incorporating "cultural rights" provisions, conducted unsuccessfully in the early 1990s in Europe, into a layer of human rights.

Cultural Uniformity

Cultural diversity is presented as the antithesis of cultural uniformity.

Some (including UNESCO) fear this hypothesis of a trend towards cultural uniformity. To support this argument they emphasize different aspects:

- The disappearance of many languages and dialects, regarding for example the languages of France, without legal status or protection (Basque, Breton, Corsican, Occitan, Catalan, Alsatian, Flemish, Poitou, Saintonge, etc.).
- Anxiety of people on the preservation of their traditions as in New Zealand, coastal regions in Australia, North America, Central America;
- Increasing cultural preeminence of the United States through the distribution of its products in film, television, music, clothing and nutritional products promoted in audio-visual media, consumer products virtually standardized on the planet (pizza, restaurants, fast food, etc..).

There are several international organizations that work towards protecting threatened societies and cultures, including Survival International and UNESCO. The UNESCO Universal Declaration on Cultural Diversity, adopted by 185 Member States in 2001, represents the first international standard-setting instrument aimed at preserving and promoting cultural diversity and intercultural dialogue. The European Commission-funded *Network of Excellence on "Sustainable Development in a Diverse World"* (known as "SUS.DIV") builds upon the UNESCO Declaration to investigate the relationship between cultural diversity and sustainable development.

Solidarity

Solidarity is the integration, and degree and type of integration, shown by a society or group with people and their neighbours. It refers to the ties in a society-social relations-that bind people to one another. The term is generally employed in sociology and the other social sciences.

What forms the basis of solidarity varies between societies. In simple societies it may be mainly based around kinship and shared values. In more complex societies there are various theories as to what contributes to a sense of social solidarity.

Ibn Khaldun

'Asabiyyah refers to social solidarity with an emphasis on unity, group consciousness, and social cohesion, originally in a context of "tribalism" and "clanism", but sometimes used for modern nationalism as well. Ibn Khaldun's *Muqaddimah* described it as the fundamental bond of human society and the basic motive force of history. 'Asabiyyah is neither necessarily nomadic nor based on blood relations. In the modern period, the term is generally analogous to solidarity.

Ibn Khaldun argues, effectively, that each dynasty has within itself the seeds of its own downfall. He explains that ruling houses tend to emerge on the peripheries of great empires and use the unity presented by those areas to their advantage in order to bring about a change in leadership. As the new rulers establish themselves at the centre of their empire, they become increasingly lax and more concerned with maintaining their lifestyles. Thus, a new dynasty can emerge at the periphery of their control and effect a change in leadership, beginning the cycle anew.

It can be compared to Emile Durkheim's mechanical solidarity as opposed to the organic solidarity which he suggests can be found in modern societies.

Durkheim

According to Emile Durkheim, the types of social solidarity correlate with types of society. Durkheim introduced the terms "mechanical" and "organic solidarity" as part of his theory of the development of societies in *The Division of Labour in Society* (1893). In a society exhibiting mechanical solidarity, its cohesion and integration comes from the homogeneity cf individuals—people feel connected through similar work, educational and religious training, and lifestyle. Mechanical solidarity normally operates in "traditional" and small scale societies. In simpler societies (e.g., tribal), solidarity is usually based on kinship ties of familial networks. Organic solidarity comes from the interdependence that arises from specialization of work and the complementarities between people—a development which occurs in "modern" and "industrial" societies. Definition: it is social cohesion based upon the dependence individuals have on each other in more advanced societies. Although individuals perform different tasks and often have different values and interest, the order and very solidarity of society depends on their reliance on each other to perform their specified tasks. Organic here is referring to the interdependence of the component parts. Thus, social solidarity is maintained in more complex societies through the interdependence of its component parts (e.g., farmers produce the food to feed the factory workers who produce the tractors that allow the farmer to produce the food).

The two types of solidarity can be distinguished by morphological and demographic features, type of norms in existence, and the intensity and content of the *conscience collective*.

"...if I have properly understood gesellschaft is supposed to be characterised by a progressive development of individualism, the dispersive effects of which can only be prevented for a time, and by artificial means by the action of the state, it is essentially a mechanical aggregate."

- Durkheim believed that Ferdinand Tonnies saw individualism as working against moral order, people become unattached like atoms flowing in space suggesting that the only thing holding people together, prevented relationships from fracturing, and holds people to society was the imposition of order and coherence of the state.
- Durkheim asserted that the life of social agglomerates is just as natural, and is no less internal as that of small groupings.
- He characterised preindustrial societies as mechanical and industrial societies as organic (thus opposing Toennies theories by using opposite terminology)

- Although the bonds of mechanical solidarity were based on "a more or less organized totality of beliefs and sentiments common to all the members of the group," this gave way in industrial society to potent new forces that were characterised by heightened complexity and differentiation, an increased dependence on society, and, seemingly paradoxically at first glance, a growing level of individual autonomy.

Quotes

International solidarity is "not an act of charity but an act of unity between allies fighting on different terrains toward the same objectives."-Samora Machel

> *"Unlike solidarity, which is horizontal and takes place between equals, charity is top-down, humiliating those who receive it and never challenging the implicit power relations."-Eduardo Galeano*

> *"Solidarity is not a matter of altruism. Solidarity comes from the inability to tolerate the affront to our own integrity of passive or active collaboration in the oppression of others, and from the deep recognition of our most expansive self-interest. From the recognition that, like it or not, our liberation is bound up with that of every other being on the planet, and that politically, spiritually, in our heart of hearts we know anything else is unaffordable."-Aurora Levins Morales*

> *"No man is an island, entire of itself; every man is a piece of the continent, a part of the main. If a clod be washed away by the sea, Europe is the less, as well as if a promontory were, as well as if a manor of thy friend's or of thine own were: any man's death diminishes me, because I am involved in mankind, and therefore never send to know for whom the bells tolls; it tolls for thee. Neither can we call this a begging of misery, or a borrowing of misery, as though we were not miserable enough of ourselves, but must fetch in more from the next house, in taking upon us the misery of our neighbours. Truly it were an excusable covetousness if we did, for affliction is a treasure, and scarce any man*

hath enough of it. No man hath affliction enough that is not matured and ripened by and made fit for God by that affliction. If a man carry treasure in bullion, or in a wedge of gold, and have none coined into current money, his treasure will not defray him as he travels. Tribulation is treasure in the nature of it, but it is not current money in the use of it, except we get nearer and nearer our home, heaven, by it. Another man may be sick too, and sick to death, and this affliction may lie in his bowels, as gold in a mine, and be of no use to him; but this bell, that tells me of his affliction, digs out and applies that gold to me: if by this consideration of another's danger I take mine own into contemplation, and so secure myself, by making my recourse to my God, who is our only security." John Donne, Meditation XVII

False Consciousness

False consciousness is the Marxist thesis that material and institutional processes in capitalist society are misleading to the proletariat, and to other classes. These processes betray the true relations of forces between those classes, and the real state of affairs regarding the development of pre-socialist society (relative to the secular development of human society in general).

This is essentially a result of ideological control which the proletariat either do not know they are under or disregard with a view to their own POUM (probability/possibility of upward mobility). POUM (not to be confused with the Workers' Party of Marxist Unification, POUM) or something like it is required in economics with its presumption of rational agency; otherwise wage labourers would be the conscious supporters of social relations antithetical to their own interests, violating that presumption.

Theory

The concept flows from the theory of commodity fetishism — that people experience social relationships as value relations between things, e.g., between the cash in their wage packet and the shirts they want. The cash and the shirt appear to conduct social relations independently of the humans involved, determining who gets what by their inherent values. This leaves the person who earned the cash and the people who made the shirt ignorant of and alienated from their social relationship with each other. So the individual "resolves" the experiences of alienation and oppression through a false conception based on a "natural law" argument that there is a fundamental need to compete with others for commodities.

In Marxist terms, not only is there no such objective need separate from the formulation of the general problem of production and distribution for a given society, moreover, Marx said each against all competition is antithetical to the very concept of society and therefore sets up a contradiction or historical dynamic which over time is resolved in favour of the class with the greatest ability to act in its own rational self interest. Ruling elites, traditional or otherwise, suffer from false consciousness to the extent that they see the social orders they command as predetermined or inevitable.

Engels

Although Marx frequently denounced ideology in general, there is no evidence that he ever actually used the phrase "false consciousness." It appears to have been used — at least in print— only by Friedrich Engels.

Engels wrote :

"Ideology is a process accomplished by the so-called thinker. Consciously, it is true, but with a false consciousness. The real motive forces impelling him remain unknown to him; otherwise it simply would not be an ideological process. Hence he imagines false or apparent motives....

It is above all this appearance of an independent history of state constitutions, of systems of law, of ideological conceptions in every separate domain, which dazzles most people. If Luther and Calvin "overcome" the official Catholic religion, or Hegel "overcomes" Fichte and Kant, or if the constitutional Montesquieu is indirectly "overcome" by Rousseau with his "Social Contract," each of these events remains within the sphere of theology, philosophy or political science, represents a stage in the history of these particular spheres of thought and never passes outside the sphere of thought. And since the bourgeois illusion of the eternity and the finality of capitalist production has been added as well, even the victory of the physiocrats and Adam Smith over the mercantilists is accounted as a sheer victory of thought; not as the reflection in thought of changed economic facts but as the finally achieved correct understanding of actual conditions subsisting always and everywhere..."

Here Engels expresses semantic baggage associated with the term *Ideology*, i.e. that it implies a lack of objectivity, which the term had at the time of its introduction from German (due in no small part to a reaction to Hegelianism). This has somewhat substantially been lost over the nearly two centuries since then as *Ideology* has come to be equivocated with *World View* or *Philosophy*. False consciousness is theoretically linked with the concepts of the dominant ideology and cultural hegemony. The idea of false consciousness has also been used by Marxist feminists and radical feminists in regard to women's studies.

Interpretations

The notion of false consciousness has been a focus for some critics of Marxism, because in this instance simplistic interpretations of Marxist theory can appear to be implicated in the worst cases of states such as the DPRK or former Soviet Union. Within the USSR, the state deployed the concept of false consciousness to justify authoritarian measures against the working class. Marxist critics of Stalinism, such as Trotsky and his followers, provide an account by which the theory is excused, on the basis that a corrupt regime is capable of perverting any theory. The concept of ideology as false consciousness, even where it is accepted that Marx did not use the term, has tended to dominate interpretations of Marx's statements on ideology, although arguably this in fact involves a misunderstanding of Marx.

Enlightenment as Mass Deception

The sociological theory that the loss of the support of objectively established religion, the dissolution of the last remnants of pre-capitalism, together with technological and social differentiation or specialisation, have led to cultural chaos is disproved every day; for culture now impresses the same stamp on everything.

Films, radio and magazines make up a system which is uniform as a whole and in every part. Even the aesthetic activities of political opposites are one in their enthusiastic obedience to the rhythm of the iron system. The decorative industrial management buildings and exhibition centres in authoritarian countries are much the same as anywhere else. The huge gleaming towers that shoot up everywhere are outward signs of the ingenious planning of international concerns, toward which the unleashed entrepreneurial system (whose monuments are a mass of gloomy houses and business premises in grimy, spiritless cities) was already hastening. Even now the older houses just outside the concrete city centres look like slums, and the new bungalows on the outskirts are at one with the flimsy structures of world fairs in their praise of technical progress and their built-in demand to be discarded after a short while like empty food cans.

Yet the city housing projects designed to perpetuate the individual as a supposedly independent unit in a small hygienic dwelling make him all the more subservient to his adversary – the absolute power of capitalism. Because the inhabitants, as producers and as consumers, are drawn into the centre in search of work and pleasure, all the living units crystallise into well-organised complexes. The striking unity of microcosm and macrocosm presents men with a model of their culture: the false identity of the general and the particular. Under monopoly all mass culture is identical, and the lines of its artificial framework begin to show through. The people at the top are no longer so interested in concealing monopoly: as its violence becomes more open, so its power grows. Movies and radio need no longer pretend to be art. The truth that they are just business is made into an ideology in order to justify the rubbish they deliberately produce. They call themselves industries; and when their directors' incomes are published, any doubt about the social utility of the finished products is removed.

Interested parties explain the culture industry in technological terms. It is alleged that because millions participate in it, certain reproduction processes are necessary that inevitably require identical needs in innumerable places to be satisfied with identical goods. The technical contrast between the few production centres and the large number of widely dispersed consumption points is said to demand organisation and planning by management. Furthermore, it is claimed that standards were based in the first place on consumers' needs, and for that reason were accepted with so little resistance. The result is the circle of manipulation and retroactive need in which the unity of the system grows ever stronger. No mention is made of the fact that the basis on which technology acquires power over society is the power of those whose economic hold over society is greatest. A technological rationale is the rationale of domination itself. It is the coercive nature of society alienated from itself. Automobiles, bombs, and movies keep the whole thing together until their leveling element shows its strength in the very wrong which it furthered. It has made the technology of the culture industry no more than the achievement of standardisation and mass production, sacrificing whatever involved a distinction between the logic of the work and that of the social system.

This is the result not of a law of movement in technology as such but of its function in today's economy. The need which might resist central control has already been suppressed by the control of the individual consciousness. The step from the telephone to the radio has clearly distinguished the roles. The former still allowed the subscriber to play the role of subject, and was liberal. The latter is democratic: it turns all participants into listeners and authoritatively subjects them to broadcast programs which are all exactly the same. No machinery of rejoinder has been devised, and private broadcasters are denied any freedom. They are confined to the apocryphal field of the "amateur," and also have to accept organisation from above.

But any trace of spontaneity from the public in official broadcasting is controlled and absorbed by talent scouts, studio competitions and official programs of every kind selected by professionals. Talented performers belong to the industry long before it displays them; otherwise they would not be so eager to fit in. The attitude of the public, which ostensibly and actually favours the system of the culture industry, is a part of the system and not an excuse for it. If one branch of art follows the same formula as one with a very different medium and content; if the dramatic intrigue of broadcast soap operas becomes no more than useful material for showing how to master technical problems at both ends of the scale of musical experience – real jazz or a cheap imitation; or if a movement from a Beethoven symphony is crudely "adapted" for a film sound-track in the same way as a Tolstoy novel is garbled in a film script: then the claim that this is done to satisfy the spontaneous wishes of the public is no more than hot air.

We are closer to the facts if we explain these phenomena as inherent in the technical and personnel apparatus which, down to its last cog, itself forms part of the economic mechanism of selection. In addition there is the agreement – or at least the determination – of all executive authorities not to produce or sanction anything that in any way differs from their own rules, their own ideas about consumers, or above all themselves.

In our age the objective social tendency is incarnate in the hidden subjective purposes of company directors, the foremost among whom are in the most powerful sectors of industry – steel, petroleum, electricity, and chemicals. Culture monopolies are weak and dependent in comparison. They cannot afford to neglect their appeasement of the real holders of power if their sphere of activity in mass society (a sphere producing a specific type of commodity which anyhow is still too closely bound up with easy-going liberalism and Jewish intellectuals) is not to undergo a series of purges. The dependence of the most powerful broadcasting company on the electrical industry, or of the motion picture industry on the banks, is characteristic of the whole sphere, whose individual branches are themselves economically interwoven. All are in such close contact that the extreme concentration of mental forces allows demarcation lines between different firms and technical branches to be ignored.

The ruthless unity in the culture industry is evidence of what will happen in politics. Marked differentiations such as those of A and B films, or of stories in magazines in different price ranges, depend not so much on subject matter as on classifying, organising, and labelling consumers. Something is provided for all so that none may escape; the distinctions are emphasised and extended. The public is catered for with a hierarchical range of mass-produced products of varying quality, thus advancing the rule of complete quantification. Everybody must behave (as if spontaneously) in accordance with his previously determined and indexed level, and choose the category of mass product turned out for his type. Consumers appear as statistics on research organisation charts, and are divided by income groups into red, green, and blue areas; the technique is that used for any type of propaganda.

How formalised the procedure is can be seen when the mechanically differentiated products prove to be all alike in the end. That the difference between the Chrysler range and General Motors products is basically illusory strikes every child with a keen interest in varieties. What connoisseurs discuss as good or bad points serve only to perpetuate the semblance of competition and range of choice. The same applies to the Warner Brothers and Metro Goldwyn Mayer productions. But even the differences between the more expensive and cheaper models put out by the same firm steadily diminish: for automobiles, there are such differences as the number of cylinders, cubic capacity, details of patented gadgets; and for films there are the number of stars, the extravagant use of technology, labor, and equipment, and the introduction of the latest psychological formulas. The universal criterion of merit is the amount of "conspicuous production," of blatant cash investment. The varying budgets in the culture industry do not bear the slightest relation to factual values, to the meaning of the products themselves.

Even the technical media are relentlessly forced into uniformity. Television aims at a synthesis of radio and film, and is held up only because the interested parties have not yet reached agreement, but its consequences will be quite enormous and promise to intensify the impoverishment of aesthetic matter so drastically, that by tomorrow the thinly veiled identity of all industrial culture products can come triumphantly out into the open, derisively fulfilling the Wagnerian dream of the *Gesamtkunstwerk* – the fusion of all the arts in one work.

The alliance of word, image, and music is all the more perfect than in Tristan because the sensuous elements which all approvingly reflect the surface of social reality are in principle embodied in the same technical process, the unity of which becomes its distinctive content. This process integrates all the elements of the production, from the novel (shaped with an eye to the film) to the last sound effect. It is the triumph of invested capital, whose title as absolute master is etched deep into the hearts of the dispossessed in the employment line; it is the meaningful content of every film, whatever plot the production team may have selected.

The man with leisure has to accept what the culture manufacturers offer him. Kant's formalism still expected a contribution from the individual, who was thought to relate the varied experiences of the senses to fundamental concepts; but industry robs the individual of his function. Its prime service to the customer is to do his schematising for him.

Kant said that there was a secret mechanism in the soul which prepared direct intuitions in such a way that they could be fitted into the system of pure reason. But today that secret has been deciphered. While the mechanism is to all appearances planned by those who serve up the data of experience, that is, by the culture industry, it is in fact forced upon the latter by the power of society, which remains irrational, however we may try to rationalise it; and this inescapable force is processed by commercial agencies so that they give an artificial impression of being in command.

There is nothing left for the consumer to classify. Producers have done it for him. Art for the masses has destroyed the dream but still conforms to the tenets of that dreaming idealism which critical idealism baulked at. Everything derives from consciousness: for Malebranche and Berkeley, from the consciousness of God; in mass art, from the consciousness of the production team. Not only are the hit songs, stars, and soap operas cyclically recurrent and rigidly invariable types, but the specific content of the entertainment itself is derived from them and only appears to change. The details are interchangeable. The short interval sequence which was effective in a hit song, the hero's momentary fall from grace (which he accepts as good sport), the rough treatment which the beloved gets from the male star, the latter's rugged defiance of the spoilt heiress, are, like all the other details, ready-made clichés to be slotted in anywhere; they never do anything more than fulfil the purpose allotted them in the overall plan. Their whole *raison d'etre* is to confirm it by being its constituent parts. As soon as the film begins, it is quite clear how it will end, and who will be rewarded, punished, or forgotten. In light music, once the trained ear has heard the first notes of the hit song, it can guess what is coming and feel flattered when it does come. The average length of the short story has to be rigidly adhered to. Even gags, effects, and jokes are calculated like the setting in which they are placed. They are the responsibility of special experts and their narrow range makes it easy for them to be apportioned in the office.

The development of the culture industry has led to the predominance of the effect, the obvious touch, and the technical detail over the work itself – which once expressed an idea, but was liquidated together with the idea. When the detail won its freedom, it became rebellious and, in the period from Romanticism to Expressionism, asserted itself as free expression, as a vehicle of protest against the organisation. In music the single harmonic effect obliterated the awareness of form as a whole; in painting the individual colour was stressed at the expense of pictorial composition; and in the novel psychology became more important than structure. The totality of the culture industry has put an end to this.

Though concerned exclusively with effects, it crushes their insubordination and makes them subserve the formula, which replaces the work. The same fate is inflicted on whole and parts alike. The whole inevitably bears no relation to the details – just like the career of a successful man into which everything is made to fit as an illustration or a proof, whereas it is nothing more than the sum of all those idiotic events. The so-called dominant idea is like a file which ensures order but not coherence. The whole and the parts are alike; there is no antithesis and no connection. Their prearranged harmony is a mockery of what had to be striven after in the great bourgeois works of art. In Germany the graveyard stillness of the dictatorship already hung over the gayest films of the democratic era.

The whole world is made to pass through the filter of the culture industry. The old experience of the movie-goer, who sees the world outside as an extension of the film he has just left (because the latter is intent upon reproducing the world of everyday perceptions), is now the producer's guideline. The more intensely and flawlessly his techniques duplicate empirical objects, the easier it is today for the illusion to prevail that the outside world is the straightforward continuation of that presented on the screen. This purpose has been furthered by mechanical reproduction since the lightning takeover by the sound film.

Real life is becoming indistinguishable from the movies. The sound film, far surpassing the theatre of illusion, leaves no room for imagination or reflection on the part of the audience, who is unable to respond within the structure of the film, yet deviate from its precise detail without losing the thread of the story; hence the film forces its victims to equate it directly with reality. The stunting of the mass-media consumer's powers of imagination and spontaneity does not have to be traced back to any psychological mechanisms; he must ascribe the loss of those attributes to the objective nature of the products themselves, especially to the most characteristic of them, the sound film. They are so designed that quickness, powers of observation, and experience are undeniably needed to apprehend them at all; yet sustained thought is out of the question if the spectator is not to miss the relentless rush of facts.

Even though the effort required for his response is semi-automatic, no scope is left for the imagination. Those who are so absorbed by the world of the movie – by its images, gestures, and words – that they are unable to supply what really makes it a world, do not have to dwell on particular points of its mechanics during a screening. All the other films and products of the entertainment industry which they have seen have taught them what to expect; they react automatically.

The might of industrial society is lodged in men's minds. The entertainments manufacturers know that their products will be consumed with alertness even when the customer is distraught, for each of them is a model of the huge economic machinery which has always sustained the masses, whether at work or at leisure – which is akin to work. From every sound film and every broadcast program the social effect can be inferred which is exclusive to none but is shared by all alike. The culture industry as a whole has moulded men as a type unfailingly reproduced in every product. All the agents of this process, from the producer to the women's clubs, take good care that the simple reproduction of this mental state is not nuanced or extended in any way.

The art historians and guardians of culture who complain of the extinction in the West of a basic style-determining power are wrong. The stereotyped appropriation of everything, even the inchoate, for the purposes of mechanical reproduction surpasses the rigour and general currency of any "real style," in the sense in which cultural cognoscenti celebrate the organic pre-capitalist past. No Palestrina could be more of a purist in eliminating every unprepared and unresolved discord than the jazz arranger in suppressing any development which does not conform to the jargon. When jazzing up Mozart he changes him not only when he is too serious or too difficult but when he harmonises the melody in a different way, perhaps more simply, than is customary now. No medieval builder can have scrutinised the subjects for church windows and sculptures more suspiciously than the studio hierarchy scrutinises a work by Balzac or Hugo before finally approving it. No medieval theologian could have determined the degree of the torment to be suffered by the damned in accordance with the order of divine love more meticulously than the producers of shoddy epics calculate the torture to be undergone by the hero or the exact point to which the leading lady's hemline shall be raised. The explicit and implicit, exoteric and esoteric catalogue of the forbidden and tolerated is so extensive that it not only defines the area of freedom but is all-powerful inside it. Everything down to the last detail is shaped accordingly.

Like its counterpart, avant-garde art, the entertainment industry determines its own language, down to its very syntax and vocabulary, by the use of anathema. The constant pressure to produce new effects (which must conform to the old pattern) serves merely as another rule to increase the power of the conventions when any single effect threatens to slip through the net. Every detail is so firmly stamped with sameness that nothing can appear which is not marked at birth, or does not meet with approval at first sight. And the star performers, whether they produce or reproduce, use this jargon as freely and fluently and with as much gusto as if it were the very language which it silenced long ago. Such is the ideal of what is natural in this field of activity, and its influence becomes all the more powerful, the more technique is perfected and diminishes the tension between the finished product and everyday life. The paradox of this routine, which is essentially travesty, can be detected and is often predominant in everything that the culture industry turns out. A jazz musician who is playing a piece of serious music, one of Beethoven's simplest minuets, syncopates it involuntarily and will smile superciliously when asked to follow the normal divisions of the beat. This is the "nature" which, complicated by the ever-present and extravagant demands of the specific medium, constitutes the new style and is a "system of non-culture, to which one might even concede a certain 'unity of style' if it really made any sense to speak of stylised barbarity."

The universal imposition of this stylised mode can even go beyond what is quasi-officially sanctioned or forbidden; today a hit song is more readily forgiven for not observing the 32 beats or the compass of the ninth than for containing even the most clandestine melodic or harmonic detail which does not conform to the idiom. Whenever Orson Welles offends against the tricks of the trade, he is forgiven because his departures from the norm are regarded as calculated mutations which serve all the more strongly to confirm the validity of the system. The constraint of the technically-conditioned idiom which stars and directors have to produce as "nature" so that the people can appropriate it, extends to such fine nuances that they almost attain the subtlety of the devices of an avant-garde work as against those of truth. The rare capacity minutely to fulfil the obligations of the natural idiom in all branches of the culture industry becomes the criterion of efficiency. What and how they say it must be measurable by everyday language, as in logical positivism.

The producers are experts. The idiom demands an astounding productive power, which it absorbs and squanders. In a diabolical way it has overreached the culturally conservative distinction between genuine and artificial style. A style might be called artificial which is imposed from without on the refractory impulses of a form. But in the culture industry every element of the subject matter has its origin in the same apparatus as that jargon whose stamp it bears. The quarrels in which the artistic experts become involved with sponsor and censor about a lie going beyond the bounds of credibility are evidence not so much of an inner aesthetic tension as of a divergence of interests. The reputation of the specialist, in which a last remnant of objective independence sometimes finds refuge, conflicts with the business politics of the Church, or the concern which is manufacturing the cultural commodity. But the thing itself has been essentially objectified and made viable before the established authorities began to argue about it. Even before Zanuck acquired her, Saint Bernadette was regarded by her latter-day hagiographer as brilliant propaganda for all interested parties. That is what became of the emotions of the character. Hence the style of the culture industry, which no longer has to test itself against any refractory material, is also the negation of style. The reconciliation of the general and particular, of the rule and the specific demands of the subject matter, the achievement of which alone gives essential, meaningful content to style, is futile because there has ceased to be the slightest tension between opposite poles: these concordant extremes are dismally identical; the general can replace the particular, and vice versa.

Nevertheless, this caricature of style does not amount to something beyond the genuine style of the past. In the culture industry the notion of genuine style is seen to be the aesthetic equivalent of domination. Style considered as mere aesthetic regularity is a romantic dream of the past. The unity of style not only of the Christian Middle Ages but of the Renaissance expresses in each case the different structure of social power, and not the obscure experience of the oppressed in which the general was enclosed. The great artists were never those who embodied a wholly flawless and perfect style, but those who used style as a way of hardening themselves against the chaotic expression of suffering, as a negative truth. The style of their works gave what was expressed that force without which life flows away unheard. Those very art forms which are known as classical, such as Mozart's music, contain objective trends which represent something different to the style which they incarnate.

As late as Schönberg and Picasso, the great artists have retained a mistrust of style, and at crucial points have subordinated it to the logic of the matter. What Dadaists and Expressionists called the untruth of style as such triumphs today in the sung jargon of a crooner, in the carefully contrived elegance of a film star, and even in the admirable expertise of a photograph of a peasant's squalid hut. Style represents a promise in every work of art. That which is expressed is subsumed through style into the dominant forms of generality, into the language of music, painting, or words, in the hope that it will be reconciled thus with the idea of true generality. This promise held out by the work of art that it will create truth by lending new shape to the conventional social forms is as necessary as it is hypocritical. It unconditionally posits the real forms of life as it is by suggesting that fulfilment lies in their aesthetic derivatives. To this extent the claim of art is always ideology too.

However, only in this confrontation with tradition of which style is the record can art express suffering. That factor in a work of art which enables it to transcend reality certainly cannot be detached from style; but it does not consist of the harmony actually realised, of any doubtful unity of form and content, within and without, of individual and society; it is to be found in those features in which discrepancy appears: in the necessary failure of the passionate striving for identity. Instead of exposing itself to this failure in which the style of the great work of art has always achieved self-negation, the inferior work has always relied on its similarity with others – on a surrogate identity.

In the culture industry this imitation finally becomes absolute. Having ceased to be anything but style, it reveals the latter's secret: obedience to the social hierarchy. Today aesthetic barbarity completes what has threatened the creations of the spirit since they were gathered together as culture and neutralised. To speak of culture was always contrary to culture. Culture as a common denominator already contains in embryo that schematisation and process of cataloguing and classification which bring culture within the sphere of administration. And it is precisely the industrialised, the consequent, subsumption which entirely accords with this notion of culture. By subordinating in the same way and to the same end all areas of intellectual creation, by occupying men's senses from the time they leave the factory in the evening to the time they clock in again the next morning with matter that bears the impress of the labor process they themselves have to sustain throughout the day, this subsumption mockingly satisfies the concept of a unified culture which the philosophers of personality contrasted with mass culture.

And so the culture industry, the most rigid of all styles, proves to be the goal of liberalism, which is reproached for its lack of style. Not only do its categories and contents derive from liberalism – domesticated naturalism as well as operetta and revue – but the modern culture monopolies form the economic area in which, together with the corresponding entrepreneurial types, for the time being some part of its sphere of operation survives, despite the process of disintegration elsewhere.

It is still possible to make one's way in entertainment, if one is not too obstinate about one's own concerns, and proves appropriately pliable. Anyone who resists can only survive by fitting in. Once his particular brand of deviation from the norm has been noted by the industry, he belongs to it as does the land-reformer to capitalism. Realistic dissidence is the trademark of anyone who has a new idea in business. In the public voice of modern society accusations are seldom audible; if they are, the perceptive can already detect signs that the dissident will soon be reconciled. The more immeasurable the gap between chorus and leaders, the more certainly there is room at the top for everybody who demonstrates his superiority by well-planned originality. Hence, in the culture industry, too, the liberal tendency to give full scope to its able men survives.

To do this for the efficient today is still the function of the market, which is otherwise proficiently controlled; as for the market's freedom, in the high period of art as elsewhere, it was freedom for the stupid to starve. Significantly, the system of the culture industry comes from the more liberal industrial nations, and all its characteristic media, such as movies, radio, jazz, and magazines, flourish there. Its progress, to be sure, had its origin in the general laws of capital. Gaumont and Pathe, Ullstein and Hugenberg followed the international trend with some success; Europe's economic dependence on the United States after war and inflation was a contributory factor. The belief that the barbarity of the culture industry is a result of "cultural lag," of the fact that the American consciousness did not keep up with the growth of technology, is quite wrong. It was pre-Fascist Europe which did not keep up with the trend toward the culture monopoly.

But it was this very lag which left intellect and creativity some degree of independence and enabled its last representatives to exist – however dismally. In Germany the failure of democratic control to permeate life had led to a paradoxical situation. Many things were exempt from the market mechanism which had invaded the Western countries. The German educational system, universities, theatres with artistic standards, great orchestras, and museums enjoyed protection. The political powers, state and municipalities, which had inherited such institutions from absolutism, had left them with a measure of the freedom from the forces of power which dominates the market, just as princes and feudal lords had done up to the nineteenth century. This strengthened art in this late phase against the verdict of supply and demand, and increased its resistance far beyond the actual degree of protection. In the market itself the tribute of a quality for which no use had been found was turned into purchasing power; in this way, respectable literary and music publishers could help authors who yielded little more in the way of profit than the respect of the connoisseur.

But what completely fettered the artist was the pressure (and the accompanying drastic threats), always to fit into business life as an aesthetic expert. Formerly, like Kant and Hume, they signed their letters "Your most humble and obedient servant," and undermined the foundations of throne and altar. Today they address heads of government by their first names, yet in every artistic activity they are subject to their illiterate masters.

The analysis Tocqueville offered a century ago has in the meantime proved wholly accurate. Under the private culture monopoly it is a fact that "tyranny leaves the body free and directs its attack at the soul. The ruler no longer says: You must think as I do or die. He says: You are free not to think as I do; your life, your property, everything shall remain yours, but from this day on you are a stranger among us." Not to conform means to be rendered powerless, economically and therefore spiritually – to be "self-employed." When the outsider is excluded from the concern, he can only too easily be accused of incompetence.

Whereas today in material production the mechanism of supply and demand is disintegrating, in the superstructure it still operates as a check in the rulers' favour. The consumers are the workers and employees, the farmers and lower middle class. Capitalist production so confines them, body and soul, that they fall helpless victims to what is offered them. As naturally as the ruled always took the morality imposed upon them more seriously than did the rulers themselves, the deceived masses are today captivated by the myth of success even more than the successful are. Immovably, they insist on the very ideology which enslaves them. The misplaced love of the common people for the wrong which is done them is a greater force than the cunning of the authorities. It is stronger even than the rigorism of the Hays Office, just as in certain great times in history it has inflamed greater forces that were turned against it, namely, the terror of the tribunals. It calls for Mickey Rooney in preference to the tragic Garbo, for Donald Duck instead of Betty Boop. The industry submits to the vote which it has itself inspired. What is a loss for the firm which cannot fully exploit a contract with a declining star is a legitimate expense for the system as a whole. By craftily sanctioning the demand for rubbish it inaugurates total harmony. The connoisseur and the expert are despised for their pretentious claim to know better than the others, even though culture is democratic and distributes its privileges to all. In view of the ideological truce, the conformism of the buyers and the effrontery of the producers who supply them prevail. The result is a constant reproduction of the same thing.

A constant sameness governs the relationship to the past as well. What is new about the phase of mass culture compared with the late liberal stage is the exclusion of the new. The machine rotates on the same spot. While determining consumption it excludes the untried as a risk. The movie-makers distrust any manuscript which is not reassuringly backed by a bestseller. Yet for this very reason there is never-ending talk of ideas, novelty, and surprise, of what is taken for granted but has never existed. Tempo and dynamics serve this trend. Nothing remains as of old; everything has to run incessantly, to keep moving. For only the universal triumph of the rhythm of mechanical production and reproduction promises that nothing changes, and nothing unsuitable will appear. Any additions to the well-proven culture inventory are too much of a speculation. The ossified forms – such as the sketch, short story, problem film, or hit song – are the standardised average of late liberal taste, dictated with threats from above. The people at the top in the culture agencies, who work in harmony as only one manager can with another, whether he comes from the rag trade or from college, have long since reorganised and rationalised the objective spirit. One might think that an omnipresent authority had sifted the material and drawn up an official catalogue of cultural commodities to provide a smooth supply of available mass-produced lines. The ideas are written in the cultural firmament where they had already been numbered by Plato – and were indeed numbers, incapable of increase and immutable.

Amusement and all the elements of the culture industry existed long before the latter came into existence. Now they are taken over from above and brought up to date. The culture industry can pride itself on having energetically executed the previously clumsy transposition of art into the sphere of consumption, on making this a principle, on divesting amusement of its obtrusive naïvetes and improving the type of commodities. The more absolute it became, the more ruthless it was in forcing every outsider either into bankruptcy or into a syndicate, and became more refined and elevated – until it ended up as a synthesis of Beethoven and the Casino de Paris. It enjoys a double victory: the truth it extinguishes without it can reproduce at will as a lie within. "Light" art as such, distraction, is not a decadent form. Anyone who complains that it is a betrayal of the ideal of pure expression is under an illusion about society. The purity of bourgeois art, which hypostasised itself as a world of freedom in contrast to what was happening in the material world, was from the beginning bought with the exclusion of the lower classes – with whose cause, the real universality, art keeps faith precisely by its freedom from the ends of the false universality. Serious art has been withheld from those for whom the hardship and oppression of life make a mockery of seriousness, and who must be glad if they can use time not spent at the production line just to keep going. Light art has been the shadow of autonomous art. It is the social bad conscience of serious art. The truth which the latter necessarily lacked because of its social premises gives the other the semblance of legitimacy. The division itself is the truth: it does at least express the negativity of the culture which the different spheres constitute. Least of all can the antithesis be reconciled by absorbing light into serious art, or vice versa. But that is what the culture industry attempts.

The eccentricity of the circus, peepshow, and brothel is as embarrassing to it as that of Schönberg and Karl Kraus. And so the jazz musician Benny Goodman appears with the Budapest string quartet, more pedantic rhythmically than any philharmonic clarinettist, while the style of the Budapest players is as uniform and sugary as that of Guy Lombardo. But what is significant is not vulgarity, stupidity, and lack of polish.

The culture industry did away with yesterday's rubbish by its own perfection, and by forbidding and domesticating the amateurish, although it constantly allows gross blunders without which the standard of the exalted style cannot be perceived. But what is new is that the irreconcilable elements of culture, art and distraction, are subordinated to one end and subsumed under one false formula: the totality of the culture industry. It consists of repetition. That its characteristic innovations are never anything more than improvements of mass reproduction is not external to the system. It is with good reason that the interest of innumerable consumers is directed to the technique, and not to the contents – which are stubbornly repeated, outworn, and by now half-discredited. The social power which the spectators worship shows itself more effectively in the omnipresence of the stereotype imposed by technical skill than in the stale ideologies for which the ephemeral contents stand in.

Nevertheless the culture industry remains the entertainment business. Its influence over the consumers is established by entertainment; that will ultimately be broken not by an outright decree, but by the hostility inherent in the principle of entertainment to what is greater than itself. Since all the trends of the culture industry are profoundly embedded in the public by the whole social process, they are encouraged by the survival of the market in this area. Demand has not yet been replaced by simple obedience. As is well known, the major reorganisation of the film industry shortly before World War I, the material prerequisite of its expansion, was precisely its deliberate acceptance of the public's needs as recorded at the box-office – a procedure which was hardly thought necessary in the pioneering days of the screen. The same opinion is held today by the captains of the film industry, who take as their criterion the more or less phenomenal song hits but wisely never have recourse to the judgment of truth, the opposite criterion. Business is their ideology. It is quite correct that the power of the culture industry resides in its identification with a manufactured need, and not in simple contrast to it, even if this contrast were one of complete power and complete powerlessness.

Amusement under late capitalism is the prolongation of work. It is sought after as an escape from the mechanised work process, and to recruit strength in order to be able to cope with it again. But at the same time mechanisation has such power over a man's leisure and happiness, and so profoundly determines the manufacture of amusement goods, that his experiences are inevitably after-images of the work process itself. The ostensible content is merely a faded foreground; what sinks in is the automatic succession of standardised operations. What happens at work, in the factory, or in the office can only be escaped from by approximation to it in one's leisure time.

All amusement suffers from this incurable malady. Pleasure hardens into boredom because, if it is to remain pleasure, it must not demand any effort and therefore moves rigorously in the worn grooves of association. No independent thinking must be expected from the audience: the product prescribes every reaction: not by its natural structure (which collapses under reflection), but by signals. Any logical connection calling for mental effort is painstakingly avoided. As far as possible, developments must follow from the immediately preceding situation and never from the idea of the whole. For the attentive movie-goer any individual scene will give him the whole thing. Even the set pattern itself still seems dangerous, offering some meaning – wretched as it might be – where only meaninglessness is acceptable. Often the plot is maliciously deprived of the development demanded by characters and matter according to the old pattern. Instead, the next step is what the script writer takes to be the most striking effect in the particular situation. Banal though elaborate surprise interrupts the story-line.

The tendency mischievously to fall back on pure nonsense, which was a legitimate part of popular art, farce and clowning, right up to Chaplin and the Marx Brothers, is most obvious in the unpretentious kinds. This tendency has completely asserted itself in the text of the novelty song, in the thriller movie, and in cartoons, although in films starring Greer Garson and Bette Davis the unity of the socio-psychological case study provides something approximating a claim to a consistent plot. The idea itself, together with the objects of comedy and terror, is massacred and fragmented. Novelty songs have always existed on a contempt for meaning which, as predecessors and successors of psychoanalysis, they reduce to the monotony of sexual symbolism. Today, detective and adventure films no longer give the audience the opportunity to experience the resolution. In the non-ironic varieties of the genre, it has also to rest content with the simple horror of situations which have almost ceased to be linked in any way.

Cartoons were once exponents of fantasy as opposed to rationalism. They ensured that justice was done to the creatures and objects they electrified, by giving the maimed specimens a second life. All they do today is to confirm the victory of technological reason over truth. A few years ago they had a consistent plot which only broke up in the final moments in a crazy chase, and thus resembled the old slapstick comedy. Now, however, time relations have shifted. In the very first sequence a motive is stated so that in the course of the action destruction can get to work on it: with the audience in pursuit, the protagonist becomes the worthless object of general violence. The quantity of organised amusement changes into the quality of organised cruelty. The self-elected censors of the film industry (with whom it enjoys a close relationship) watch over the unfolding of the crime, which is as drawn-out as a hunt. Fun replaces the pleasure which the sight of an embrace would allegedly afford, and postpones satisfaction till the day of the pogrom. Insofar as cartoons do any more than accustom the senses to the new tempo, they hammer into every brain the old lesson that continuous friction, the breaking down of all individual resistance, is the condition of life in this society. Donald Duck in the cartoons and the unfortunate in real life get their thrashing so that the audience can learn to take their own punishment.

The enjoyment of the violence suffered by the movie character turns into violence against the spectator, and distraction into exertion. Nothing that the experts have devised as a stimulant must escape the weary eye; no stupidity is allowed in the face of all the trickery; one has to follow everything and even display the smart responses shown and recommended in the film. This raises the question whether the culture industry fulfils the function of diverting minds which it boasts about so loudly. If most of the radio stations and movie theatres were closed down, the consumers would probably not lose so very much. To walk from the street into the movie theatre is no longer to enter a world of dream; as soon as the very existence of these institutions no longer made it obligatory to use them, there would be no great urge to do so. Such closures would not be reactionary machine wrecking.

The disappointment would be felt not so much by the enthusiasts as by the slow-witted, who are the ones who suffer for everything anyhow. In spite of the films which are intended to complete her integration, the housewife finds in the darkness of the movie theatre a place of refuge where she can sit for a few hours with nobody watching, just as she used to look out of the window when there were still homes and rest in the evening.

The unemployed in the great cities find coolness in summer and warmth in winter in these temperature-controlled locations. Otherwise, despite its size, this bloated pleasure apparatus adds no dignity to man's lives. The idea of "fully exploiting" available technical resources and the facilities for aesthetic mass consumption is part of the economic system which refuses to exploit resources to abolish hunger.

The culture industry perpetually cheats its consumers of what it perpetually promises. The promissory note which, with its plots and staging, it draws on pleasure is endlessly prolonged; the promise, which is actually all the spectacle consists of, is illusory: all it actually confirms is that the real point will never be reached, that the diner must be satisfied with the menu. In front of the appetite stimulated by all those brilliant names and images there is finally set no more than a commendation of the depressing everyday world it sought to escape. Of course works of art were not sexual exhibitions either. However, by representing deprivation as negative, they retracted, as it were, the prostitution of the impulse and rescued by mediation what was denied.

The secret of aesthetic sublimation is its representation of fulfilment as a broken promise. The culture industry does not sublimate; it represses. By repeatedly exposing the objects of desire, breasts in a clinging sweater or the naked torso of the athletic hero, it only stimulates the unsublimated forepleasure which habitual deprivation has long since reduced to a masochistic semblance. There is no erotic situation which, while insinuating and exciting, does not fail to indicate unmistakably that things can never go that far. The Hays Office merely confirms the ritual of Tantalus that the culture industry has established anyway. Works of art are ascetic and unashamed; the culture industry is pornographic and prudish. Love is downgraded to romance. And, after the descent, much is permitted; even license as a marketable speciality has its quota bearing the trade description "daring." The mass production of the sexual automatically achieves its repression. Because of his ubiquity, the film star with whom one is meant to fall in love is from the outset a copy of himself. Every tenor voice comes to sound like a Caruso record, and the "natural" faces of Texas girls are like the successful models by whom Hollywood has typecast them. The mechanical reproduction of beauty, which reactionary cultural fanaticism wholeheartedly serves in its methodical idolisation of individuality, leaves no room for that unconscious idolatry which was once essential to beauty.

The triumph over beauty is celebrated by humour -- the Schadenfreude that every successful deprivation calls forth. There is laughter because there is nothing to laugh at. Laughter, whether conciliatory or terrible, always occurs when some fear passes. It indicates liberation either from physical danger or from the grip of logic. Conciliatory laughter is heard as the echo of an escape from power; the wrong kind overcomes fear by capitulating to the forces which are to be feared. It is the echo of power as something inescapable.

Fun is a medicinal bath. The pleasure industry never fails to prescribe it. It makes laughter the instrument of the fraud practised on happiness. Moments of happiness are without laughter; only operettas and films portray sex to the accompaniment of resounding laughter. But Baudelaire is as devoid of humour as Hölderlin. In the false society laughter is a disease which has attacked happiness and is drawing it into its worthless totality. To laugh at something is always to deride it, and the life which, according to Bergson, in laughter breaks through the barrier, is actually an invading barbaric life, self-assertion prepared to parade its liberation from any scruple when the social occasion arises. Such a laughing audience is a parody of humanity. Its members are monads, all dedicated to the pleasure of being ready for anything at the expense of everyone else.

Their harmony is a caricature of solidarity. What is fiendish about this false laughter is that it is a compelling parody of the best, which is conciliatory. Delight is austere: *res severa verum gaudium*. The monastic theory that not asceticism but the sexual act denotes the renunciation of attainable bliss receives negative confirmation in the gravity of the lover who with foreboding commits his life to the fleeting moment. In the culture industry, jovial denial takes the place of the pain found in ecstasy and in asceticism. The supreme law is that they shall not satisfy their desires at any price; they must laugh and be content with laughter. In every product of the culture industry, the permanent denial imposed by civilisation is once again unmistakably demonstrated and inflicted on its victims. To offer and to deprive them of something is one and the same. This is what happens in erotic films. Precisely because it must never take place, everything centres upon copulation. In films it is more strictly forbidden for an illegitimate relationship to be admitted without the parties being punished than for a millionaire's future son-in-law to be active in the labour movement. In contrast to the liberal era, industrialised as well as popular culture may wax indignant at capitalism, but it cannot renounce the threat of castration. This is fundamental. It outlasts the organised acceptance of the uniformed seen in the films which are produced to that end, and in reality. What is decisive today is no longer puritanism, although it still asserts itself in the form of women's organisations, but the necessity inherent in the system not to leave the customer alone, not for a moment to allow him any suspicion that resistance is possible.

The principle dictates that he should be shown all his needs as capable of-fulfilment, but that those needs should be so predetermined that he feels himself to be the eternal consumer, the object of the culture industry. Not only does it make him believe that the deception it practices is satisfaction, but it goes further and implies that, whatever the state of affairs, he must put up with what is offered. The escape from everyday drudgery which the whole culture industry promises may be compared to the daughter's abduction in the cartoon: the father is holding the ladder in the dark. The paradise offered by the culture industry is the same old drudgery. Both escape and elopement are pre-designed to lead back to the starting point. Pleasure promotes the resignation which it ought to help to forget.

Even today the culture industry dresses works of art like political slogans and forces them upon a resistant public at reduced prices; they are as accessible for public enjoyment as a park. But the disappearance of their genuine commodity character does not mean that they have been abolished in the life of a free society, but that the last defence against their reduction to culture goods has fallen. The abolition of educational privilege by the device of clearance sales does not open for the masses the spheres from which they were formerly excluded, but, given existing social conditions, contributes directly to the decay of education and the progress of barbaric meaninglessness. Those who spent their money in the nineteenth or the early twentieth century to see a play or to go to a concert respected the performance as much as the money they spent. The bourgeois who wanted to get something out of it tried occasionally to establish some rapport with the work. Evidence for this is to be found in the literary "introductions" to works, or in the commentaries on *Faust*. These were the first steps toward the biographical coating and other practices to which a work of art is subjected today.

Even in the early, prosperous days of business, exchange-value did carry use value as a mere appendix but had developed it as a prerequisite for its own existence; this was socially helpful for works of art. Art exercised some restraint on the bourgeois as long as it cost money. That is now a thing of the past. Now that it has lost every restraint and there is no need to pay any money, the proximity of art to those who are exposed to it completes the alienation and assimilates one to the other under the banner of triumphant objectivity. Criticism and respect disappear in the culture industry; the former becomes a mechanical expertise, the latter is succeeded by a shallow cult of leading personalities. Consumers now find nothing expensive. Nevertheless, they suspect that the less anything costs, the less it is being given them.

The double mistrust of traditional culture as ideology is combined with mistrust of industrialised culture as a swindle. When thrown in free, the now debased works of art, together with the rubbish to which the medium assimilates them, are secretly rejected by the fortunate recipients, who are supposed to be satisfied by the mere fact that there is so much to be seen and heard. Everything can be obtained. The screenos and vaudevilles in the movie theatre, the competitions for guessing music, the free books, rewards and gifts offered on certain radio programs, are not mere accidents but a continuation of the practice obtaining with culture products. The symphony becomes a reward for listening to the radio, and – if technology had its way-the film would be delivered to people's homes as happens with the radio.

It is moving toward the commercial system. Television points the way to a development which might easily enough force the Warner Brothers into what would certainly be the unwelcome position of serious musicians and cultural conservatives. But the gift system has already taken hold among consumers. As culture is represented as a bonus with undoubted private and social advantages, they have to seize the chance. They rush in lest they miss something. Exactly what, is not clear, but in any case the only ones with a chance are the participants. Fascism, however, hopes to use the training the culture industry has given these recipients of gifts, in order to organise them into its own forced battalions.

Culture is a paradoxical commodity. So completely is it subject to the law of exchange that it is no longer exchanged; it is so blindly consumed in use that it can no longer be used. Therefore it amalgamates with advertising. The more meaningless the latter seems to be under a monopoly, the more omnipotent it becomes. The motives are markedly economic.

One could certainly live without the culture industry, therefore it necessarily creates too much satiation and apathy. In itself, it has few resources itself to correct this. Advertising is its elixir of life. But as its product never fails to reduce to a mere promise the enjoyment which it promises as a commodity, it eventually coincides with publicity, which it needs because it cannot be enjoyed. In a competitive society, advertising performed the social service of informing the buyer about the market; it made choice easier and helped the unknown but more efficient supplier to dispose of his goods. Far from costing time, it saved it.

Today, when the free market is coming to an end, those who control the system are entrenching themselves in it. It strengthens the firm bond between the consumers and the big combines. Only those who can pay the exorbitant rates charged by the advertising agencies, chief of which are the radio networks themselves; that is, only those who are already in a position to do so, or are co-opted by the decision of the banks and industrial capital, can enter the pseudo-market as sellers. The costs of advertising, which finally flow back into the pockets of the combines, make it unnecessary to defeat unwelcome outsiders by laborious competition. They guarantee that power will remain in the same hands – not unlike those economic decisions by which the establishment and running of undertakings is controlled in a totalitarian state. Advertising today is a negative principle, a blocking device: everything that does not bear its stamp is economically suspect. Universal publicity is in no way necessary for people to get to know the kinds of goods – whose supply is restricted anyway. It helps sales only indirectly. For a particular firm, to phase out a current advertising practice constitutes a loss of prestige, and a breach of the discipline imposed by the influential clique on its members. In wartime, goods which are unobtainable are still advertised, merely to keep industrial power in view. Subsidising ideological media is more important than the repetition of the name.

Because the system obliges every product to use advertising, it has permeated the idiom – the "style" – of the culture industry. Its victory is so complete that it is no longer evident in the key positions: the huge buildings of the top men, floodlit stone advertisements, are free of advertising; at most they exhibit on the rooftops, in monumental brilliance and without any self-glorification, the firm's initials. But, in contrast, the nineteenth-century houses, whose architecture still shamefully indicates that they can be used as a consumption commodity and are intended to be lived in, are covered with posters and inscriptions from the ground right up to and beyond the roof: until they become no more than backgrounds for bills and sign-boards. Advertising becomes art and nothing else, just as Goebbels – with foresight – combines them: *l'art pour l'art*, advertising for its own sake, a pure representation of social power. In the most influential American magazines, Life and Fortune, a quick glance can now scarcely distinguish advertising from editorial picture and text. The latter features an enthusiastic and gratuitous account of the great man (with illustrations of his life and grooming habits) which will bring him new fans, while the advertisement pages use so many factual photographs and details that they represent the ideal of information which the editorial part has only begun to try to achieve.

The assembly-line character of the culture industry, the synthetic, planned method of turning out its products (factory-like not only in the studio but, more or less, in the compilation of cheap biographies, pseudo-documentary novels, and hit songs) is very suited to advertising: the important individual points, by becoming detachable, interchangeable, and even technically alienated from any connected meaning, lend themselves to ends external to the work. The effect, the trick, the isolated repeatable device, have always been used to exhibit goods for advertising purposes, and today every monster close-up of a star is an advertisement for her name, and every hit song a plug for its tune. Advertising and the culture industry merge technically as well as economically. In both cases the same thing can be seen in innumerable places, and the mechanical repetition of the same culture product has come to be the same as that of the propaganda slogan. In both cases the insistent demand for effectiveness makes technology into psycho-technology, into a procedure for manipulating men. In both cases the standards are the striking yet familiar, the easy yet catchy, the skilful yet simple; the object is to overpower the customer, who is conceived as absent-minded or resistant.

By the language he speaks, he makes his own contribution to culture as publicity. The more completely language is lost in the announcement, the more words are debased as substantial vehicles of meaning and become signs devoid of quality; the more purely and transparently words communicate what is intended, the more impenetrable they become.

The demythologisation of language, taken as an element of the whole process of enlightenment, is a relapse into magic. Word and essential content were distinct yet inseparable from one another. Concepts like melancholy and history, even life, were recognised in the word, which separated them out and preserved them. Its form simultaneously constituted and reflected them. The absolute separation, which makes the moving accidental and its relation to the object arbitrary, puts an end to the superstitious fusion of word and thing.

Anything in a determined literal sequence which goes beyond the correlation to the event is rejected as unclear and as verbal metaphysics. But the result is that the word, which can now be only a sign without any meaning, becomes so fixed to the thing that it is just a petrified formula. This affects language and object alike. Instead of making the object experiential, the purified word treats it as an abstract instance, and everything else (now excluded by the demand for ruthless clarity from expression – itself now banished) fades away in reality. A left-half at football, a black-shirt, a member of the Hitler Youth, and so on, are no more than names. If before its rationalisation the word had given rise to lies as well as to longing, now, after its rationalisation, it is a straitjacket for longing more even than for lies. The blindness and dumbness of the data to which positivism reduces the world pass over into language itself, which restricts itself to recording those data.

Terms themselves become impenetrable; they obtain a striking force, a power of adhesion and repulsion which makes them like their extreme opposite, incantations. They come to be a kind of trick, because the name of the prima donna is cooked up in the studio on a statistical basis, or because a welfare state is anathematised by using taboo terms such as "bureaucrats" or "intellectuals," or because base practice uses the name of the country as a charm.

In general, the name – to which magic most easily attaches – is undergoing a chemical change: a metamorphosis into capricious, manipulable designations, whose effect is admittedly now calculable, but which for that very reason is just as despotic as that of the archaic name. First names, those archaic remnants, have been brought up to date either by stylisation as advertising trade-marks (film stars' surnames have become first names), or by collective standardisation.

In comparison, the bourgeois family name which, instead of being a trade-mark, once individualised its bearer by relating him to his own past history, seems antiquated. It arouses a strange embarrassment in Americans. In order to hide the awkward distance between individuals, they call one another "Bob" and "Harry," as interchangeable team members. This practice reduces relations between human beings to the good fellowship of the sporting community and is a defence against the true kind of relationship.

Signification, which is the only function of a word admitted by semantics, reaches perfection in the sign. Whether folk-songs were rightly or wrongly called upper-class culture in decay, their elements have only acquired their popular form through a long process of repeated transmission. The spread of popular songs, on the other hand, takes place at lightning speed. The American expression "fad," used for fashions which appear like epidemics – that is, inflamed by highly-concentrated economic forces – designated this phenomenon long before totalitarian advertising bosses enforced the general lines of culture. When the German Fascists decide one day to launch a word – say, "intolerable" – over the loudspeakers the next day the whole nation is saying "intolerable." By the same pattern, the nations against whom the weight of the German *blitzkrieg* was thrown took the word into their own jargon. The general repetition of names for measures to be taken by the authorities makes them, so to speak, familiar, just as the brand name on everybody's lips increased sales in the era of the free market. The blind and rapidly spreading repetition of words with special designations links advertising with the totalitarian watchword.

The layer of experience which created the words for their speakers has been removed; in this swift appropriation language acquires the coldness which until now it had only on billboards and in the advertisement columns of newspapers. Innumerable people use words and expressions which they have either ceased to understand or employ only because they trigger off conditioned reflexes; in this sense, words are trade-marks which are finally all the more firmly linked to the things they denote, the less their linguistic sense is grasped. The minister for mass education talks incomprehendingly of "dynamic forces," and the hit songs unceasingly celebrate "reverie" and "rhapsody," yet base their popularity precisely on the magic of the unintelligible as creating the thrill of a more exalted life. Other stereotypes, such as memory, are still partly comprehended, but escape from the experience which might allow them content. They appear like enclaves in the spoken language. On the radio of Flesch and Hitler they may be recognised from the affected pronunciation of the announcer when he says to the nation, "Good night, everybody!" or "This is the Hitler Youth," and even intones "the Fuehrer" in a way imitated by millions. In such cliches the last bond between sedimentary experience and language is severed which still had a reconciling effect in dialect in the nineteenth century. But in the prose of the journalist whose adaptable attitude led to his appointment as an all-German editor, the German words become petrified, alien terms. Every word shows how far it has been debased by the Fascist pseudo-folk community.

By now, of course, this kind of language is already universal, totalitarian. All the violence done to words is so vile that one can hardly bear to hear them any longer. The announcer does not need to speak pompously; he would indeed be impossible if his inflection were different from that of his particular audience. But, as against that, the language and gestures of the audience and spectators are coloured more strongly than ever before by the culture industry, even in fine nuances which cannot yet be explained experimentally.

Today the culture industry has taken over the civilising inheritance of the entrepreneurial and frontier democracy – whose appreciation of intellectual deviations was never very finely attuned. All are free to dance and enjoy themselves, just as they have been free, since the historical neutralisation of religion, to join any of the innumerable sects.

But freedom to choose an ideology – since ideology always reflects economic coercion – everywhere proves to be freedom to choose what is always the same. The way in which a girl accepts and keeps the obligatory date, the inflection on the telephone or in the most intimate situation, the choice of words in conversation, and the whole inner life as classified by the now somewhat devalued depth psychology, bear witness to man's attempt to make himself a proficient apparatus, similar (even in emotions) to the model served up by the culture industry.

The most intimate reactions of human beings have been so thoroughly reified that the idea of anything specific to themselves now persists only as an utterly abstract notion: personality scarcely signifies anything more than shining white teeth and freedom from body odour and emotions. The triumph of advertising in the culture industry is that consumers feel compelled to buy and use its products even though they see through them.

Base and Superstructure

In Marxist theory, human society consists of two parts: the base and superstructure; the base comprehends the forces and relations of production — employer-employee work conditions, the technical division of labour, and property relations — into which people enter to produce the necessities and amenities of life. These relations determine society's other relationships and ideas, which are described as its superstructure. The superstructure of a society includes its culture, institutions, political power structures, roles, rituals, and state. The base *determines* (conditions) the superstructure, yet their relation is *not* strictly causal, because the superstructure often influences the base; the influence of the base, however, predominates.

The Model and its Qualification

In developing Alexis de Tocqueville's observations, Marx identified civil society as the economic base and political society as the political superstructure. Marx postulated the essentials of the base–superstructure concept in his Preface to *A Contribution to the Critique of Political Economy* (1859):

"In the social production of their existence, men inevitably enter Into definite relations, which are independent of their will, namely [the] relations of production appropriate to a given stage in the development of their material forces of production.

The totality of these relations of production constitutes the economic structure of society, the real foundation, on which arises a legal and political superstructure, and to which correspond definite forms of consciousness. The mode of production of material life conditions the general process of social, political, and intellectual life. It is not the consciousness of men that determines their existence, but their social existence that determines their consciousness.

At a certain stage of development, the material productive forces of society come into conflict with the existing relations of production or — this merely expresses the same thing in legal terms — with the property relations within the framework of which they have operated hitherto. From forms of development of the productive forces, these relations turn into their fetters. Then begins an era of social revolution. The changes in the economic foundation lead, sooner or later, to the transformation of the whole, immense, superstructure. In studying such transformations, it is always necessary to distinguish between the material transformation of the economic conditions of production, which can be determined with the precision of natural science, and the legal, political, religious, artistic, or philosophic — in short, ideological forms in which men become conscious of this conflict and fight it out. Just as one does not judge an individual by what he thinks about himself, so one cannot judge such a period of transformation by its consciousness, but, on the contrary, this consciousness must be explained from the contradictions of material life, from the conflict existing between the social forces of production and the relations of production."

Marx's "base determines superstructure" axiom, however, requires qualification:

1. the base is the whole of productive relationships, not only a given economic element, e.g. the working class
2. historically, the superstructure varies and develops unevenly in society's different activities; for example, art, politics, economics, etc.
3. the base–superstructure relationship is *reciprocal*; Engels explains that the base determines the superstructure *only in the last instance.*

Contemporary Marxist interpretations, such as those of critical theory, criticise this conception of the base–superstructure interaction and examine how each affects and conditions the other. Raymond Williams, for example, argues against loose, "popular" usages of base and superstructure as discrete entities, which, he explains, are not the intention of Marx and Engels:

> *"So, we have to say that when we talk of 'the base', we are talking of a process, and not a state [....] We have to revalue 'superstructure' towards a related range of cultural practices, and away from a reflected, reproduced, or specifically-dependent content. And, crucially, we have to revalue 'the base' away from [the] notion[s] of [either] a fixed economic or [a] technological abstraction, and towards the specific activities of men in real, social and economic relationships, containing fundamental contradictions and variations, and, therefore, always in a state of dynamic process.*

2

Toward an Interpretive Theory

Interpretive theory is a general category of theory including symbolic interactionism, labelling, ethnomethodology, phenomenology and social constructionism.

Interpretive theory is typically contrasted with structural theories which claim to remove the subjectivity of the actor and the researcher and assume that human behaviour can best be understood as determined by the pushes and pulls of structural forces.

Interpretive theory is more accepting of free will and sees human behaviour as the outcome of the subjective interpretation of the environment.

Structural theory focuses on the situation in which people act while interpretive theory focuses on the actor's definition of the situation in which they act.

Interpretive theory seeks reciprocal inter-subjective understanding of subjects.

In her book, *Philosophy in a New Key*, Susanne Langer remarks that certain ideas burst upon the intellectual landscape with a tremendous force. They resolve so many fundamental problems at once that they seem also to promise that they will resolve all fundamental problems, clarify all obscure issues. Everyone snaps them up as the open sesame of some new positive science, the conceptual centre-point around which a comprehensive system of analysis can be built. The sudden vogue of such a *grande ideé*, crowding out almost everything else for a while, is due, she says, "to the fact that all sensitive and active minds turn at once to exploiting it. We try it in every connection, for every purpose, experiment with possible stretches of its strict meaning, with generalizetions and derivatives."

After we have become familiar with the new idea, however, after it has become part of our general stock of theoretical concepts, our expectations are brought more into balance with its actual uses, and its excessive popularity is ended. A few zealots persist in the old key-to-the-universe view of it; but less driven thinkers settle down after a while to the problems the idea has really generated. They try to apply it and extend it where it applies and where it is capable of extension; and they desist where it does not apply or cannot be extended. It becomes, if it was, in truth, a seminal idea in the first place, a permanent and enduring part of our intellectual armory. But it no longer has the grandiose, all-promising scope, the infinite versatility of apparent application, it once had.

The second law of thermodynamics, or the principle of natural selection, or the notion of unconscious motivation, or the organization of the means of production does not explain everything, not even everything human, but it still explains something; and our attention shifts to isolating just what that something is, to disentangling ourselves from a lot of pseudoscience to which, in the first flush of its celebrity, it has also given rise.

Whether or not this is, in fact, the way all centrally important scientific concepts develop, I don't know. But certainly this pattern fits the concept of culture, around which the whole discipline of anthropology arose, and whose domination that discipline has been increasingly concerned to limit, specify, focus, and contain. It is to this cutting of the culture concept down to size, therefore actually insuring its continued importance rather than undermining it, that the essays below are all, in their several ways and from their several directions, dedicated. They all argue, sometimes explicitly, more often merely through the particular analysis they develop, for a narrowed, specialized, and, so I imagine, theoretically more powerful concept of culture to replace E. B. Tylor's famous "most complex whole," which, its originative power not denied, seems to me to have reached the point where it obscures a good deal more than it reveals. The conceptual morass into which the Tylorean kind of *pot-au-feu* theorizing about culture can lead, is evident in what is still one of the better general introductions to anthropology, Clyde Kluckhohn's *Mirror for Man*. In some twenty-seven pages of his chapter on the concept, Kluckhohn managed to define culture in turn as:

1. "the total way of life of a people";
2. "the social legacy the individual acquires from his group";
3. a "way of thinking, feeling, and believing";
4. an "abstraction from behaviour";
5. a "theory on the part of the anthropologist about the way in which a group of people in fact behave";
6. a "storehouse of pooled learning";
7. a "set of standardized orientations to re-current problems";
8. "learned behaviour";
9. a "mechanism for the normative regulation of behaviour";
10. a "set of techniques for adjusting both to the external environment and to other men";
11. "a precipitate of history"; and turning, perhaps in desperation, to similes, as a map, as a sieve, and as a matrix.

In the face of this sort of theoretical diffusion, even a somewhat constricted and not entirely standard concept of culture, which is at least internally coherent and, more important, which has a definable argument to make is (as, to be fair, Kluckhohn himself keenly realized) an improvement. Eclecticism is self-defeating not because there is only one direction in which it is useful to move, but because there are so many: it is necessary to choose.

The concept of culture I espouse, and whose utility the essays below attempt to demonstrate, is essentially a semiotic one. Believing, with Max Weber, that man is an animal suspended in webs of significance he himself has spun, I take culture to be those webs, and the analysis of it to be therefore not an experimental science in search of law but an iterpretive one in search of meaning. It is explication I am after, construing social expressions on their surface enigmatical. But this pronouncement, a doctrine in a clause, demands itself some explication.

Operationalism as a methodological dogma never made much sense so far as the social sciences are concerned, and except for a few rather toowell-swept corners—Skinnerian behaviourism, intelligence testing, and so on—it is largely dead now. But it had, for all that, an important point to make, which, however we may feel about trying to define charisma or alienation in terms of operations, retains a certain force: if you want to understand what a science is, you should look in the first instance not at its theories or its findings, and certainly not at what its apologists say about it; you should look at what the practitioners of it do.

In anthropology, or anyway social anthropology, what the practioners do is ethnography. And it is in understanding what ethnography is, or more exactly *what doing ethnography* is, that a start can be made toward grasping what anthropological analysis amounts to as a form of knowledge. This, it must immediately be said, is not a matter of methods. From one point of view, that of the textbook, doing ethnography is establishing rapport, selecting informants, transcribing texts, taking genealogies, mapping fields, keeping a diary, and so on. But it is not these things, techniques and received procedures, that define the enterprise.

What defines it is the kind of intellectual effort it is: an elaborate venture in, to borrow a notion from Gilbert Ryle, "thick description."

Ryle's discussion of "thick description" appears in two recent essays of his (now reprinted in the second volume of his *Collected Papers* addressed to the general question of what, as he puts it, "*Le Penseur*" is doing: "*Thinking and Reflecting*" and "*The Thinking of Thoughts.*" Consider, he says, two boys rapidly contracting the eyelids of their right eyes. In one, this is an involuntary twitch; in the other, a conspiratorial signal to a friend. The two movements are, as movements, identical; from an l-am-a-camera, "phenomenalistic" observation of them alone, one could not tell which was twitch and which was wink, or indeed whether both or either was twitch or wink. Yet the difference, however unphotographable, between a twitch and a wink is vast; as anyone unfortunate enough to have had the first taken for the second knows.

The winker is communicating, and indeed communicating in a quite precise and special way: (1) deliberately, (2) to someone in particular, (3) to impart a particular message, (4) according to a socially established code, and (5) without cognizance of the rest of the company. As Ryle points out, the winker has not done two things, contracted his eyelids and winked, while the twitcher has done only one, contracted his eyelids. Contracting your eyelids on purpose when there exists a public code in which so doing counts as a conspiratorial signal is winking. That's all there is to it: a speck of behaviour, a fleck of culture, and—*voilà!*—a gesture.

That, however, is just the beginning. Suppose, he continues, there is a third boy, who, "to give malicious amusement to his cronies," parodies the first boy's wink, as amateurish, clumsy, obvious, and so on. He, of course, does this in the same way the second boy winked and the first twitched: by contracting his right eyelids. Only this boy is neither winking nor twitching, he is parodying someone else's, as he takes it, laughable, attempt at winking. Here, too, a socially established code exists (he will "wink" laboriously, over-obviously, perhaps adding a grimace—the usual artifices of the clown); and so also does a message. Only now it is not conspiracy but ridicule that is in the air. If the others think he is actually winking, his whole project misfires as completely, though with somewhat different results, as if they think he is twitching. One can go further: uncertain of his mimicking abilities, the would-be satirist may practice at home before the mirror, in which case he is not twitching, winking, or parodying, but rehearsing; though so far as what a camera, a radical behaviourist, or a believer in protocol sentences would record: he is just rapidly contracting his right eyelids like all the others. Complexities are possible, if not practically without end, at least logically so.

The original winker might, for example, actually have been fake-winking, say, to mislead outsiders into imagining there was a conspiracy afoot when there in fact was not, in which case our descriptions of what the parodist is parodying and the rehearser is rehearsing of course shift accordingly. But the point is that between what Ryle calls the "thin description" of what the rehearser (parodist, winker, twitcher...) is doing ("rapidly contracting his right eyelids") and the "thick description" of what he is doing ("practicing a burlesque of a friend faking a wink to deceive an innocent into thinking a conspiracy is in motion") lies the object of ethnography: a stratified hierarchy of meaningful structures in terms of which twitches, winks, fake-winks, parodies, rehearsals of parodies are produced, perceived, and interpreted, and without which they would not (not even the zero-form twitches, which, as a *cultural category*, are as much non-winks as winks are non-twitches) in fact exist, no matter what anyone did or didn't do with his eyelids.

Like so many of the little stories Oxford philosophers like to makeup for themselves, all this winking, fake-winking, burlesque-fake-winking, rehearsed-burlesque-fake-winking, may seem a bit artificial. In way of adding a more empirical note, let me give, deliberately unpreceded by any prior explanatory comment at all, a not untypical excerpt from my own field journal to demonstrate that, however evened off for didactic purposes, Ryle's example presents an image only too exact of the sort of piled-up structures of inference and implication through which an ethnographer is continually trying to pick his way:

"The French (the informant said) had only just arrived. They set up twenty or so small forts between here, the town, and the Marmusha area up in the middle of the mountains, placing them on promontories so they could survey the countryside. But for all this they couldn't guarantee safety, especially at night, so although the *mezrag* (trade-pact-system) was supposed to be legally abolished it in fact continued as before.

One night, when Cohen (who speaks fluent Berber) was up there (at Marmusha) two other Jews who were traders to a neighbouring tribe came by to purchase some goods from him. Some Berbers—from yet another neighbouring tribe—tried to break into Cohen's place, but he fired his rifle in the air. (Traditionally, Jews were not allowed to carry weapons; but at this period things were so unsettled many did so anyway.) This attracted the attention of the French and the marauders fled. The next night, however, they came back, and one of them disguised as a woman who knocked on the door with some sort of a story. Cohen was suspicious and didn't want to let "her" in, but the other Jews said: "oh, it's all right, it's only a woman." So they opened the door and the whole lot came pouring in. They killed the two visiting Jews, but Cohen managed to barricade himself in an adjoining room. He heard the robbers planning to burn him alive in the shop after they removed his goods, and so he opened the door and—laying about him wildly with a club—managed to escape through a window.

He went up to the fort (then) to have his wounds dressed, and complained to the local commandant, one Captain Dumari, saying he wanted his "ar-ie", four or five times the value of the merchandise stolen from him. The robbers were from a tribe which had not yet submitted to French authority and were in open rebellion against it, and he wanted authorization to go with his *mezrag*-holder, the Marmusha tribal *sheikh*, to collect the indemnity that, under traditional rules, he had coming to him. Captain Dumari couldn't officially give him permission to do this—because of the French prohibition of the mezrag relationship—but he gave him verbal authorization saying, "If you get killed, it's your problem."

So the *sheikh*, the Jew, and a small company of armed Marmushans went off ten or fifteen kilometers up into the rehellious area, where there were of course no French, and, sneaking up, captured the thief-tribe's shepherd and stole its herds. The other tribe soon came riding out on horses after them armed with rifles and ready to attack. But when they saw who the "sheep thieves" were, they thought better of it and said, "all right, we'll talk." They couldn't really deny what had happened—that some of their men had robbed Cohen and killed the two visitors—and they weren't prepared to start the serious feud with the Marmusha, a scuffle with the invading party would bring on. So the two groups talked, and talked, and talked, there on the plain amid the thousands of sheep, and decided finally on five-hundred-sheep damagee. The two armed Berber groups then lined up on their horse at opposite ends of the plain with the sheep herded between them, and Cohen, in his black gown, pillhox hat, and flapping slippers, went out alone among the sheep, picking out, one by one and at his own good speed, the best ones for his payment.

So Cohen got his sheep and drove them back to Marmusha. The French, up in their fort, heard them coming from some distance ("Ba, ba, ba" said Cohen, happily, recalling the image) and said, "What the hell is that?" Cohen said "That is my *'ar'*." The French couldn't believe he had actually done what he said he had done, and accused him of being a spy for the rebellious Berbers, put him in prison, and took his sheep. In the town, his family, not having heard from him in so long a time, thought he was dead. But after a while the French released him and he came back home, but without his sheep. He then went to the Colonel in the town, the Frenchman in charge of the whole region, to complain. But the Colonel said, "I can't do anything about the matter. It's not my problem."

Quoted raw, a note in a bottle, this passage conveys, as any similar one similarly presented would do, a fair sense of how much goes into ethnographic description of even the most elemental sort—how extraordinarily "thick" it is. In finished anthropological writings, including those collected here, this fact—that what we call our data are really our own constructions of other people's constructions of what they and their compatriots are up to—is obscured because most of what we need to comprehend a particular event, ritual, custom, idea, or whatever is insinuated as background information before the thing itself is directly examined. (Even to reveal that this little drama took place in the highlands of central Morocco in 1912—and was recounted there in 1968—is to determine much of our understanding of it. There is nothing particularly wrong with this, and it is in any case inevitable. But it does lead to a view of anthropological research as rather more of an observational and rather less of an interpretive activity than it really is.

Right down at the factual base, the hard rock, insofar as there is any, of the whole enterprise, we are already explicating: and worse, explicating explications. Winks upon winks upon winks. Analysis, then, is sorting out the structures of signification—what Ryle called established codes, a somewhat misleading expression, for it makes the enterprise sound too much like that of the cipher clerk when it is much more like that of the literary critic—and determining their social ground and import. Here, in our text, such sorting would begin with distinguishing the three unlike frames of interpretation ingredient in the situation Jewish, Berber, and French, and would then move on to show how (and why) at that time, in that place, their copresence produced a situation in which systematic misunderstanding reduced traditional form to social farce. What tripped Cohen up, and with him the whole, ancient pattern of social and economic relationships within which he functioned, was a confusion of tongues.

I shall come back to this too-compacted aphorism later, as well as to the details of the text itself. The point for now is only that ethnography is thick description. What the ethnographer is in fact faced with—except when (as, of course, he must do) he is pursuing the more automatized routines of data collection—is a multiplicity of complex conceptual structures, many of them superimposed upon or knotted into one another, which are at once strange, irregular, and inexplicit, and which he must contrive somehow first to grasp and then to render. And this is true at the most down-to-earth, jungle field work levels of his activity: interviewing informants, observing rituals, eliciting kin terms, tracing property lines, censusing households... writing his journal.

Doing ethnography is like trying to read (in the sense of "construct a reading of') a manuscript—foreign, faded, full of ellipses, incoherencies, suspicious emendations, and tendentious commentaries, but written not in conventionalized graphs of sound but in transient examples of shaped behaviour.

Culture, this acted document, thus is public, like a burlesqued wink or a mock sheep raid. Though ideational it does not exist in someone's head; though unphysical is not an occult entity. The interminable, because unterminable, debate within anthropology as to whether culture is "subjective" or "objective," together with the mutual exchange of intellectual insults ("idealist!"—"materialist!"; "mentalist!"—"behaviourist!"; "impressionist!"—"positivist!") which accompanies it, is wholly misconceived. Once human behaviour is seen as (most of the time; there are true twitches) symbolic action which, like phonation in speech, pigment in painting, line in writing, or sonance in music, signifies, the question as to whether culture is patterned conduct or a frame of mind, or even the two somehow mixed together, loses sense. The thing to ask about a burlesqued wink or a mock sheep raid is not what their ontological status is. It is the same as that of rocks on the one hand and dreams on the other—they are things of this world. The thing to ask is what their import is: what it is, ridicule or challenge, irony or anger, snobbery or pride, that in their occurrence and through their agency, is getting said.

This may seem like an obvious truth, but there are a number of ways to obscure it. One is to imagine that culture is a self-contained "super-organic" reality with forces and purposes of its own; that is, to reify it.

Another is to claim that it consists in the brute pattern of behavioural events we observe in fact to occur in some identifiable community or other; that is, to reduce it.

But though both these confusions still exist, and doubtless will be always with us, the main source of theoretical muddlement in contemporary anthropology is a view which developed in reaction to them and is right now very widely held—namely, that, to quote Ward Goodenough, perhaps its leading proponent, "culture [is located] in the minds and hearts of men."

Variously called ethnoscience, componential analysis, or cognitive anthropology (a terminological wavering which reflects a deeper uncertainty), this school of thought holds that culture is composed of psychological structures by means of which individuals or groups of individuals guide their behaviour. "A society's culture," to quote Goodenough again, this time in a passage which has become the locus classicus of the whole movement, "consists of whatever it is one has to know or believe in order to operate in a manner acceptable to its members." And from this view of what culture is follows a view, equally assured, of what describing it is —the writing out of systematic rules, an ethnographic algorithm, which, if followed, would make it possible so to operate, to pass (physical appearance aside) for a native. In such a way, extreme subjectivism is married to extreme formalism, with the expected result: an explosion of debate as to whether particular analyses (which come in the form of taxonomies, paradigms, tables, trees, and other ingenuities) reflect what the natives "really" think or are merely clever simulations, logically equivalent but substantively different, of what they think.

As, on first glance, this approach may look close enough to the one being developed here to be mistaken for it, it is useful to be explicit as to what divides them. If, leaving our winks and sheep behind for the moment, we take, say, a Beethoven quartet as an, admittedly rather special but, for these purposes, nicely illustrative sample of culture, no one would, I think, identify it with its score, with the skills and knowledge needed to play it, with the understanding of it possessed by its performers or auditors, nor, to take care, *en passant*, by the view of the reductionists and reifiers: with a particular performance of it or with some mysterious entity transcending material existence. The "no one" is perhaps too strong here, for there are always incorrigibles. But that a Beethoven quartet is a temporally developed tonal structure, a coherent sequence of musical sound—in a word, music—and not anybody's knowledge c-f or belief about anything, including how to play it, is a proposition to which most people are, upon reflection, likely to assent. To play the violin it is necessary to possess certain habits, skills, knowledge, and talents, to be in the mood to play, and (as the old joke goes) to have a violin. But violin playing is neither the habits, skills, knowledge, and so on, nor the mood, nor (the notion believers in "material culture" apparently embrace) the violin. To make a trade pact in Morocco, you have to do certain things in certain ways (among others, cut, while chanting Quranic Arabic, the throat of a lamb before the assembled, undeformed, adult male members of your tribe) and to be possessed of certain psychological characteristics (among others, a desire for distant things). But a trade pact is neither the throat cutting nor the desire, though it is real enough, as seven kinsmen of our Marmusha sheikh discovered when, on an earlier occasion, they were executed by him following the theft of one mangy, essentially valueless sheepskin from Cohen.

Culture is public because meaning is. You can't wink (or burlesque one) without knowing what counts as winking or how, physically, to contract your eyelids, and you can't conduct a sheep raid (or mimic one) without knowing what it is to steal a sheep and how practically to go about it. But to draw from such truths the conclusion that knowing how to wink is winking and knowing how to steal a sheep is sheep raiding is to betray as deep a confusion as, taking thin descriptions for thick, to identify winking with eyelid contractions or sheep raiding with chasing woolly animals out of pastures. The cognitivist fallacy—that culture consists (to quote another spokesman for the movement, Stephen Tyler) of "mental phenomena which can [he means "should"] be analyzed by normal methods similar to those of mathematics and logic"—is as destructive of an effective use of the concept as are the behaviourist and idealist fallacies to which it is a misdrawn correction. Perhaps, as its errors are more sophisticated and its distortions subtler, it is even more so.

The generalized attack on privacy theories of meaning is, since early Husserl and late Wittgenstein, so much a part of modern thought that it need not be developed once more here. What is necessary is to see to it that the news of it reaches anthropology; and in particular that it is made clear that to say that culture consists of socially established structures of meaning in terms of which people do such things as signal conspiracies and join them or perceive insults and answer them, is no moreto say that it is a psychological phenomenon, a characteristic of someone's mind, personality, cognitive structure, or whatever, than to say that Tantrism, genetics, the progressive form of the verb, the classification of wines, the Common Law, or the notion of "a conditional curse" (as Westermarck defined the concept of 'ar in terms of which Cohen pressed his claim to damages) is. What, in a place like Morocco, most prevents those of us who grew up winking other winks or attending other sheep from grasping what people are up to is not ignorance as to how cognition works (though, especially as, one assumes, it works the same among them as it does among us, it would greatly help to have less of that too) as a lack of familiarity with the imaginative universe within which their acts are signs. As Wittgenstein has been invoked, he may as well be quoted:

> *"We... say of some people that they are transparent to us. It is, however important as regards this observation, that one human being can be a complete enigma to another. We learn this when we come into a strange country with entirely strange traditions; and. what is*

> *more, even given a mastery of the country's language. We do not* understand *the people. (And not because of not knowing what they are saying to themselves.) We cannot find our feet with them."*

Finding our feet, an unnerving business which never more than distantly succeeds, is what ethnographic research consists of as a personal experience; trying to formulate the basis on which one imagines, always excessively, one has found them is what anthropological writing consists of as a scientific endeavour. We are not, or at least I am not, seeking either to become natives (a compromised word in any case) or to mimic them. Only romantics or spies would seem to find point in that. We are seeking, in the widened sense of the term in which it encompasses very much more than talk, to converse with them, a matter a great deal more difficult, and not only with strangers, than is commonly recognized. "If speaking *for* someone else seems to be a mysterious process," Stanley Cavell has remarked, "that may be because speaking *to* someone does not seem mysterious enough".

Looked at in this way, the aim of anthropology is the enlargement of the universe of human discourse. That is not, of course, its only aim—instruction, amusement, practical counsel, moral advance, and the discovery of natural order in human behaviour are others; nor is anthropology the only discipline which pursues it. But it is an aim to which a semiotic concept of culture is peculiarly well adapted. As interworked systems of construable signs (what, ignoring provincial usages, I would call symbols), culture is not a power, something to which social events, behaviours, institutions, or processes can be causally attributed; it is a context, something within which they can be intelligibly—that is, thickly—described.

The famous anthropological absorption with the (to us) exotic Berber horsemen, Jewish peddlers, French Legionnaires—is, thus, essentially a device for displacing the dulling sense of familiarity with which the mysteriousness of our own ability to relate perceptively to one another is concealed from us. Looking at the ordinary in places where it takes unaccustomed forms brings out not, as has so often been claimed, the arbitrariness of human behaviour (there is nothing especially arbitrary about taking sheep theft for insolence in Morocco), but the degree to which its meaning varies according to the pattern of life by, which it is informed. Understanding a people's culture exposes their normalness without reducing their particularity. (The more I manage to follow what the Moroccans are up to, the more logical, and the more singular, they seem.) It renders them accessible: setting them in the frame of their own banalities, it dissolves their opacity.

It is this manoeuvre, usually too casually referred to as "seeing things from the actor's point of view," too bookishly as "the *verstehen* approach," or too technically as "emic analysis," that so often leads to the notion that anthropology is a variety of either long-distance mind reading or cannibal-isle fantasizing, and which, for someone anxious to navigate past the wrecks of a dozen sunken philosophies, must therefore be executed with a great deal of care. Nothing is more necessary to comprehending what anthropological interpretation is, and the degree to which it is interpretation, than an exact understanding of what it means—and what it does not mean—to say that our formulations of other peoples' symbol systems must be actor-oriented.

"Not only other peoples": anthropology can be trained on the culture of which it is itself a part, and it increasingly is; a fact of profound importance, but which, as it raises a few tricky and rather special second order problems, I shall put to the side for the moment. What it means is that descriptions of Berber, Jewish, or French culture must be cast in terms of the constructions we imagine Berbers, Jews, or Frenchmen to place upon what they live through, the formulae they use to define what happens to them.

What it does not mean is that such descriptions are themselves Berber, Jewish, or French—that is, part of the reality they are ostensibly describing; they are anthropological —that is, part of a developing system of scientific analysis. They must be cast in terms of the interpretations to which persons of a particular denomination subject their experience, because that is what they profess to be descriptions of; they are anthropological because it is, in fact, anthropologists who profess them. Normally, it is not necessary to point out quite so laboriously that the object of study is one thing and the study of it another. It is clear enough that the physical world is not physics and *A Skelton Key to Finnegan's Wake* is not Finnegan's *Wake*. But, as, in the study of culture, analysis penetrates into the very body of the object—that is, *we begin with our own interpretations of what our informants are up to, or think they are up to, and then systematize those*—the line between (Moroccan) culture as a natural fact and (Moroccan) culture as a theoretical entity tends to get blurred. All the more so, as the latter is presented in the form of an actor's-eye description of (Moroccan) conceptions of everything from violence, honor, divinity, and justice, to tribe, property, patronage, and chiefship.

In short, anthropological writings are themselves interpretations, and second and third order ones to boot. (By definition, only a "native" makes first order ones: it's *his* culture.) They are, thus, fictions; fictions, in the sense that they are "something made," "something fashioned"—the original meaning of *fictio*—not that they are false, unfactual, or merely "as if" thought experiments. To construct actor-oriented descriptions of the involvements of a Berber chieftain, a Jewish merchant, and a French soldier with one another in 1912 Morocco is clearly an imaginative act, not all that different from constructing similar descriptions of, say, the involvements with one another of a provincial French doctor, his silly, adulterous wife, and her feckless lover in nineteenth century France. In the latter case, the actors are represented as not having existed and the events as not having happened, while in the former they are represented as actual, or as having been so. This is a difference of no mean importance; indeed, precisely the one Madame Bovary had difficulty grasping. But the importance does not lie in the fact that her story was created while Cohen's was only noted. The conditions of their creation, all "the point of it (to say nothing of the manner and the quality) differ. But the one is as much a *fictio*—a making"—as the other.

Anthropologists have not always been as aware as they might be of this fact: that although culture exists in the trading post, the hill fort, or the sheep run, anthropology exists in the book, the article, the lecture, the museum display, or, sometimes nowadays, the film. To become aware of it is to realize that the line between mode of representation and substantive content is as undrawable in cultural analysis as it is in painting; and that fact in turn seems to threaten the objective status of anthropological knowledge by suggesting that its source is not social reality but scholarly artifice.

It does threaten it, but the threat is hollow. The claim to attention of an ethnographic account does not rest on its author's ability to capture primitive facts in faraway places and carry them home like a mask or a carving, but on the degree to which he is able to clarify what goes on in such places, to reduce the puzzlement—what manner of men are these?—to which unfamiliar acts emerging out of unknown backgrounds naturally give rise. This raises some serious problems of verification, all right—or, if "verification" is too strong a word for so soft a science (I, myself, would prefer "appraisal"), of how you can tell a better account from a worse one. But that is precisely the virtue of it. If ethnography is thick description and ethnographers those who are doing the describing, then the determining question for any given example of it, whether a field journal squib or a Malinowski-sized monograph, is whether it sorts winks from twitches and real winks from mimicked ones. It is not against a body of uninterpreted data, radically thinned descriptions, that we must measure the cogency of our explications, but against the power of the scientific imagination to bring us into touch with the lives of strangers. It is not worth it, as Thoreau said, to go round the world to count the cats in Zanzibar.

Now, this proposition, that it is not in our interest to bleach human behaviour of the very properties that interest us before we begin to examine it, has sometimes been escalated into a larger claim: namely, that as it is only those properties that interest us, we need not attend, save cursorily, to behaviour at all. Culture is most effectively treated, the argument goes, purely as a symbolic system (the catch phrase is, "in its own terms"), by isolating its elements, specifying the internal relationships among those elements, and then characterizing the whole system in some general way—according to the core symbols around which it is organized, the underlying structures of which it is a surface expression, or the ideological principles upon which it is based. Though a distinct improvement over "learned behaviour" and "mental phenomena" notions of what culture is, and the source of some of the most powerful theoretical ideas in contemporary anthropology, this hermetical approach to things seems to me to run the danger (and increasingly to have been overtaken by it) of locking cultural analysis away from its proper object, the informal logic of actual life. There is little profit in extricating a concept from the defects of psychologism only to plunge it immediately into those of schematicism.

Behaviour must be attended to, and with some exactness, because it is through the flow of behaviour—or, more precisely, social action—that cultural forms find articulation. They find it as well of course, in various sorts of artifacts, and various states of consciousness; but these draw their meaning from the role they play (Wittgenstein would say their "use") in an ongoing pattern of life, not from any intrinsic relationships they bear to one another. It is what Cohen, the sheikh, and "Captain Dumari" were doing when they tripped over one another's purposes--pursuing trade, defending honor, establishing dominance—that created our pastoral drama, and that is what the drama is, therefore, "about." Whatever, or wherever, symbol systems "in their own terms" may be, we gain empirical access to them by inspecting events, not by arranging abstracted entities into unified patterns.

A further implication of this is that coherence cannot be the major test of validity for a cultural description. Cultural systems must have a minimal degree of coherence, else we would not call them systems; and, by observation, they normally have a great deal more. But there is nothing so coherent as a paranoid's delusion or a swindler's story. The force of our interpretations cannot rest, as they are now so often made to do, on the tightness with which they hold together, or the assurance with which they are argued. Nothing has done more, I think, to discredit cultural analysis than the construction of impeccable depictions of formal order in whose actual existence nobody can quite believe.

If anthropological interpretation is constructing a reading of what happens, then to divorce it from what happens—from what, in this time or that place, specific people say, what they do, what is done to them, from the whole vast business of the world—is to divorce it from its applications and render it vacant. A good interpretation of anything—a poem, a person, a history, a ritual, an institution, a society—takes us into the heart of that of which it is the interpretation. When it does not do that, but leads us instead somewhere else—into an admiration of its own elegance, of its author's cleverness, or of the beauties of Euclidean order—it may have its intrinsic charms; but it is something else than what the task at hand—figuring out what all that rigamarole with the sheep is about—calls for.

The rigamarole with the sheep—the sham theft of them, the reparative transfer of them, the political confiscation of them—is (or was) essentially a social discourse, even if, as I suggested earlier, one conducted in multiple tongues and as much in action as in words.

Claiming his *'ar*, Cohen invoked the trade pact; recognizing the claim, the sheikh challenged the offenders' tribe; accepting responsibility, the offenders' tribe paid the indemnity; anxious to make clear to sheikhs and peddlers alike who was now in charge here, the French showed the imperial hand. As in any discourse, code does not determine conduct, and what was actually said need not have been. Cohen might not have, given its illegitimacy in Protectorate eyes, chosen to press his claim. The sheikh might, for similar reasons, have rejected it. The offenders' tribe, still resisting French authority, might have decided to regard the raid as "real" and fight rather than negotiate. The French, were they more *habilé* and less *dur* (as, under Mareschal Lyautey's seigniorial tutelage, they later in fact became), might have permitted Cohen to keep his sheep, winking—as we say—at the continuance of the trade pattern and its limitation to their authority. And there are other possibilities: the Marmushans might have regarded the French action as to great an insult to bear and gone into dissidence themselves; the French might have attempted not just to clamp down on Cohen but to bring the sheikh himself more closely to heel; and Cohen might have concluded that between renegade Berbers and Beau Geste soldiers, driving trade in the Atlas highlands was no longer worth the candle and retired to the better-governed confines of the town. This, indeed, is more or less what happened, somewhat further along, as the Protectorate moved toward genuine sovereignty. But the point here is not to describe what did or did not take place in Morocco. (From this simple incident one can widen out into enormous complexities of social experience.) It is to demonstrate what a piece of anthropological interpretation consists in tracing the curve of a social discourse; fixing it into inspectable form.

The ethnographer "inscribes" social discourse; *he writes it down*. In so doing, he turns it from a passing event, which exists only in its own moment of occurrence, into an account, which exists in its inscriptions and can be reconsulted. The sheikh is long dead, killed in the process of being, as the French called it, "pacified"; "Captain Dumari," his pacifier, lives, retired to his souvenirs, in the south of France; and Cohen went last year, part refugee, part pilgrim, part dying patriarch, "home" to Israel. But what they, in my extended sense, "said" to one another on an Atlas plateau sixty years ago is—very far from perfectly—preserved for study. "What," Paul Ricoeur, from whom this whole idea of the inscription of action is borrowed and somewhat twisted, asks, "what does writing fix?"

Not the event of speaking, but the "said" of speaking, where we understand by the "said" of speaking that intentional exteriorization constitutive of the aim of discourse thanks to which the '*Sagen*'—the saying—wants to become the '*Aussage*': the enunciated. In short, what we write is the *noema* ["thought", "content," "gist"] of the speaking. It is the meaning of the speech event, not the event as event.

This is not itself so very "said"—if Oxford philosophers run to little stories, phenomenological ones run to large sentences; but it brings us anyway to a more precise answer to our generative question, "What does the ethnographer do?"—he writes. This, too, may seem a less than startling discovery, and to someone familiar with the current "literature," an implausible one. But as the standard answer to our question has been: "He observes, he records, he analyses"—a kind of "*veni-vidi-vici*"-conception of the matter—it may have more deep-going consequences than are at first apparent,—not the least of which is that distinguishing these three phases of knowledge-seeking may not, as a matter of fact, normally be possible; and, indeed, as autonomous "operations" they may not in fact exist.

The situation is even more delicate, because, as already noted, what we inscribe (or try to) is not raw social discourse, to which, because save very marginally or very specially, we are not actors, we do not have direct access, but only that small part of it which our informants can lead us into understanding. This is not as fatal as it sounds, for, in fact, not all Cretans are liars, and it is not necessary to know everything in order to understand something. But it does make the view of anthropological analysis as the conceptual manipulation of discovered facts, a logical reconstruction of a mere reality, seem rather lame. To set forth symmetrical crystals of significance, purified of the material complexity in which they were located, and then attribute their existence to autogenous principles of order, universal properties of the human mind, or vast, a priori *weltanschauungen* is to pretend a science that does not exist and imagine a reality that cannot be found. Cultural analysis is (or should be) guessing at meanings, assessing the guesses, and drawing explanatory conclusions from the better guesses, not discovering the *Continent of Meaning* and mapping out its bodiless landscape.

So, there are three characteristics of ethnographic description: it is interpretive; what it is interpretive of is the flow of social discourse; and the interpreting involved consists in trying to rescue the "said" of such discourse from its perishing occasions and fix it in perusable terms. The *kula* is gone or altered; but, for better or worse, *The Argonauts of the Western Pacific* remains.

So far as it has reinforced the anthropologist's impulse to engage himself with his informants as persons rather than as objects, the notion of "participant observation" has been a valuable one. But, to the degree it has lead the anthropologist to block from his view the very special, culturally bracketed nature of his own role and to imagine himself something more than an interested (in both senses of that word) sojourner, it has been our most powerful source of bad faith.

Western Pacific remains. But there is, in addition, a fourth characteristic of such description, at least as I practice it: it is microscopic.

This is not to say that there are no large-scale anthropological interpretations of whole societies, civilizations, world events, and so on. Indeed, it is such extension of our analyses to wider contexts that, along with their theoretical implications, recommends them to general attention and justifies our constructing them. No one really cares anymore, not even Cohen (well... maybe, Cohen), about those sheep as such.

History may have its unobtrusive turning points, "great noises in a little room"; but this little go-round was surely not one of them. It is merely to say that the anthropologist characteristically approaches such broader interpretations and more abstract analyses from the direction of exceedingly extended acquaintances with extremely small matters. He confronts the same grand realities that others—historians, economists, political scientists, sociologists—confront in more fateful settings: Power, Change, Faith, Oppression, Work, Passion, Authority, Beauty, Violence, Love, Prestige; but he confronts them in contexts obscure enough —places like Marmusha and lives like Cohen's—to take the capital letters off them. These all-too-human constancies, "those big words that make us all afraid," take a homely form in such homely contexts. But that is exactly the advantage. There are enough profundities in the world already. Yet, the problem of how to get from a collection of ethnographic miniatures on the order of our sheep story—an assortment of remarks and anecdotes—to wall-sized culturescapes of the nation, the epoch, the continent, or the civilization is not so easily passed over with vague allusions to the virtues of concreteness and the down-to-earth mind. For a science born in Indian tribes, Pacific islands, and African lineages and subsequently seized with grander ambitions, this has come to be a major methodological problem, and for the most part a badly handled one.

The models that anthropologists have themselves worked out to justify their moving from local truths to general visions have been, in fact, as responsible for undermining the effort as anything their critics—sociologists obsessed with sample sizes, psychologists with measures, or economists with aggregates—have been able to devise against them.

Of these, the two main ones have been: the Jonesville-is-the-USA "microcosmic" model; and the Easter-Island-is-a-testing-case "natural experiment" model. Either heaven in a grain of sand, or the farther shores of possibility. The Jonesville-is-America writ small (or America-is-Jonesville writ large) fallacy is so obviously one that the only thing that needs explanation is how people have managed to believe it and expected others to believe it. The notion that one can find the essence of national societies, civilizations, great religions, or whatever summed up and simplified in so-called "typical" small towns and villages is palpable nonsense. What one finds in small towns and villages is (alas) small-town or village life.

If localized, microscopic studies were really dependent for their greater relevance upon such a premise—that they captured the great world in the little—they wouldn't have any relevance.

But, of course, they are not. The locus of study is not the object of study. Anthropologists don't study villages (tribes, towns, neighbourhoods...); they study in villages. You can study different things in different places, and some things—for example, what colonial domination does to established frames of moral expectation you can best study in confined localities. But that doesn't make the place what it is you are studying. In the remoter provinces of Morocco and Indonesia I have wrestled with the same questions other social scientists have wrestled with in more central locations—for example, how comes it that men's most importunate claims to humanity are cast in the accents of group pride? and with about the same conclusiveness. One can add a dimension—one much needed in the present climate of size-up-and-solve social science; but that is all. There is a certain value, if you are going to run on about the exploitation of the masses in having seen a Javanese sharecropper turning earth in a tropical downpour or a Morrocan tailor embroidering kaftans by the light of a twenty-watt bulb.

But the notion that this gives you the thing entire (and elevates you to some moral vantage ground from which you can look down upon the ethically less privileged) is an idea which only someone too long in the bush could possibly entertain.

The "natural laboratory" notion has been equally pernicious, not only because the analogy is false—what kind of a laboratory is it where none of the parameters are manipulated?—but because it leads to a notion that the data derived from ethnographic studies are purer, or more fundamental, or more solid, or less conditioned (the most favoured word is "elementary") than those derived from other sorts of social inquiry.

The great natural variation of cultural forms is, of course, not only anthropology's great (and wasting) resource, but the ground of its deepest theoretical dilemma: how is such variation to be squared with the biological unity of the human species? But it is not, even metaphorically, experimental variation, because the context in which it occurs varies along with it, and it is not possible (though there are those who try) to isolate the y's from x's to write a proper function.

The famous studies purporting to show that the Oedipus complex was backwards in the Trobriands, sex roles were upside down in Tchambuli, and the Pueblo Indians lacked aggression (it is characteristic that they were all negative—"but not in the South"), are, whatever their empirical validity may or may not be, not "scientifically tested and approved" hypotheses.

They are interpretations, or misinterpretations, like any others, arrived at in the same way as any others, and as inherently inconclusive as any others, and the attempt to invest them with the authority of physical experimentation is but methodological sleight of hand. Ethnographic findings are not privileged, just particular: another country heard from. To regard them as anything more (*or anything* less) than that distorts both them and their implications, which are far profounder than mere primitivity, for social theory.

Another country heard from: the reason that protracted descriptions of distant sheep raids (and a really good ethnographer would have gone into what kind of sheep they were) have general relevance is that they present the sociological mind with bodied stuff on which to feed. The important thing about the anthropologist's findings is their complex specificness, their circumstantiality. It is with the kind of material produced by long-term, mainly (though not exclusively) qualitative, highly participative, and almost obsessively fine-comb field study in confined contexts that the mega-concepts with which contemporary social science is afflicted—legitimacy, modernization, integration, conflict, charisma, structure,... meaning—can be given the sort of sensible actuality that makes it possible to think not only realistically and *concretely* about them, but, what is more important, creatively and imaginatively *with* them.

The methodological problem which the microscopic nature of ethnography presents is both real and critical. But it is not to be resolved by regarding a remote locality as the world in a teacup or as the sociological equivalent of a cloud chamber. It is to be resolved—or, anyway, decently kept at bay—by realizing that social actions are comments on more than themselves; that where an interpretation comes from does not determine where it can be impelled to go. Small facts speak to large issues, winks to epistemology, or sheep raids to revolution, because they are made to.

Which brings us, finally, to theory. The besetting sin of interpretive approaches to anything—literature, dreams, symptoms, culture—is that they tend to resist, or to be permitted to resist, conceptual articulation and thus to escape systematic modes of assessment. You either grasp an interpretation or you do not, see the point of it or you do not, accept it or you do not. Imprisoned in the immediacy of its own detail, it is presented as self-validating, or, worse, as validated by the supposedly developed sensitivities of the person who presents it; any attempt to cast what it says in terms other than its own is regarded as a travesty—as, the anthropologist's severest term of moral abuse, ethnocentric.

For a field of study which, however timidly (though I, myself, am not timid about the matter at all), asserts itself to be a science, this just will not do. There is no reason why the conceptual structure of a cultural interpretation should be any less formulable, and thus less susceptible to explicit canons of appraisal, than that of, say, a biological observation or a physical experiment—no reason except that the terms in which such formulations can be cast are, if not wholly nonexistent, very nearly so. We are reduced to insinuating theories because we lack the power to state them.

At the same time, it must be admitted that there are a number of characteristics of cultural interpretation which make the theoretical development of it more than usually difficult. The first is the need for theory to stay rather closer to the ground than tends to be the case in sciences more able to give themselves over to imaginative abstraction. Only short flights of ratiocination tend to be effective in anthropology; longer ones tend to drift off into logical dreams, academic bemusements with formal symmetry. The whole point of a semiotic approach to culture is, as I have said, to aid us in gaining access to the conceptual world in which our subjects live so that we can, in some extended sense of the term, converse with them. The tension between the pull of this need to penetrate an unfamiliar universe of symbolic action and the requirements of technical advance in the theory of culture, between the need to grasp and the need to analyse, is, as a result, both necessarily great and essentially irremovable. Indeed, the further theoretical development goes, the deeper the tension gets. This is the first condition for cultural theory: it is not its own master. As it is unseverable from the immediacies thick description presents, its freedom to shape itself in terms of its internal logic is rather limited. What generality it contrives to achieve grows out of the delicacy of its distinctions, not the sweep of its abstractions.

And from this follows a peculiarity in the way, as a simple matter of empirical fact, our knowledge of culture (cultures, a culture) grows: in spurts. Rather than following a rising curve of cumulative findings, cultural analysis breaks up into a disconnected yet coherent sequence of bolder and bolder sorts. Studies do build on other studies, not in the sense that they take up where the others leave off, but in the sense that, better informed and better conceptualized, they plunge more deeply into the same things. Every serious cultural analysis starts from a sheer beginning and ends where it manages to get before exhausting its intellectual impulse. Previously discovered facts are mobilized, previously developed concepts used, previously formulated hypotheses tried out; but the movement is not from already proven theorems to newly proven ones, it is from an awkward fumbling for the most elementary understanding to a supported claim that one has achieved that and surpassed it. A study is an advance if it is more incisive—whatever that may mean—than those that preceded it; but it less stands on their shoulders than, challenged and challenging, runs by their side.

It is for this reason, among others, that the essay, whether of thirty pages or three hundred, has seemed the natural genre in which to present cultural interpretations and the theories sustaining them, and why, if one looks for systematic treatises in the field, one is so soon disappointed, the more so if one finds any. Even inventory articles are rare here, and anyway of hardly more than bibliographical interest. The major theoretical contributions not only lie in specific studies—that is true in almost any field—but they are very difficult to abstract from such studies and integrate into anything one might call "culture theory" as such. Theoretical formulations hover so low over the interpretations they govern that they don't make much sense or hold much interest apart from them.. This is so, not because they are not general (if they are not general, they are not theoretical), but because, stated independently of their applications, they seem either commonplace or vacant.

One can, and this in fact is how the field progresses conceptually, take a line of theoretical attack developed in connection with one exercise in ethnographic interpretation and employ it in another, pushing it forward to greater precision and broader relevance; but one cannot write a "General Theory of Cultural Interpretation." Or, rather, one can, but there appears to be little profit in it, because the essential task of theory building here is not to codify abstract regularities but to make thick description possible, not to generalize across cases but to generalize within them.

To generalize within cases is usually called, at least in medicine and depth psychology, clinical inference. Rather than beginning with a set of observations and attempting to subsume them under a governing law, such inference begins with a set of (presumptive) signifies and attempts to place them within an intelligible frame. Measures are matched to theoretical predictions, but symptoms (even when they are measured) are scanned for theoretical peculiarities—that is, they are diagnosed. In the study of culture the signifies are not symptoms or clusters of symptoms, but symbolic acts or clusters of symbolic acts, and the aim is not therapy but the analysis of social discourse. But the way in which theory is used—to ferret out the unapparent import of things—is the same.

Thus we are lead to the second condition of cultural theory: it is not, at least in the strict meaning of the term, predictive. The diagnostician doesn't predict measles; he decides that someone has them, or at the very most clincially decides that someone is rather likely shortly to get them. But this limitation, which is real enough, has commonly been both misunderstood and exaggerated, because it has been taken to mean that cultural interpretation is merely post facto: that, like the peasant in the old story, we first shoot the holes in the fence and then paint the bull's-eyes around them. It is hardly to be denied that there is a good deal of that sort of thing around, some of it in prominent places. It is to be denied, however, that it is the inevitable outcome of a clinical approach to the use of theory.

It is true that in the clinical style of theoretical formulation, conceptualization is directed toward the task of generating interpretations of matters already in hand, not toward projecting outcomes of experimental manipulations or deducing future states of a determined system. But that does not mean that theory has only to fit (or, more carefully, to generate cogent interpretations of) realities past; it has also to survive—intellectually survive—realities to come. Although we formulate our interpretation of an outburst of winking or an instance of sheep-raiding after its occurrence, sometimes long after, the theoretical framework in terms of which such an interpretation is made must be capable of continuing to yield defensible interpretations as new social phenomena swim into view. Although one starts any effort at thick description, beyond the obvious and superficial, from a state of general bewilderment as to what the devil is going on—trying to find one's feet—one does not start (or ought not) intellectually empty-handed. Theoretical ideas are not created wholly anew in each study; as I have said, they are adopted from other, related studies, and, refined in the process, applied to new interpretive problems. If they cease being useful with respect to such problems, they tend to stop being used and are more or less abandoned. If they continue being useful, throwing up new understandings, they are further elaborated and go on being used.

Such a view of how theory functions in an interpretive science suggests that the distinction, relative in any case, that appears in the experimental or observational sciences between "description" and "explanation" appears here as one, even more relative, between "inscription" ("thick description") and "specification" ("diagnosis")—between setting down the meaning particular social actions have for the actors whose actions they are, and stating, as explicitly as we can manage, what the knowledge thus attained demonstrates about the society in which it is found and, beyond that, about social life as such. Our double task is to uncover the conceptual structures that inform our subjects' acts, the "said" of social discourse, and to construct a system of analysis in whose terms what is generic to those structures, what belongs to them because they are what they are, will stand out against the other determinants of human behaviour. In ethnography, the office of theory is to provide a vocabulary in which what symbolic action has to say about itself—that is, about the role of culture in human life—can be expressed.

Aside from a couple of orienting pieces concerned with more foundational matters, it is in such a manner that theory operates in the essays collected here. A repertoire of very general, made-in-the-academy concepts and systems of concepts—"integration?" "rationalization," "symbol," "ideology," "ethos," "revolution," "identity," "metaphor," "structure," "ritual," "world view," "actor," "function," "sacred," and, of course, "culture" itself—is woven into the body of thick-description ethnography in the hope of rendering mere occurrences scientifically eloquent. The aim is to draw large conclusions from small, but very densely textured facts; to support broad assertions about the role of culture in the construction of collective life by engaging them exactly with complex specifics.

Thus it is not only interpretational that goes all the way down to the most immediate observational level: the theory upon which such interpretation conceptually depends does so also. My interest in Cohen's story, like Ryle's in winks, grew out of some very general notions indeed. The "confusion of tongues" model the view that social conflict is not something that happens when, out of weakness, indefiniteness, obsolescence, or neglect, cultural forms cease to operate, but rather something which happens when, like burlesqued winks, such forms are pressed by unusual situations or unusual intentions to operate in unusual ways—is not an idea I got from Cohen's story. It is one, instructed by colleagues, students, and predecessors, I brought to it.

Our innocent-looking "note in a bottle" is more than a portrayal of the frames of meaning of Jewish peddlers, Berber warriors, and French proconsuls, or even of their mutual interference. It is an argument that to rework the pattern of social relationships is to rearrange the coordinates of the experienced world. Society's forms are culture's substance.

There is an Indian story—at least I heard it as an Indian story—about an Englishman who, having been told that the world rested on a platform which rested on the back of an elephant which rested in turn on the back of a turtle, asked (perhaps he was an ethnographer; it is the way they behave), what did the turtle rest on? Another turtle. And that turtle ? "Ah, Sahib, after that it is turtles all the way down."

Such, indeed, is the condition of things. I do not know how long it would be profitable to meditate on the encounter of Cohen, the sheikh, and "Dumari" (the period has perhaps already been exceeded); but I do know that however long I did so I would not get anywhere near to the bottom of it. Nor have I ever gotten anywhere near to the bottom of anything I have ever written about, either in the essays below or elsewhere. Cultural analysis is intrinsically incomplete. And, worse than that, the more deeply it goes the less complete it is. It is a strange science whose most telling assertions are its most tremulously based, in which to get somewhere with the matter at hand is to intensify the suspicion, both your own and that of others, that you are not quite getting it right. But that, along with plaguing subtle people with obtuse questions, is what being an ethnographer is like.

There are a number of ways to escape this—turning culture into folklore and collecting it, turning it into traits and counting it, turning it into institutions and classifying it, turning it into structures and toying with it. But they are escapes. The fact is that to commit oneself to a semiotic concept of culture and an interpretive approach to the study of it is to commit oneself to a view of ethnographic assertion as, to borrow. B. Gallie's by now famous phrase, "essentially contestable." Anthropology, or at least interpretive anthropology, is a science whose progress is marked less by a perfection of consensus than by a refinement of debate. What gets better is the precision with which we vex each other.

This is very difficult to see when one's attention is being monopolized by a single party to the argument. Monologues are of little value here, because there are no conclusions to be reported; there is merely a discussion to be sustained. Insofar as the essays here collected have any importance, it is less in what they say than what they are witness to: an enormous increase in interest, not only in anthropology, but in social studies generally, in the role of symbolic forms in human life. Meaning, this elusive and ill-defined pseudoentity we were once more than content to leave philosophers and literary critics to fumble with, has now come back into the heart of our discipline. Even Marxists are quoting Cassirer; even positivists, Kenneth Burke.

My own position in the midst of all this has been to try to resist subjectivism on the one hand and cabbalism on the other, to try to keep the analysis of symbolic forms as closely tied as I could to concrete social events and occasions, the public world of common life, and to organize it in such a way that the connections between theoretical formulations and descriptive interpretations were unobscured by appeals to dark sciences. I have never been impressed by the argument that, as complete objectivity is impossible in these matters (as, of course, it is), one might as well let one's sentiments run loose. As Robert Solow has remarked, that is like saying that as a perfectly aseptic environment is impossible, one might as well conduct surgery in a sewer. Nor, on the other hand, have I been impressed with claims that structural linguistics, computer engineering, or some other advanced form of thought is going to enable us to understand men without knowing them. Nothing will discredit a semiotic approach to culture more quickly than allowing it to drift into a combination of intuitionism and alchemy, no matter how elegantly the intuitions are expressed or how modern the alchemy is made to look.

The danger that cultural analysis, in search of all-too-deep-lying turtles, will lose touch with the hard surfaces of life—with the political, economic, stratificatory realities within which men are everywhere contained—and with the biological and physical necessities on which those surfaces rest, is an ever-present one. The only defence against it, and against, thus, turning cultural analysis into a kind of sociological aestheticism, is to train such analysis on such realities and such necessities in the first place. It is thus that I have written about nationalism, about violence, about identity, about human nature, about legitimacy, about revolution, about ethnicity, about urbanization, about status, about death, about time, and most of all about particular attempts by particular peoples to place these things in some sort of comprehensible, meaningful frame.

To look at the symbolic dimensions of social action—art, religion, ideology, science, law, morality, common sense—is not to turn away from the existential dilemmas of life for some empyrean realm of deemotionalized forms; it is to plunge into the midst of them. The essential vocation of interpretive anthropology is not to answer our deepest questions, but to make available to us answers that others, guarding other sheep in other valleys, have given, and thus to include them in the consultable record of what man has said.

3

Cultural Power

Cultural power, also called cultural hegemony, cultural imperialism and cultural colonialism, is generally referred to as imposed cultural values between states and between ethnic groups. This concept first put forward by Gramsci in the 1930s revealed the "super-political veil" of the traditional concept of culture. He held that cultural hegemony was an indispensable ruling form.

To rule civil society, the ruling class must draw support from intellectuals and cultural institutions to make its ethics, politics and cultural values a universally accepted code of conduct and make the broad masses of the people freely agree with the social lifestyle of the basic ruling group. In fact, before that, Western colonialists used cultural power as their powerful weapon in the international arena. Wherever they went, they recklessly destroyed local civilizations, denied or changed local moral norms and forcibly judged the destiny of other countries and ethnic groups by their own cultural values. History is developing, the times are forging ahead and peace and development have become the themes of the current age. But cultural power as a phenomenon contrary to the times has not yet disappeared from the scene. Though it has come by the barbarous and bloody means the colonialists had adopted, its essence remains as before.

The Historical Background of Cultural Power

Cultural power has not emerged and developed accidentally, but has a certain background in the times.

An Age of the Emergence of Culture

The end of the Cold War has entailed a softening of fierce military threats in international relations and a relaxation of ideological confrontation between blocs. Many countries have begun economic reforms and contacts between countries and between ethnic groups have increasingly been strengthened, thus enhancing awareness of civilization. Whether a country is strong or weak is measured no longer only from the political and military perspective, but in terms of its comprehensive national strength. This includes not only such factors as economy and military affairs, science and technology, and natural resources, but also the essential spiritual factors of national culture, will, character and spirit. It includes also the integration and balance of those essential factors.

This clearly enhances the importance of culture, which now becomes one of the main factors determining a country's strength, along with politics, economy, military affairs, science and technology. Because of changes in world political and military situations, countries with a strong "hegemonic awareness" have turned their attention to the cultural field and attempted to unify the world with their cultural values in order to achieve results they cannot reach through political struggles and military force. The modernized media have facilitated this enabling cultural power to emerge at this historical moment and become a very prominent post-Cold War cultural phenomenon between countries and ethnic groups.

The New World Pattern Demands New Cultural Values

At present, the world pattern is moving towards multi-polarization. First, the position of the U.S. as the sole superpower is declining. Although it has tried to move from leadership of the West to that of the world, its internal and external contradictions are numerous and its abilities fall short of its wishes. Second, Western Europe has formed a community to save the central position of the West; it has moved from being a follower to being a competitor of the U.S. Third, Japan has continued to say "no" to the U.S.; it has competed fiercely with the U.S. economically and displayed remarkable politically ability. Fourth, Russia has inherited most of the assets of the former Soviet Union, especially its military force; it remains strong, though its vitality has been sapped due to the disintegration of the former Soviet Union. Fifth, China has developed rapidly since the beginning of its reform and opening and is gradually manifesting its strength. In the world, from the perspective of comprehensive national strength, the U.S. ranks first; militarily, the U.S. and Russia predominate; in economy, the U.S., Japan and Europe form a tripod; politically, there are five power centres, the U.S., Russia, Europe, Japan and China. The above pattern has appeared in embryonic form; it is difficult to determine how many poles the world will be divided into in the future.

Under the situation of a multi-polar world pattern, mutual respect and tolerance between countries appear especially important. As early as 1988, when meeting Indian Prime Minister Rajiv Gandhi, Deng Xiaoping pointed out, "Two things have to be done at the same time. One is to establish a new international political order; the other is to establish a new international economic order." As for establishing a new international order, we should take the Five Principles of Peaceful Coexistence as norms for international relations. However, the U.S. has not abandoned the effort to establish a "uni-polar" world dominated by itself. It assumes the responsibility of leading the world, promoting U.S. values and safeguarding U.S. interests all over the world. The essence of the so-called U.S. responsibility for leadershipis to continue to establish U.S. hegemonic position in the world. Maintaining this position and advancing U.S. values, including cultural values, are twin aims. Maintaining the former is beneficial to promoting the latter, while promoting the latter maintains the former. At the moment when a new world pattern is in the shaping, the U.S. is stepping up pursuit of cultural power as part of its plan for acting as a "world leader".

Historical Source of Cultural Power

Deep-rooted Western Centralism

In research on world civilizations, many Western philosophers and historians have elaborated the following view: In the world, there is only one real civilization, that is, Western civilization. Other civilizations either lack vitality or have converged into Western civilization, which is a "universal civilization suiting everyone" just as Western values are global values. For instance, the great philosopher, Hegel once stood on the "holy" world philosophic rostrum in Europe and solemnly foretold with European pride that the development of the heart of the history of humankind like the route of the sun, rises in the East and falls in the West. But after falling in the West, it will no longer rise in the East, for the West occupies the centre of the world. British writer Rudyard Kipling nakedly declared that the burden of the whites lies in subjecting the East to the high British civilization either by belief or by violence.

The dissemination of modern Western civilization accompanied the imperialist aggression and expansion. Western centralists deny that the development of any cultural type is the result of choice according to its own distinct cultural background, conditions and needs. They hold stubbornly that only their approach to the world, value standard and pattern of behaviour is correct and civil.

They have never seriously listened to the voice from the East and have always sized up the East at a distance and from a height. Even in the face of the fact that in recent years East Asian countries have risen one after another and accomplished economic miracles, some Western thinkers still hold a suspicious and negative attitude to East Asia's important role on the world. They even think that this is the result of importing Western culture.

The formation of Western centralism is based first on the sense of superiority resulting from the development of Western industrial revolution. Then it reflects the fact that Western Christians consider themselves to be the chosen of God who must shoulder the mission of disseminating civilization to the whole world. Hence, they are always overweening, like to play the role of "Savior," and cannot tolerate any phenomenon contrary to Western cultural values. As early as 90 years ago, Sun Yat-sen acutely pointed out that Europeans regarded themselves as disseminators of orthodox cultures and posed as cultural masters. Any cultural development or independent thinking outside the European was regarded as a revolt. This was an "overbearing culture".

Lingering Cold War "Customs"

In the Cold War period hegemonic countries confronted each other as enemies. Since then geopolitical enemies no longer existed, but by habit and out of their political and economic needs, countries accustomed to the Cold War shifted their struggles to the more extensive field of civilization and culture, and extended their target to the whole Third World. They vowed to conduct "a war without gun smoke" with all non-Western civilizations and attempted to use their value standards to unify the world; they have raised civilizational and cultural issues as a new excuse for interfering in other countries' internal affairs.

The U.S. regards the drastic changes in East Europe and the disintegration of the former Soviet Union as a victory of the tactics of peaceful evolution or of U.S. cultural values. In his agenda, Bush wrote that political and economic ties have been favoured by the attraction of U.S. culture for the whole world; this is a new "soft power". Some important U.S. Government officials have also put forward in their speeches about foreign policy an "expansion strategy" of spreading the market-oriented family of democratic countries to the rest of the world. Under this thinking, the U.S. has actively intervened into Latin America to build a so-called "democratized hemisphere"; it has also set up "Radio Free Asia" based on the earlier "Radio Free Europe" with ulterior motives. The U.S. has made it clear that Radio Free Asia will also play a proper role in the ideological field. Its motive in pushing cultural power and making Cold War noises is all too clear: the Cold War has passed away as an era, but its habits remain.

Cultural Power Contrary to the Trend of World Cultural Development

World Cultural Pluralism

Cultural connotations are very rich. Its central content is a deep value system, a characteristic national psychology evolved over a long history, and a kind of lifestyle. Different economic, political, historical and geographic environments, climate conditions and "genetic codes" have caused many differences between various ethnic groups in custom, habit, ideology and concept. In this view a cultural historical typology takes the expression of the diversity of the human lifestyles as its mission and holds that culture is plural. Development of any cultural type is the result of choice and is created according to its own cultural law, cultural background, historical conditions and realistic needs; this develops various cultural modes in reality. However, some Western centralist scholars often mechanically look on and analyse the complicated reality of other cultural types according to the Western model of cultural development, and deny the diversity of various cultures and their ability to choose their own development road. This is quite absurd and not in conformity with objective facts.

As all know, four countries with ancient civilizations of different cultural types have made great contributions to world culture. Other countries' national cultures have also more or less enriched the cultural treasure house. Since modern times, because of the industrial revolution in the West, "Western centred theory" and "Western cultural superiority theory" have prevailed for a time. Western cultural values long occupied a dominant position in the world. Modernization became almost a synonym for Westernization. Western culture naturally has its own strong points, but is not universally applicable and cannot be imposed on countries and peoples with different national conditions.

"East Asian economic miracles" have presented a development road different from the West. Though much influenced by Western culture, some countries are quite different on a series of issues such as ideology, concept and interrelations between individuals, family, the collective and the state. Even Japan actively absorbing Western culture has always combined the Japanese spirit with Western learning and tenaciously defended its national spirit. Under the leadership of the Communist Party of China, guided by Marxism, China has had as its objective the realization of socialism with Chinese characteristics. Especially since the beginning of its reform and opening China has insisted on the road of building socialism with Chinese characteristics. It has made giant strides in socialist modernization and formulated socialist culture and values with Chinese characteristics, attracting world attention. These facts strongly prove that in contrast to the opinion of

Western scholars, it is not only Western culture that can help bring about a sole successful mode of modernization in the history of humankind.

Economic success has strengthened the cultural self-confidence of East Asian and Southeast Asian countries, which no longer consider that the "Western moon seems more full" and have clearly recognized that Western values are not adapted to Asia. But they do not rule out an absorption of the strong points of Western cultures. Some insightful Western personages have begun to realize the limitations and drawbacks of Western culture. Some have pointed out that the problem of Western culture is that it can successfully reduce mortality from diseases, but it can not reduce the suicide rate from the collapse of values. They advocate learning from ancient Oriental culture, resulting in an "Oriental fad" in some regions.

Each culture has its inherent value. There is only difference between cultures, but no distinction between the good and the bad. Taking Western cultural values as the sole choice of the whole of humankind is unrealistic, unscientific and unreasonable. The world is developing towards a multi-polarization that promotes cultural pluralism. With the world economic centre moving eastward, it is fully possible for East Asia to become the third largest cultural centre in the world, following North America and West Europe.

Cultural Blend and Conflict

Each culture has its own national characteristics. With the construction and hookup of information superhighways and the close interrelation between the economies of the world, different countries and ethnic groups have forged unprecedented interrelations. This greatly increases the chance of exchange and collision between different countries.

Generally speaking, in contacts with different cultures, one ethnic group always measures the others by its own value standards, either deepening understanding and blending or broadening the divergence and causing friction and conflict. Neither blend nor conflict is absolute; there is conflict in the process of blending, while there is slow mutual infiltration tending towards blending even in the process of conflict. This is an unavoidable phenomenon in contacts between different cultures. One major advance in the modern cultural theory is that people universally realize that cultures are mixed, different, interrelated and interdependent. Edward Said held that the development and maintenance of each culture needs another different and competitive culture, that is, the existence of an alter ego. Undifferentiated culture is unrealistic and can be said to be lopsided.

Divergence does not mean conflict, while blend does not mean the elimination of national individuality. Correct realization of blend and conflict in cultural development lies in exploring how to make different cultures blend and avoid conflict; this is the requirement of peaceful development in human society. Historically, there have existed many civilizations such as Islam, Confucianism and Buddhism on the Asian continent. Over thousands of years they have been marked by exchange and coexistence. Only after meeting with Western civilization, have relations between rule and subjection appeared. Since the beginning of its reform and opening, China has felt that it can absorb advanced technology and managerial experience favourable to its modernization drive in contact with other (including Western) civilizations. Facts have proved the coexistence of different civilizations to be possible. Here the key lies in the attitude of mutual respect, the position of equality, and in the full realization that this is a two-way choice. Marx showed how history transfers into world history by bringing to light from the angle of productive forces the importance of the extension of universal human contacts to cultural accumulation and evolution. We must realize that the interaction between Eastern and Western civilizations is the fundamental condition for the progress of humankind. The 21 century is an era pf the globalization of the coexistence of plural cultures and requires a corresponding "global awareness". The whole world cannot have but one kind of cultural values and one voice. Exchanges, learning from each other's strong points and blending between different cultures will promote friendship between peoples of various countries and ethnic groups. But taking an overweening attitude to push cultural power goes against the trend of the times; it is bound to trigger or intensify contradictions and conflicts between different cultures and to create a tense international situation.

The "Clash of Civilizations" Theory is a Cultural Power Theory

After the Cold War, some Western scholars have actively cooperated with U.S.-led Western countries in pushing cultural power on developing countries and put forward in succession such theories as "the end of history", "the clash of civilizations" and "post-colonialism". They have attempted to create theoretical foundations for their cultural infiltration and expansion under the cloak of rationality and legality. Among these views, the "clash of civilizations" theory has had the most extensive influence. It holds that in the next century, conflict between civilizations will supplant ideological and other forms of conflict as the dominant form of global conflict. We must analyse this theory in order to detect its crux.

Behind Heavy Heartedness

First of all, it must be noted that here the concept of civilization is basically equal to the concept of culture. The two can be interchanged. For example, "Confucian civilization" can also be called "Confucian culture". Civilization is an existential form of culture. Then to what does the "clash of civilizations" theory specifically refer? Professor Samuel Huntington of Harvard University wrote in the article "The Clash of Civilizations?" that non-Western civilizations no longer remain objects, but have become actors. The centerpiece of international politics will become the interaction between the West and non-Western civilizations. In the near future, the focus of conflict will concentrate on relations between the West and some Islamic-Confucian countries. He means that non-Western civilizations have gone up on the international stage and stood up to the West as equals, leading to cultural conflict.

In essence, this is entirely a cultural power theory that regards Western civilization as the orthodox one which embodies the "absolute spirit", to which other civilizations should be subjected. Once non-Western civilizations have an independent spirit and move from being "objects" to "actors", there will be a deluge of rebellion which should be "contained" and struck down. This thinking represents the aspirations of some Western centralists. For instance, an article in the German newspaper *Frankfurter Allgemeine Zeitung* said that the clash of civilizations between Islam and the West is obvious and that political Islam seeks to replace Western civilization so that Islamic civilization occupies the world's leading position. An article in German *Die Welt* also held that Oriental culture is weakening the infiltration of Western ideology. It pointed out that with the end of the Cold War various civilized societies outside the West seem to emit a new radiant force, which is crippling the imported principles of Western life and strengthening local cultural awareness.

As described above, world culture is moving towards diversification. There is not only conflict, but also a blending of different cultures in their exchanges and interchanges. The key lies in mutual respect and inclusiveness, which is beneficial to cultural blending and coexistence. The "clash of civilizations" theory has absolutized local ethnic and religious cultural conflicts in history and reality. It has turned a blind eye to the megatrend of peaceful coexistence, exchange and development between ethnic groups and cultures. In cultural development history, while Western culture has made great contributions to human civilization, Oriental culture is also a gem of human ideology. They should exchange with each other and learn from each other's strong points in order to benefit humankind, rather than be used to repel each other and contend for hegemony.

If Not Power, What?

The "clash of civilizations" theory has naturally been criticized in many quarters. For this reason, S. Huntington wrote another article entitled "If Not Civilization, What?: Paradigms of the Post-Cold War World", reiterating that civilization is the source of post-Cold War conflicts.

Cultural power is bound to accompany political power. For example, U.S. foreign policy has always included a plan of disseminating U.S. cultural values to the rest of the world, of which exporting the mode of U.S. political development is one of the major elements. In the international political arena, the U.S. has always brandished a menacing club, now sanctioning this country, now punishing that country. The world has on occasion been divided into four types of countries — "law-abiding," "newly-emerging," "barbarous" and "gloomy". To guarantee U.S. interests, it has been considered imperative to have an operable international system in conformity with U.S. standards. The U.S. has been regarding China as its potential rival and after the "clash of civilizations" theory very many pages about the so-called "China threat" theory have appeared in some overseas newspapers and periodicals. China has always adhered to the Five Principles of Peaceful Coexistence and advocated settling international disputes through peaceful means. In its modern process of seeking national and ethnic interests, it has never expanded to other regions and fields outside its homeland. Where did the "China threat" come from?

The so-called human rights issue is a political slogan of which the U.S. is most fond and a main means by which the U.S. pursues its cultural power. It accuses Singapore of being an Oriental authoritarian state on the grounds of infringing on human rights. For this reason, Lee Kuan Yew has made a series of statements. On the one hand, he expounds the divergence between concepts of family, society and state in Oriental civilization and those in Western civilization. On the other hand, he criticizes Western values based upon individualism and various problems occurring in U.S. society.

However, the U.S. has managed with difficulty to subject other countries to its cultural values. Time and again it has issued human rights reports with vicious slanders and charges against human rights situations in Eastern countries, especially China, interfering in other countries' internal affairs. This has aroused dissatisfaction and resistance from many countries. In reply to the question: "if not civilization, what?" aimed at establishing the dominant position of Western civilization, we would counter with a question "if not power, what?".

Marxist cultural theory, based on the fundamentals of historical materialism, fully affirms the diversity of various ethnic and social cultures and firmly opposes an absolutization of any culture. It opposes cultural expansionism and rejects cultural relativism. As early as the *Communist Manifesto*, Marx and Engels predicted the trend of world integration:

In place of the old local and national seclusion and self-sufficiency, we have intercourse in every direction, universal interdependence of nations. And as in material, so also in intellectual production. The intellectual creations of individual nations become common property. National one-sidedness and narrow-mindedness become more and more impossible and from the numerous national and local literatures, there arises a world literature.

Today, when the world has become a "global village", all ethnic cultures should join hands in creating a more rational and healthy world culture based on maintaining and developing individuality.

If you are a woman and you have ever walked into a men's meeting, or a person of colour and have walked into a white organization, or a child who walked into the principal's office, or a Jew or Muslim who entered a Christian space then you know what it is like to walk into a culture of power that is not your own. You may feel insecure, unsafe, disrespected, unseen or marginalized. You know you have to tread carefully.

Whenever one group of people accumulates more power than another group, the more powerful group creates an environment that places its members at the cultural centre and other groups at the margins.

People in the more powerful group (the "in-group") are accepted as the norm, so if you are in that group it can be very hard for you to see the benefits you receive.

Since I'm male and I live in a culture in which men have more social, political, and economic power than women, I often don't notice that women are treated differently than I am. I'm inside a male culture of power. I expect to be treated with respect, to be listened to, and to have my opinions valued. I expect to be welcomed. I expect to see people like me in positions of authority. I expect to find books and newspapers that are written by people like me, that reflect my perspective, and that show me in central roles. I don't necessarily notice that the women around me are treated less respectfully, ignored, or silenced; that they are not visible in positions of authority nor welcomed in certain spaces; and that they are charged more for a variety of goods and services and are not always safe in situations where I feel perfectly comfortable.

Remember when you were a young person entering a space that reflected an adult culture of power a classroom, store, or office where adults were in charge? What let you know that you were on adult turf, that adults were at the centre of power? Some of the things I remember are that adults were in control. They made the decisions. They might be considerate enough to ask me what I thought, but they did not have to take my concerns into account. I could be dismissed at any time, so I learned to be cautious. I could look around and see what was on the walls, what music was being played, what topics were being discussed, and most important, who made those decisions, and I knew that this was an adult culture of power.

I felt I was under scrutiny. I had to change my behaviour how I dressed ("pull up your pants", "tuck in your shirt"), how I spoke ("speak up", "don't mumble"), even my posture ("Sit up, don't slouch", "look me in the eye when I'm talking to you") so that I would be accepted and heard. I couldn't be as smart as I was or I'd be considered a smart aleck. I had to learn the adults' code, talk about what they wanted to talk about, and find allies among them adults who would speak up for my needs in my absence. Sometimes I had to cover up my family background and religion in order to be less at risk from adult disapproval. And if there was any disagreement or problem between an adult and myself, I had little credibility. The adult's word was almost always believed over mine.

The effects on young people of an adult culture of power are similar to the effects on people of colour of a white culture of power or the effects on women of a male culture of power. As an adult I rarely notice that I am surrounded by an adult culture of power, which often puts young people and their cultures at a severe disadvantage as they are judged, valued, and given credibility or not by adults on adult terms. Similarly, as a white person, when I'm driving on the freeway I am unlikely to notice that people of colour are being pulled over based on skin colour. Or when I am in a store I am unlikely to notice that people of colour are being followed, not being served as well, or being charged more for the same items. I assume that everyone can vote as easily as I can and that everyone's vote counts. I am never asked where I am from (and this would be true even if I had stepped off the boat yesterday). In a society that proclaims equal opportunity I may not even believe that other people are being paid less than I am for the same work, or being turned away from jobs and housing because of the colour of their skin. When I am in public spaces, the music played in the background, the art on the walls, the language spoken, the layout of the space, the design of the buildings are all things I might not even notice because, as a white person, I am so comfortable with them. If I did notice them I would probably consider them bland, culturally neutral items. Most of the time I am so much inside the white culture of power, it is so invisible to me, that I have to rely on people of colour to point out to me what it looks like, what it feels like, and what impact it has on them.

We can learn to notice the culture of power around us. Recently I was giving a talk at a large Midwestern university and was shown to my room in the hotel run by the university's hotel management department. When I had put my suitcase down and hung up my clothes, I looked around the room. There were two pictures on the wall. One was of a university baseball team from many years ago 22 white men wearing their team uniforms. The other picture was of a science lab class 14 students, 13 white men and 1 white woman dressed in lab coats and working at lab benches. In total I had 35 white men and 1 white woman on the walls of my room. "This clearly tells me who's in charge at this university," I said to myself, and it would probably send an unwelcoming, cautionary message to many people of colour and white women who stayed in that room that they could expect to be excluded from the culture of power in this institution. I mentioned the composition of the pictures to the hotel management and referred to it again in my talk the next day.

The problem with a culture of power is that it reinforces the prevailing hierarchy. When we are inside a culture of power we expect to have things our way, the way we are most comfortable with. We may go through life complacent in our monoculturalism, not even aware of the limits of our perspectives, the gaps in our knowledge, the inadequacy of our understanding. We remain unaware of the superior status and opportunities we have simply because we're white, or male, or ablebodied, or heterosexual. Of course a culture of power also dramatically limits the ability of those on the margins to participate in an event, a situation, or an organization. They are only able to participate on unfavorable terms, at others' discretion, which puts them at a big disadvantage. They often have to give up or hide much of who they are to participate in the dominant culture. And if there are any problems it becomes very easy to identify the people on the margins as the source of those problems and blame or attack them rather than the problem itself.

Every organization has work to do to become more inclusive. I want to focus on some ways that groups often fail to include members of our country's most marginalized membersthose marginalized by economic status, physical ability, and English language ability.

Often, when groups talk about diversity issues, they address those issues of race, gender, and sexual orientation that are most visible. Without an understanding of how class limits people's ability to participate in organizations a group may end up with a remarkably diverse group of middle class participants. Those who are homeless, poor, single parents, working two jobs, or poorly educated (and many people fall into more than one of these categories) are unable to attend meetings or events because they cannot afford the time, the fees, the childcare, or the energy.

When they do make it they may feel unwelcome because they have not been as able to participate previously, because they do not speak the language (or the jargon) of the organizers, or because they are unfamiliar or uncomfortable with the middle class values and styles of the group.

People with disabilities can be similarly excluded when meetings are held in rooms and buildings which are not accessible, when signing is not provided, when accessible public transportation is not available, or when the pace and organization of the meeting does not allow them to participate.

People for whom English is not their primary language may face comparable barriers to finding out about meetings, attending events, becoming part of the leadership of an organization, or simply participating as a member when interpretation is not provided, when non-English media and communication networks are not utilized, or, again, when the pace and style of the group does not allow for the slower pace that a multilingual process calls for.

Assessing the Culture of Power

What does the culture of power look like in your organization? In your office or area where you work? In your school or classroom? In your living room or living space? In your congregation? Where you shop for clothes? In agencies whose services you use?

The following questions can be used to identity cultures of power based on gender, class, sexual orientation, religion, age, race, language, physical ability, immigrant status, or education.

1. Who is in authority?
2. Who has credibility (whose words and ideas are listened to with most attention and respect)?
3. Who is treated with full respect?
4. Whose experience is valued?
5. Whose voices are heard?
6. Who has access to or is given important information?
7. Who talks most at meetings?
8. Whose ideas are given importance?
9. Who is assigned to or expected to take on background roles?
10. How is the space designed? Who has physical access?
11. What is on the walls?
12. What language(s) are used? Which are acceptable?
13. What music and food is available? Who provides it?
14. How much are different people paid? How are prices determined?
15. Who cleans up?
16. Who decides?

Every person has the right to complete respect, equitable access, and full participation. Anything less limits the effectiveness of an organization by denying it the contributions the experiences, insights and creative input—of those individuals and groups excluded or discriminated against.

Those inside the culture of power rarely notice it, while those excluded are often acutely sensitive to how they and others are being marginalized. Therefore leadership in efforts to eliminate the culture of power need to come from those in excluded or marginalized groups.

Unless they are in leadership positions, with sufficient respect, status, and authority, the organization's efforts to change will be token, insufficient, and have limited effectiveness.

As they become better at identifying patterns of exclusion, people from within the culture of power can learn to take leadership in identifying marginalizing practices so that the organization doesn't have to rely as much on people at the margins to do this work for it. Although groups will always need to look to the insights of people at the margins to completely identify how systems of oppression are currently operating, there is an important role for those inside the culture of power to take leadership as allies to those excluded. They can challenge the status quo and can educate other "insiders" who are resistant to change. It is precisely because they have more credibility, status, and access that people on the inside make good allies. They can do this best not by speaking for or representing those marginalized, but by challenging the status quo and opening up opportunities for others to step forward and speak for themselves.

Every institution of higher education has a culture of power. And each department, division, school, program, and office within it has its own subculture of power. These may not be consistent or overlapping.

To be in opposition to the prevailing culture of power does not preclude us from creating subcultures of power that, in turn, exclude others who are even more marginalized than we are.

We have a responsibility, as people who have had access to educational opportunities, not to let the fact of our being on the inside of a culture of power allow us to deny educational opportunity to those who are on the outside. We need to fight for equal opportunity and full access and inclusion not just for those groups that we are a part of, but also for those groups we are not. For most of us that means listening to those on the margins, acknowledging our insider status compared to some other groups, and acknowledging our access to power, our resources, and our privileges. Then we can work with others to use our power, resources, and privileges to open up the educational structures to those who continue to knock on the doors.

Corporate Culture

Corporate culture needs careful attention – establishing the correct and appropriate corporate culture is an essential process of managing an organization.

What is corporate culture? It is something that managers have to establish and run all the way through a business, with clear values and beliefs, successful business principles and operations, and a suitable emphasis on human resources and customer satisfaction.

To a large extent, those at the very top, with their example, words and actions, determine the goals, philosophy and principles of the organization.

How many times have you seen clients with the perfect job having the whole experience turn sour because of corporate culture and internal politics? It is our responsibility to help our clients appraise the corporate culture as much as the job description, salary and benefits, acknowledging that understanding the culture of an organization before working there is a challenge, teach them these tips for uncovering it.

Encourage clients to keep the corporate culture in mind while networking and interviewing. Listening for informal comments and being very observant may prevent taking a job in a toxic environment. Clients should try to assess support for professional growth, rate of turnover, leadership styles, employee morale, style of dress, length of the work day, support for life work balance, and the ease and frequency of internal communication.

Besides looking and listening to clues, clients should also look at the public relations material and the company's web site. Does the information seem forthright or withholding? Are people in the organization featured? Are the values and goals espoused by the organization ones that they can support? Encourage clients to trust their impressions.

Asking for a tour of the facility including the cafeteria and staff room can be worth more than information on the web site or public relations materials. If they get one message from the physical environment while being told something very different, they should take notice.

As you know so well, corporate culture should not be confused with the corporate mission. But your clients may not know that working for a non-profit will NOT insure working with nice people, a kind atmosphere, fair reviews and less emphasis on the bottom line. Encourage them to check out the philosophy and leadership style of the CEO. They will be much better indications of corporate culture than the mission of the company. Ask clients to find out everything they can about the CEO. Show them how to conduct an internet search for articles about her. Have them ask for a press kit which usually contains biographical material. The CEO's beliefs and values will permeate the organization.

Finding the right organizational culture is very important to your clients' futures. Their progress in an organization will depend a great deal on their compatibility with it. They will be rewarded for "fitting in" as much as for what they do.

Ask clients to write their impressions in the following after each interview.

Impressions of Corporate Culture

- Professional Growth
- Rate of Turnover
- Leadership Style
- Dress
- Length of day
- Life/work balance
- Internal Communication
- Values of Organization
- Value for Employees
- Physical Plant
- Reputation of CEO.

Corporate culture is a term used to describe the collective beliefs, value systems, and processes that provide a company with its own unique flavour and attitude. Businesses of all sizes posses some type of corporate culture, in that every company has a set of values and goals that help to define what the business is all about. Here are some examples of elements that go into creating and defining a corporate culture.

At the foundation of any company culture are the standards that govern the operation of the business. These standards are usually expressed in terms of the policies and procedures that define how the company will operate. This will include how different departments or functions relate to one another in the production process, the line of communication established between management and departmental employees, and rules governing acceptable conduct of everyone who is part of the company. This basic organizational culture makes it possible to develop other layers of corporate culture based on these foundational factors.

Above and beyond organizational and procedural factors, corporate culture is further informed by the attitude of everyone involved with the organization. When executives, managers, and rank and file employees are all on the same page as far as basic corporate values, it becomes possible to have general agreement on the relationships that must be in place to accurately reflect the desired corporate culture. For example, when employees are provided with ways to make suggestions that could improve the productivity or the general working environment of the company, it can be said that the corporate culture is inclusive, as it allows for free communication between everyone employed by the business.

As with many types of cultures, corporate culture usually involves the inclusions of some rites or rituals. This can be something as simple as the annual holiday bonus, a week in the summer when the entire company shuts down, or even the naming of an employee of the month. These rites help to bond people together and provide some sense of collective identity, which is very important to the creation of a positive corporate culture.

It is important to note that a particular corporate culture may be positive or negative. Businesses where the rules constantly change, employee input is not encouraged, and rites tend to change constantly could be said to have a negative or counter-effective corporate culture. Since most companies cannot survive without the support of all employees and a dedication to core values, any business that develops negative corporate attitudes and culture is likely to be extremely limited in growth, or will fail to survive.

In six words, corporate culture is "How we do things around here."

Corporate culture is the collective behaviour of people using common corporate vision, goals, shared values, beliefs, habits, working language, systems, and symbols. It is interwoven with processes, technologies, learning and significant events. In addition, different individuals bring to the workplace their own uniqueness, knowledge, and ethnic culture. So corporate culture encompasses moral, social, and behavioural norms of your organization based on the values, beliefs, attitudes, and priorities of its members.

Corporate culture can be transformed, but leadership to sustain anything that sweeping has to come from "the top."

Adaptive Cultures

Your corporate culture is good only if it fits its context, i.e. your business space and your business strategy. In today's rapidly changing economy, "only cultures that can help organizations anticipate and adapt to environmental change will be associated with superior performance over the long time." Research findings show that cultures that are externally oriented (e.g. risk taking, readiness to meet new challenges) tend to be more strongly associated with organizational performance (operationalized using a range of measures) than do those cultures which are bureaucratic and predominantly internally focused.

Corporate Culture: The Three Levels

Edgar Shein describes the three levels of a corporate culture:

1. Surface Level: At this level, culture is both enacted and reinforced through visible appearances and behaviours, such as physical layouts, dress codes, organizational structure, company policies, procedures and programs, and attitudes.
2. Middle Level: Here, culture is manifested through our beliefs and values.

3. Deepest Level: At this level, culture is manifested through basic assumptions – our long-learned, automatic responses and established opinions.

Case in Point Toyota

The spiritual centre of Toyota is Toyota City, a huge company town of 400,000 people outside the industrial city of Nagoya. Once in a while, Toyota employees from around the globe come to the company's Toyota City plant near Nagoya, Japan for indoctrination in the "Toyota Way."

The company's commitment to teamwork is exemplified on the factory floor, where workers grab parts from trolleys that move with the line, one of many timesaving innovations proposed by the workers themselves. Slogans written by employees hang from the ceiling, and each production team has its own melody that rings out when a member needs to catch management's attention. Toyota's devotion to "Kaizen," or continuous improvement, shows up throughout the company and is a lesson that will serve all managers.

Toyota's global competitive advantage is based on a corporate philosophy known as the Toyota Production System. Toyota's philosophy of empowering its workers is the centrepiece of a human resources management system that fosters creativity, continuous improvement, and innovation by encouraging employee participation, and that likewise engenders high levels of employee loyalty.

4

Symbolic Boundaries and Status

Symbolic boundaries are a theory of how people form social groups proposed by cultural sociologists.

Symbolic boundaries are "conceptual distinctions made by social actors...that separate people into groups and generate feelings of similarity and group membership." Symbolic boundaries are distinct from "social boundaries" that are "objectified forms of social differences manifested in unequal access to an unequal distribution of resources... and social opportunities."

Symbolic boundaries are a "necessary but insufficient" condition for social change. "Only when symbolic boundaries are widely agreed upon can they take on a constraining character... and become social boundaries."

Consider three examples of tactics from disparate social movements: The 19th century antislavery movement's primary logo depicted a black man in chains with the question, "Am I not a man and a brother?" The contemporary antiabortion movement uses bumper stickers that claim, "I'm a survivor of the American Holocaust: Roe v Wade." And the animal rights movement often displays a poster of a pig and a cat, with the caption, "Which do you pet and which do you eat? Why?" What, if anything, do these three examples have in common? They all work for the rights, broadly speaking, of various groups. But more than that, they all exemplify social movements engaging in symbolic boundary deconstruction.

Symbolic boundaries are "conceptual distinctions that we make to categorize objects, people, practices, and even time and space". Previously existing research has largely focused on the cultural strategies, content, and outcomes of creating and maintaining symbolic boundaries. Understanding these processes is important, but unfortunately, researchers have largely ignored the complementary process of deconstructing symbolic boundaries.

Understanding symbolic boundary deconstruction should be of utter importance to social movement scholars, as nearly all movements strive for and/or achieve cultural change, to greater or lesser extents. Citing Nina Eliasoph's (1999) study of country-western dancers' racist discourse, Laura Desfor Edles (2002) maintains that "eliminating racism in the United States necessitates not only establishing new, antiracist institutional structures, but new symbolic structures as well. For however ironic and benign the country-western dancers' 'race talk' may appear, it is based on, and it reaffirms, the same old (same old) racist symbolic framework." Though cultural and social structures are intertwined, cultural change does not simply emerge from institutional change. Understanding such cultural change should also take more of a centre stage in social movement studies.

Scholars interested in new social movements (NSMs) in particular should attend to cultural change as a goal and strategy. Although NSM scholars claim that changing cultural codes is a fundamental goal of such movements, their investigations of these ends an means is primarily relegated to the process of collective identity.

Symbolic Boundaries: Permanent Creations?

Social scientists have typically viewed shared symbols and symbolic boundaries as tools to promote social solidarity, to provide mechanisms of social control, and to maintain social order. In foundational anthropological works on symbolic boundaries, the focus largely rested on boundary maintenance in two opposing senses. On the one hand, scholars conceived of violating or crossing symbolic borders as "pollution" to be avoided (Douglas 1966). On the other hand, some theorists believed that social actors breached symbolic boundaries purposefully, as in religious rituals, with a goal of reinforcing those barriers. Thus nearly any social action towards a symbolic boundary—avoidance or transgression—merely served to preserve the boundary. Social actors who aspire or attempt to dismantle such boundaries, rather than reinforce them, have evaded the regard of social scientists. In sociology, scholars have primarily examined the construction and maintenance of symbolic boundaries. People create symbolic boundaries to categorize and distinguish themselves from others. These boundaries separate people into groups, and give them feelings of membership in a group.

Even scholars of social movements, surprisingly, more often investigate boundary maintenance instead of boundary deconstruction. For example, Joshua Gamson (1997) studied the banning of transsexuals from the Michigan Womyn's Music Festival, focusing on how feminist activists created collective identities that excluded transsexuals from participation.

While Gamson illuminated the differences between public utterances of exclusion and private actions of inclusion, he only told half of the story. There was more than one movement taking place at the festival—not only were feminists celebrating womynhood, but transsexuals were also aiming to deconstruct the symbolic boundaries between "womyn-born womyn" and male-to-female transsexuals. For example, transsexual participants used workshops and literature tables to debunk myths and misperceptions about transsexuality at the festival.

Further, "one participant announced herself as transsexual at two workshops, later declaring her presence there 'to be in the same tradition of civil disobedience as that of African Americans who conducted sit-ins at segregated lunch counters in the early 1960s'".

Re-examining the Rhetoric of the "Cultural Border"

Constructing a topology of a multicultural society is never simple. Although cultural diversity is often defined by seemingly clear-cut categories such as ethnicity, race, class, religion, gender, sexual orientation, and exceptionality, sorting out "culture" intertwined with these multicultural categories is a complex process. I am not even sure whether anyone sees the value of taking on the challenge because different categories of people are considered syr onymous with cultural differences. It is common to hear references to Asian-American culture, Black culture, Muslim culture, female culture, homosexual culture and ADD culture as if they have clear boundaries and are distinguished entities. It is also assumed that if an Asian meets an African-American their presumed cultural differences are expected to form a cultural border. Or if a White teacher has a group of minority children in her classroom, the formation of a cultural border between them is considered inevitable. However, if the focus switches from a society (or group) to individuals, the power of the cultural border rhetoric seems to lose its potency. For example, the Korean and the African-American may share many cultural traits, so their racial and ethnic difference may not have such an enduring effect.

Cultural Border and Cultural Boundary

The terms "border" and " boundary" are physical in origin. The original imagery is not quite abandonedand is even intentionally played outwhen the terms are used in reference to culture. Cultural border and boundary often connote the border and boundary of a nation, a state or a tribal community, which are clearly identifiable markers. The equation between a culture and a territory has dominated the discourse in anthropology. The assumption is that as long as two distinct societies remain separate from each other, their boundaries exist and cultural distinctiveness is expected. It is further assumed that if two societies, identified with two distinct cultures, come in contact, a cultural border is expected to form between them. If an individual from Culture A is to voluntarily or involuntarily3 become part of Culture B, she/he is expected to literally leave his/her own society, cross the border and enter a new society. This physical implication of the cultural border is fully entertained by scholars of Mexican immigrants, for whom crossing the border is a literal as well as a figurative experience.

To many scholars a border is not a neutral demarcation line. It is a symbol of power that imposes inclusion and exclusion. The more privilegeddominant, hegemoniousside will actively control the border to keep border-crossers out. Erickson (1997) accentuated the political nature of a border by differentiating it from a boundary:

A cultural boundary refers to the presence of some kind of cultural difference cultural boundaries are characteristic of all human societies, traditional as well as modern. A border is a social construct that is political in origin. Across a border power is exercised, as in the political border between two nations.

A cultural border connotes a barrier that a more powerful side constructs to guard its own political power, cultural knowledge and privileges.

The cultural border rhetoric is grounded in the essentialist view of culture. This view makes several assumptions regarding culture: (1) a culture is viewed as a bounded system which is separate and distinguishable from others; (2) a culture is expected to be "homogeneous"; (3) a culture is expected to be shared by members of the society.

The first assumption is evident in the work of many anthropologists. The cultural boundary is viewed as coterminous with a nation, a state, a tribe, a community or an organization that is clearly defined by an identifiable markeroften physical borders. Goodenough (1981) attributed this notion of culture to Franz Boas, a pioneer German-American anthropologist:

At the end of the nineteenth century, Franz Boas began to use "culture" to refer to the distinctive body of customs, beliefs, and social institutions that seemed to characterize each separate society.

The notion of one-distinct-culture-for-each-separate-society suggests that one culture represents a society and vice versa. This close match makes the conceptual interchange of culture and society acceptable. Henze and Vanett (1993) further explore this assumption of culture in the metaphor of "walking in two worlds" in their study of native Alaskan and Native American students.

The second assumption of cultural homogeneity suggests that a homogeneous, patterned prototype of a culture can be abstracted. It implies that a "pure" form of a culture exists. Any variation from the pure form is treated as an exception, peripheral to "the culture." This assumption ignores the dynamic nature of culture, in which people of a society change at different rates for different reasons. The diffusionist view of culture argues against this notion of cultural homogeneity, for all cultures include elements borrowed from other cultures.

The third assumption of the cultural border is that a culture is "shared" by members of a society. The extent of sharedness is debatable, yet sharedness is considered a trademark of culture. This assumption suggests that people within a cultural system share a set of traits unique to their group membership. Sharedness is considered a product of cultural transmission and acquisition which often take place through personal interactions among members of physical proximity. In other words, an Asian is expected to share with other Asians traits unique to Asian culture. When a group is small and specific, the extent of sharedness among members may be higher. However, if a group presents a large, cross-sectional or cross-national cultural identity, such as "female culture," "middle-class culture" and "Muslim culture," the sharedness of that particular culture is blurred by other cultural identities. Ewing (1998) examined how the cultural identity of Muslims shifts relative to national borders and the gender line.

This territory-oriented rhetoric of culture, cultural border and boundary faces a great challenge in a multicultural society because intense contacts between various cultural carriers blur the clarity of demarcation lines.

Cultural Borderland

"Cultural borderland" is a notion created to accommodate a multicultural society. Foley (1995) explores the cultural borderland as a "space" created when two or more cultures and races occupy the same territory. He considers the space psychological and political: [According to Rosaldo and Clifford, the borderland] generally refers to a psychological space at the conjuncture of two cultures. A cultural borderland is also a political space in which ethnic groups actively fuse and blend their culture with the mainstream culture.

The borderland is viewed as a psychological space in which border-crossers struggle with their bicultural or multicultural identities. In this borderland individuals decide how much they want to identify with their cultures of origin or of adoption. Too much of either can be the subject of ridicule. Saenz (1997) compared two distinguished Mexican-American writers who try to come to terms with their ethnic identities. He argued that Gloria Anzaldua is "completely mortgaged to a nostalgia" a nostalgia to the Aztec origin of the Mexican culture. Richard Rodriguez, on the other hand, "is completely mortgaged to an ideology that privileges the category of individual". In the eyes of Saenz, Rodriguez has taken too much of his adopted culture. In between lies Saenz's Mexican-American college student who refused to read "gringo" (White) poetry and Saenz himself who insists on his identity as a Chicano writer.

The borderland is also highly political. The borderland is never on centre stage. It is often viewed as a marginal space for cultural hybrids—those who have adopted "foreign," distinctly different, cultural traits—who therefore do not fit the homogeneous prototypes of their original cultures. In Foleys Mesquaki Indian study the borderland is viewed as a threat to the integrity of the Indian culture. It was a space for Indian progressives (who proposed to modernize the Indian community and to collaborate with Whites), White "wannabes" (who tried to adopt the Indian culture) and "mixed-bloods" (biracial individuals of White and Indian parents).

The borderland rhetoric is still embedded in the essentialist view of culture. For example, Foleys notion of cultural borderlands creates an image of three separate zones: the "pure" Indian culture that is being guarded by "traditionalists" (Lets call it Culture A); the "pure" White culture that is distinguished from the Indian (Culture B); and the borderland between them, a space for border-crossers. Chang (1997) quesitons this essentialist presumption of culture by wondering, "just where the Indian culture ends and the White culture begins for border crossers".

How Real is Cultural Border

The cultural border and boundary rhetoric focuses on a societal culture. If cultural diversity is viewed at the societal level, cultural borders seem authentic and real. Skin colour, national origin, gender, religious affiliation, identification of disability, and group membership all serve as identifiable markers for subgroups. Since these categories are socially constructed and validated, cultural differences are assumed and expected. But when the cultures of individuals are under scrutiny, it becomes clear that cultural borders do not hold their dividing power. Cultural boundaries within individuals become blurred as components from diverse cultures become incorporated into their individual cultural identity, instead of remaining separate from each other.

Let us take a close look at four multicultural individuals who had a close connection with Korea but who live in the pluralistic U.S. society.

Jean Kohl, a 9-year-old daughter of a German father and a Korean mother, was born and raised in the United States. Her parents, fluent speakers of German and Korean respectively, adopted English as the primary language at home. "I am an American," proclaimed she, but she often ended her proclamation with an addendum that she was also German and Korean. For several summers she traveled to visit her maternal or paternal grandparents in Korea or Germany, during which she was exposed to her parents native cultures and languages. The German, Korean and U. S. heritage blended in her cultural repertoire. For Jean, where does the "American" cultural border end and other cultural borders begin?

Carrie Baumstein, a 20-year-old woman, was born in Korea and adopted by a Messianic Jewish-American couple when she was 2 years old. She has lived in the States ever since. She was not exposed to much Korean culture and language when she was growing up, but was instead surrounded by her parents Jewish tradition. Despite her primary identity with the Jewish culture, she was often reminded by her relatives and neighbours of her Koreanor Asianlinkage. She was in an identity search for Asianness when she was attending a small Christian college on the East Coast. For Carrie, where do the cultural borders lie between the Korean and the American and between the Messianic Jew and the Christian?

Peter Lee, a 15-year-old, was born in the States to immigrant parents from Korea. His parents own and operate a dry cleaning shop in a suburb of Philadelphia. Their English is functional for the business but they prefer speaking Korean on all other occasions. Peters family attends a Korean church regularly, which usually serves as a cultural community as much as a religious one. Peters Korean is so limited that he usually speaks English, although his parents speak Korean to him. He is definitely an American in his mind and heart, perhaps a Korean-American occasionally. But his preference of Korean-American peers to others is a curious phenomenon. Where lies the cultural border that divides the Korean and the "American" for Peter?

Elaine Sook-Ja Cho, 50 years old, immigrated to the States 30 years ago to marry a Korean bachelor 10 years her senior. Her husband came to the States as a student and found employment upon completion of his study. Elaine was a housewife for 20 years before undertaking a small grocery business. She speaks "Konglish" (a mixture of Korean sentence structure and English words) but she seems to be at ease speaking English. She is Korean in her heart but "Americanized" in her own words and by her life style. For Sook-Ja how far does the Korean cultural border stretch to meet the "American" culture?

I wonder how I would map the cultural topology (again a physical metaphor) of Jean Kohl, Carrie Baumstein, Peter Lee and Elaine Sook-Ja Cho. How would I draw up the boundary of the Korean culture for each case? Would they cross cultural borders from the Korean to the German and so on daily? How cognizant would they be of crossing? Would it be possible for one to become culturally more Korean in the morning, German for lunch, "American" in the afternoon, and back to Korean in the evening?

The early illustration of an individual leaving his/her society, crossing the border and entering a new society may shed light on the problem with the cultural border rhetoric. Once you acquire cultural traits, whether in a certain territorial context or not, leaving the territory does not make an individual "lose" the culture. Sook-Ja is not any less Korean culturally now because she left her homeland 30 years ago. Carries minimal identity as a Korean is not surprising despite her origin. Peter and Jean who were born and raised in the States have acquired Korean cultural traits from their parents. In other words, the physical proximity or distance to Korea does not serve as an accurate gauge for their Koreanness in culture. It is also hardly imaginable that Jeans notion of the Korean culture is similar to that of Sook-Ja, although both claim to be Korean. What would Peter share about the Korean culture with others and to what extent? How would I compare these peoples Korean culture with that of Koreans who have never left the country? The essentialist image of culturein particular, the Korean cultureseems to lose the clarity of its boundary as I probe into each individuals personal version of culture.

Conclusion

Everyone is cultural and multicultural: "cultural" in that culture is not a property of an exotic people but "standards" that all human beings adopt for their daily operations; "multicultural" in the sense of being competent in multiple macro or microcultural systems.

In a pluralistic society in which people from diverse cultures come in constant contact, the cultural metamorphosis takes place noticeably in individual cultures. Thus the Boas-Benedict legacy of the "plural, separate, distinct, historically homogeneous" culture offers little help in understanding the multicultural society and its residents. Rosaldo also critiqued the fallacy of cultural homogeneity, especially in the pluralistic setting:

[H]uman cultures are neither necessarily coherent nor always homogeneous. More often than we usually care to think, our everyday lives are crisscrossed by border zones, pockets and eruptions of all kinds.

It also becomes clear that a culture is not bounded by a territory as earlier anthropologists believed. Rather, people are the carriers, movers, consumers, and inventors of a culture. When they move from one place to the other, they carry their culturestheir personal outlookswith them. Goodenough (1981) coined a term, "propriospect," to refer to the "private, subjective view of the world and of its content," which includes the various standards for perceiving, evaluating, believing, and doing that an individual attributes to other persons as a result of his or her experience of their actions and admonitions. Wolcott (1991) elaborated on the meaning of the term "propriospect" to illustrate how individuals develop personal versions of a culture through personal contacts with others with different sets of standards. Through these contacts they acquire some of the new standards.

As a result, they become increasingly multicultural. This concept of culture sheds light on cultural differences. Since everyone has a unique cultural make-up, cultural differences are not really divisive and separable. Individual cultural differences are really different combinations of standards. Once different standards are embraced by individuals, the differences are incorporated into their individual cultures. In other words, the cultural differences are reframed into multiculturalism. It seems logical to me that we understand our individual multiculturalism as a pathway to understand our societal multiculturalism. The constructive view of individual cultures would be too useful and insightful to ignore.

Social Class

Social classes are economic or cultural arrangements of groups in society. Class is an essential object of analysis for sociologists, political scientists, economists, anthropologists and social historians. In the social sciences, social class is often discussed in terms of 'social stratification'. In the modern Western context, stratification typically comprises of three layers: upper class, middle class, and lower class. Each class may be further subdivided into smaller classes (e.g. occupational).

The most basic class distinction is between the powerful and the powerless. Social classes with a great deal of power are usually viewed as "the elites" within their own societies. Various social and political theories propose that social classes with greater power attempt to cement their own ranking above the lower classes in the hierarchy to the detriment of the society overall. By contrast, conservatives and structural functionalists have presented class difference as intrinsic to the structure of any society and to that extent ineradicable.

In Marxist theory, two basic class divisions owe to the fundamental economic structure of work and property: the proletariat and the bourgeoisie. The capitalists own the means of production, but this effectively includes the proletariat as they are only able to sell their own labour power. These inequalities are normalised and reproduced through cultural ideology. Max Weber critiqued historical materialism (or economic determinism), positing that stratification is not based purely on economic inequalities, but on other status and power differentials. Social class pertaining broadly to material wealth may be distinguished from status class based on honour, prestige, religious affiliation, and so on.

Theorists such as Ralf Dahrendorf have noted the tendency toward an enlarged middle class in modern Western societies, particularly in relation to the necessity of an educated work force in technological economies. Perspectives concerning globalization and neocolonialism, such as dependency theory, suggest this owes to the shift of low-level labourers to developing nations and the Third World. Developed nations have thereby become less directly active in primary industry (e.g.. basic manufacturing, agriculture, forestry, mining, etc.) and increasingly involved with "virtual" goods and services. The national concept of "social class" has therefore become increasingly complex and confused.

Causes and Outcomes of Social Class

Determinants of Class Position

In so-called non-stratified societies or acephalous societies, there is no concept of social class, power, or hierarchy beyond temporary or limited social statuses. In such societies, every individual has a roughly equal social standing in most situations.

In class societies a person's class status is a type of group membership. Theorists disagree about the elements determining membership, but common features appear in many accounts. Among these are:

- Relationships of production, ownership and consumption
- A common legal status, including ceremonial, occupational and reproductive rights
- Family, kinship or tribal group structures or membership
- Acculturation, including education.

Classes often have a distinct lifestyle that emphasizes their class. The most powerful class in a society often uses markers such as costume, grooming, manners and language codes that mark insiders and outsiders; unique political rights such as honorary titles; and, concepts of social honour or face that are claimed to only be applicable to the in group. But each class has distinctive features, often becoming defining elements of personal identity and uniting factors in group behaviour. French sociologist Pierre Bourdieu suggests a notion of high and low classes with a distinction between bourgeois tastes and sensitivities and the working class tastes and sensitivities.

Race and other large-scale groupings can also influence class standing. The association of particular ethnic groups with class statuses are common in many societies. As a result of conquest or internal ethnic differentiation, a ruling class is often ethnically homogenous and particular races or ethnic groups in some societies are legally or customarily restricted to occupying particular class positions. Which ethnicities are considered as belonging to high or low classes varies from society to society. In modern societies strict legal links between ethnicity and class have been drawn, such as in apartheid, the Caste system in Africa, and in the position of the Burakumin in Japanese society.

A distinction often made is that of Ascribed status versus Achieved status. This deals with difference between obtained class identification, and whether social standing is determined at birth or earned over a lifetime. Achieved statuses are acquired based on merit, skills, abilities, and actions. Examples of achieved status include being a doctor or even being a criminal—the status then determines a set of behaviours and expectations for the individual.

Consequences of Class Position

Different consumption of social goods is the most visible consequence of class. In modern societies, it manifests as income inequality, though in subsistence societies it manifested as malnutrition and periodic starvation. Although class status is not a causal factor for income, there is consistent data that show those in higher classes have higher incomes than those in lower classes. This inequality still persists when controlling for occupation. The conditions at work vary greatly depending on class. Those in the upper-middle class and middle class enjoy greater freedoms in their occupations. They generally are more respected, enjoy more diversity, and are able to exhibit some authority. Those in lower classes tend to feel more alienated and have lower work satisfaction overall. The physical conditions of the workplace differ greatly between classes. While middle-class workers may "suffer alienating conditions" or "lack of job satisfaction", blue-collar workers suffer alienating, often routine, work with obvious physical health hazards, injury, and even death.

In the more social sphere, class has direct consequences on lifestyle. Lifestyle includes tastes, preferences, and a general style of living. These lifestyles could quite possibly affect educational attainment, and therefore status attainment. Class lifestyle also affects how children are raised. For example, a working-class person is more likely to raise their child to be working class and middle-class children are more likely to be raised to be middle-class. This perpetuates the idea of class for future generations.

Theoretical Models

Theoretical models of class seek to explain how class relationships come into being, and why particular class relationships exist across broadly similar societies.

Marxist

The Marxist conception of class involves a collective group of individuals that share similar economic and social relations relative to each other in society. A class is a group with intrinsic tendencies and interests that are different from, and may be opposed to the interests of other groups in society. For example, it is in the laborer's best interest to maximize wages and benefits and in the capitalist's best interest to maximize profit at the expense of such, leading to a contradiction within the capitalist system, even if the labourers and capitalists themselves are unaware of these class dichotomies.

For Marx, class involves two factors:

Objective Factors

A class shares a common relationship to the means of production. That is, all people in one class make their living in a common way in terms of ownership of the things that produce social goods. A class may own things, own land, own people, be owned, own nothing but their labor. A class will extract tax, produce agriculture, enslave and work others, be enslaved and work, or work for a wage.

Subjective Factors

The members will necessarily have some perception of their similarity and common interest. Marx termed this Class consciousness. Class consciousness is not simply an awareness of one's own class interest (for instance, the maximisation of shareholder value; or, the maximization of the wage with the minimization of the working day), class consciousness also embodies deeply shared views of how society should be organized legally, culturally, socially and politically.

The first criteria divides a society into the owners and non-owners of means of production. In capitalism, these are capitalist (bourgeoisie) and proletariat. Finer divisions can be made, however: the most important subgroup in capitalism being petite bourgeoisie (small bourgeoisie), people who possess their own means of production but utilize it primarily by working on it themselves rather than hiring others to work on it. They include self-employed artisans, small shopkeepers, and many professionals. Jon Elster has found mention in Marx of 15 classes from various historical periods.

A prerequisite for classes is existence of sufficient surplus product. Marxists explain the history of "civilized" societies in terms of a war of classes between those who control production and those who produce the goods or services in society. In the Marxist view of capitalism, this is a conflict between capitalists (bourgeoisie) and wage-workers (the proletariat). For Marxists, class antagonism is rooted in the situation that control over social production necessarily entails control over the class which produces goods—in capitalism this is the exploitation of workers by the bourgeoisie.

Marx himself argued that it was the goal of the proletariat itself to displace the capitalist system with socialism, changing the social relationships underpinning the class system and then developing into a future communist society in which: "..the free development of each is the condition for the free development of all." (Communist Manifesto) This would mark the beginning of a classless society in which human needs rather than profit would be motive for production. In a society with democratic control and production for use, there would be no class, no state and no need for money.

Vladimir Lenin has defined classes as "large groups of people differing from each other by the place they occupy in a historically determined system of social production, by their relation (in most cases fixed and formulated in law) to the means of production, by their role in the social organization of labor, and, consequently, by the dimensions of the share of social wealth of which they dispose and the mode of acquiring it." *A Great Beginning*

Proletarianisation

The most important transformation of society for Marxists has been the massive and rapid growth of the proletariat the last two hundred and fifty years. Starting with agricultural and domestic textile labourers in England and Flanders, more and more occupations only provide a living through wages or salaries.

Private manufacturing, leading to self-employment, is no longer as viable as it was before the industrial revolution, because automation made manufacturing very cheap. Many people who once controlled their own labor-time were converted into proletarians through industrialization. Today groups which in the past subsisted on stipends or private wealth—like doctors, academics or lawyers—are now increasingly working as wage labourers. Marxists call this process proletarianization, and point to it as the major factor in the proletariat being the largest class in current societies in the rich countries of the "first world."

The increasing dissolution of the peasant-lord relationship, initially in the commercially active and industrializing countries, and then in the unindustrialized countries as well, has virtually eliminated the class of peasants. Poor rural labourers still exist, but their current relationship with production is predominantly as landless wage labourers or rural proletarians. The destruction of the peasantry, and its conversion into a rural proletariat, is largely a result of the general proletarianization of all work. This process is today largely complete, although it was arguably incomplete in the 1960s and 1970s.

Dialectics, or Historical Materialism, in Marxist Class

Marx saw class categories as defined by continuing historical processes. Classes, in Marxism, are not static entities, but are regenerated daily through the productive process. Marxism views classes as human social relationships which change over time, with historical commonality created through shared productive processes. A 17th century farm labourer who worked for day wages shares a similar relationship to production as an average office worker of the 21st century. In this example, it is the shared structure of wage labour that makes both of these individuals "working class."

Objective and Subjective Factors in Class in Marxism

Marxism has a rather heavily defined dialectic between objective factors (i.e., material conditions, the social structure) and subjective factors (i.e. the conscious organization of class members). While most Marxism analyses people's class based on objective factors (class structure), major Marxist trends have made greater use of subjective factors in understanding the history of the working class. E.P. Thompson's *The Making of the English Working Class* is a definitive example of this "subjective" Marxist trend. Thompson analyses the English working class as a group of people with shared material conditions coming to a positive self-consciousness of their social position. This feature of social class is commonly termed class consciousness in Marxism, a concept which became famous with Georg Lukacs' *History and Class Consciousness* (1923). It is seen as the process of a "class in itself" moving in the direction of a "class for itself," a collective agent that changes history rather than simply being a victim of the historical process. In Lukacs' words, the proletariat was the "subject-object of history", and the first class which could separate false consciousness (inherent to the bourgeois's consciousness), which reified economic laws as universal (whereas they are only a consequence of historic capitalism).

Max Weber

The seminal sociological interpretation of class was advanced by Max Weber. Weber formulated a three-component theory of stratification, with class, status and party (or politics) as subordinate to the ownership of the means of production, but for Weber how they interact is a contingent question and one that will vary from society to society. Weber is also known for his six "American Dream" Values which are: 1) Hard work, 2) Universalism, 3) Individualism, 4) Wealth, 5) Activism, and 6) Rationality.

Academic Models

Schools of sociology differ in how they conceptualize class. A distinction can be drawn between *analytical* concepts of social class, such as the Marxian and Weberian traditions, and the more *empirical* traditions such as socio-economic status approach, which notes the correlation of income, education and wealth with social outcomes without necessarily implying a particular theory of social structure. The Warnerian approach can be considered *empirical* in the sense that it is more descriptive than analytical.

The traditional 'pigeon-holing' mainstay of much of the advertising industry used to be that of social class. Recently, however, as affluence has become more widespread, the process has become much less clear. It is now argued that the new 'opinion leaders' come from within the same social class. The class groupings that were traditionally used by advertising agencies (for example in the NRS social grade schema were: AB-Managerial and professional, C1-Supervisory and clerical, C2-Skilled manual, DE-Unskilled manual and unemployed.) have been reported to be of decreasing value in recent decades, especially in the distinction between clerical workers and manual workers in education and disposable income.

Whereas some four decades ago, when these groupings were first widely used, the numbers in each of the main categories (C, D and E) were reasonably well balanced, today the C group in total (although now usually split to give C1 and C2) forms such a large sector that it dominates the whole classification system and offers less in terms of usable concentration of marketing effort.

William Lloyd Warner

An early example of a stratum class model was developed by the sociologist William Lloyd Warner in his 1949 book,

Social Class in America. For many decades, the Warnerian theory was dominant in U.S. sociological theory.

Based on social anthropology, Warner divided Americans into three classes (upper, middle, and lower), then further subdivided each of these into an "upper" and "lower" segment, with the following postulates:

- Upper upper class. "Old money." People who have been born into and raised with wealth; mostly consists of old "noble" or prestigious families (e.g., Earl of Shrewsbury, Vanderbilt, Rockefeller).
- Lower upper class. "New money." Individuals who have become rich within their own lifetimes (e.g., entrepreneurs, movie stars, top athletes, as well as some prominent professionals).
- Upper middle class. Professionals with a college education, and more often with postgraduate degrees like MBAs, Ph.D.s, MDs, JDs, MSs, etc. (e.g., doctors, engineers, dentists, lawyers, bankers, corporate executives, head teachers, university professors, scientists, pharmacists, airline pilots, ship captains, actuaries, high level civil servants, politicians, and military officers, architects, artists, writers, poets, and musicians).
- Lower middle class. Lower-paid white collar workers, but not manual labourers. Often hold Associates or Bachelor degrees. (e.g., police officers, fire fighters, primary and high school teachers, accountants, nurses, municipal office workers and low to mid-level civil servants, sales representatives, non-management office workers, clergy, technicians, small business owners).
- Upper lower class. Blue-collar workers and manual labourers. Also known as the "working class."
- Lower lower class. The homeless and permanently unemployed, as well as the "working poor."

To Warner, American social class was based more on attitudes than on the actual amount of money an individual made. For example, the richest people in America would belong to the "lower upper class" since many of them created their own fortunes; one can only be born into the highest class.

Nonetheless, members of the wealthy upper-upper class tend to be more powerful, as a simple survey of U.S. presidents may demonstrate (i.e., the Roosevelts; Kennedys; Bushes).

Another observation: members of the upper lower class might make more money than members of the lower middle class (i.e., a well-salaried factory worker vs. a secretarial worker), but the class difference is based on the type of work they perform.

In his research findings, Warner observed that American social class was largely based on these shared attitudes. For example, he noted that the lower middle class tended to be the most conservative group of all, since very little separated them from the working class. The upper-middle class, while a relatively small section of the population, usually "set the standard" for proper American behaviour, as reflected in the mass media.

Professionals with salaries and educational attainment higher than those found near the middle of the income strata (e.g. bottom rung professors, managerial office workers, architects) may also be considered as being true middle class.

Coleman and Rainwater

In 1978 sociologists Coleman and Rainwater conceived the "Metropolitan Class Structure" consisting of three social classes, each with a number sub-classes.

- Upper Americans;
    - Upper-upper class; (ca. 1%) Old money stemming from inherited wealth. Persons in this class typically have an "Ivy league college degree." Their household income in 1978 was over $500,000 ($1,673,215 in 2005 dollars)
    - Lower-upper class; (ca. 1%) This is the "Success elite" consisting of "Top professionals [and] senior corporate executives." People in this class have degrees from "Good colleges." Their household income was also commonly in excess of $77,000 ($251,000 in 2005 dollars). *Nouveau riche* (French for "new rich"), or new money, refers to a person who has acquired considerable wealth within his or

her generation. This term is generally used to emphasize that the individual was previously part of a lower socioeconomic rank, and that such wealth has provided the means for the acquisition of goods or luxuries that were previously unobtainable.

  - Upper-middle class; (ca. 19%) Also called the "Professional and Managerial" class, it consists of "Middle professionals and managers" with a college and often graduate degrees. Household incomes for this group lay between $35,000 ($114,000 in 2005 dollars) and $60,000 ($183,000 in 2005 dollars).

- Middle Americans;
  - Middle class; (ca. 31%) This class consists of "Lower-level managers; small-business owners; lower-status professionals (accountants, teachers); sales and clerical" workers. Middle class persons had a high school and some college education. Their household incomes commonly ranged between $10,000 and $20,000 ($30,000-$60,000 in 2005 dollars)
  - Working class; (ca. 35%) This class consists of "Higher blue collar (craftsman, truck drivers); lowest-paid sales and clerical" workers. Younger individuals in 1978 who were members of this class had a high school education. Their household income lay in between $7,500 and $15,000 ($23,000-$45,000 in 2005 dollars).
- Lower Americans (ca. 13%);
  - Semipoor; This class had high school education and consisted of "labor and service" workers with household incomes ranging from $4,500 to $6,000 ($14,000-$18,000 in 2005 dollars)
  - The bottom; Those who are "Often unemployed" or rely on welfare payments. Household incomes of less than $4,500 ($14,000 in 2005 dollars).

Thompson & Hickey

In their 2005 sociology textbook, *Society in Focus*, sociologists William Thompson and Joseph Hickey present a five class model in which the middle class is divided into two sections and the term working class is applied to clerical and pink collar workers. Their class system goes as follows:

- Upper class, (ca. 1%-5%) individuals with considerable power over the nation's economic and political institutions. This group owns a disproportionate share of the nation's resources. The top 1% had incomes exceeding $250,000 with the top 5% having household incomes exceeding $140,000. This group features strong group solidarity and is largely constituted by the heirs to multi-generational fortunes. Prominent government officials, CEOs and successful entrepreneurs are among the upper class even if not of elite background.
- Upper middle class, (ca. 15%) white collar professionals with advanced post-secondary education such as physicians, professors, lawyers, corporate executives, and other management. While households commonly have six figure incomes in this group, the majority of income earners do not. Only 6% of persons had six figure incomes while 15% were upper middle class. While high educational attainment commonly serves as the staple mark of this group, entrepreneurs and business owners may also be upper middle class even if lacking advanced educational attainment.
- Lower middle class, (ca. 33%) individuals who worked their way through college and commonly have a Bachelor's degree or some college education. School teachers, sales-employees and lower to mid level supervisors rank among those in this particular group. Household income is generally in the range of $30,000 to $75,000. Workers in this group are mostly white collar but have less autonomy in their work than do upper middle class professionals. Members of this class often attempt to emulate those in the two higher classes and have recently become overly indebted by their desire to have a comfortable lifestyle.
- Working class, (ca. 30%) individuals who occupy both blue and white collar occupations. Pink collar workers in predominantly female clerical positions are common in this class. Job security tends to be low for this group and unemployment as well as losing health insurance

remain potent economic threats. Household incomes typically range from $16,000 to $30,000.

- Lower class, repeated cycles of unemployment, working multiple low-level part-time jobs are common among this group. Gilbert & Kahl.

In *The American Class Structure, 6th edition* (Wadsworth 2002) as well the preceding 5th edition, Dennis Gilbert lays out an even more precise breakdown of American social classes. Dennis Gilbert stresses that "there is really no way to establish that a particular model is 'true' and another 'false.'" He furthermore states that his "model emphasizes *sources of income*" and that household income, being very dependent on the number of income earners, varies greatly within each social class. The class descriptions in quotes below are lifted from the 5th edition, pages 284 and 285.

- Capitalist class; (ca. 1%) *"Subdivided into nationals and locals, whose income is derived largely from return on assets."* However, the top 1.5% of households made $250,000 or more with only 146,000, 0.01% of households having incomes of $1,600,000 or more.
- Upper middle class; (ca. 14%) *"...college trained professionals and managers (a few of whom ascend to such heights of bureaucratic dominance or accumulated wealth that they become part of the capitalist class)."* Educational attainment is the main feature of this class. They enjoy great job autonomy and economic security. Household incomes vary greatly depending of the number of income earners." Considering US Census Bureau According to the 2005 Economic Survey, the top 15% of income earners made $62,500 or more with the top 15% of households having six figure incomes.
- Middle class; (ca. 30%) *"...members have significant skills and perform varied tasks at work, under loose supervision. They earn enough to afford a comfortable, mainstream lifestyle. Most wear white collars, but some wear blue."* In 2005 incomes for this group would have ranged from $50,000 to $90,000 for households and $27,500 to $52,500 for individuals.
- Working class; (ca. 30%) *"People who are less skilled*

than members of the middle class and work at highly routinized, closely supervised manual and clerical jobs. Their work provides them with a relatively stable income sufficient to maintain a living standard just below the mainstream." Incomes in 2005 would have ranged from $10,000 to $27,500 for individuals and $20,000 to $50,000 for households.

- Working poor; (ca. 13%) "*...people employed in low-skill jobs, often at marginal firms. The members of this class are typically labourers, service workers, or low-paid operators. Their incomes leave them well below mainstream living standards. Moreover, they cannot depend on steady employment."* In 2004 the bottom 12.2% of households made less than $12,500.
- Underclass (ca. 12%) "*...members have limited participation in the labor force and do not have wealth to fall back on. Many depend on government transfers."* The average household income is $12,000 a year, and the class makes up 12% of the population.

Chinese Model

In the Structure and Evolution of Chinese Social Stratification, sociologist Li Yi lays out a detailed model of Chinese social stratification after 1949. In China today, there is a peasant class, a working class (urban state worker and urban collective worker, urban non-state worker, and peasant worker), a capitalist class (about 15 million), and a class of cadre (about 40 million) and quasi-cadre (about 27 million).

Iranian Model

Farhad Nomani and Sohrab Behdad in their book *Class and Labor in Iran; Did the Revolution Matter?* (Syracuse University Press, 2006) define and quantify social classes in Iran and examine the changes in the configuration of social classes in the post-revolutionary Iran. Nomani and Behdad base their analysis on three dimensions of (1) property ownership, (2) possession of scarce skills/credentials, and (3) organizational assets/authority. They recognize four distinct class categories and the ambiguous category of political functionaries of the state:

1. Capitalists: Owners of physical and financial means of economic activities, who employ workers. Capitalists are divided into modern and traditional occupational categories.
2. Petty bourgeoisie: Self-employed persons who do not hire any paid worker but may rely on unpaid family labor. They, too, consist of modern and traditional categories.
3. The middle class: Employees of the state or the private sector, in administrative-managerial and professional-technical positions. They exercise some authority and enjoy relative autonomy. In this category are those who are employed in economic activities and social services of the state. Those employed in the administrative or managerial position in the political apparatus of the state are not included here.
4. The working class: Workers who do not own the means of economic activity and do not benefit from the authority and autonomy of those in the middle class. They are employees of the state or the private sector, excluding those in the lower ranks of the political apparatus of the state.

Those employed in the political apparatus of the state, engaged in political administration, national defence and domestic surveillance, constitute the ambiguous class category of political functionaries. This category includes higher rank of state administrators, managers, and military and para-military officers, the rank file of the political apparatus, and the lower rank members of the coercive forces (including the military draftees).

The post 1979 revolutionary turmoil had notable impacts on the class reconfiguration of Iran. The disruption of the accumulation process in the first revolutionary decade (Khomeini period) retarded the capitalist relations of production (structural involution). This condition gave rise to deproletarianization of labor and peasantization of agriculture, and a general expansion in petty-commodity activities and a rise of the petty bourgeoisie, alongside a huge expansion of state activities. In the post-Khomeini period, the effort toward reconstitution of capitalist relations of production via an economic liberalization policy (deinvolutionary process) reversed some of the previous trends. In the second post-revolutionary period an increase in proletarianization of labor and de-peasantization of agriculture is observed. The first (involutionary [2]) period promoted traditional capitalists and the petty bourgeoisie, whereas in the second (deinvolutionary) period the number of modern capitalists, modern petty bourgeoisie, and the middle class (especially those employed by the private sector) increased significantly.

In a comparison of the class structure in 1996 with that in 1976 one can observe that in spite of some peculiar differences, there are striking similarities between the two periods. If the changes between 1986 and 1996 may be regarded as a trend, there is a pattern toward reconstruction of the 1976 class configuration of Iran in the years ahead.

Middle Class

In about the 1770s, when the term "social class" first entered the English lexicon, the concept of a "middle class" within that structure was also becoming important. The Industrial Revolution was allowing a much greater portion of the population to have time for the kind of education and cultural pursuits once restricted to the European feudal division of aristocracy, bourgeoisie, and peasantry which in that period would have included what later became the industrial proletarians of the towns and cities.

Today, concepts of social class assume three general categories: an upper class of proprietors and senior managers; a middle class of people who may not exert power over others, but may earn a significant proportion of their income through commerce, land ownership, or professional employment; and a lower class, who rely on wages for their livelihood.

It is important, however, to highlight the distinction of such a class model from that of the British concept of class in which the terms upper, middle and working-class have different definitions. The chief difference relates to the association of inherited wealth and landed property as a defining characteristic of the upper class. This distinguishes its members from those of the middle class whose membership is more fluid and more reliant upon employment status and its income. This is a broad generalization as there are classes within the middle class, such as the upper middle class whose interest in culture, and whose manners and mores distinguish them from other ranks in the middle strata, but is nonetheless a useful marker by which to distinguish the British concept of class from that of the new world.

In the United States, the term "middle class" is applied very broadly and includes people who would elsewhere be considered working class. As the vast majority of Americans identify themselves as being middle class, there are multiple theories as to what constitutes the American middle class. The term has been used to describe people from all walks of life, from janitors to attorneys. The definition of middle class is also relevant to the perspective of the individual. Due to the high standard of living in wealthy countries such as the U.S., the term middle class is also relevant to the standard of living of the majority of people in the world.

From this perspective, the term middle class becomes more inclusive. As a result, the US middle class is often sub-divided into two or three groups. While one set of theories claim that the middle class is composed of those in the middle of the social strata, other theories maintain that professionals and managers who have a college degree make up most of the middle class. In 2005 roughly 35% of Americans worked in the professional/professional support or managerial field and 27% had a college degree. Sociologists such as Dennis Gilbert or Joseph J. Hickey argue that the middle class is divided into two sub-groups. The upper middle class consists of white collar professionals with advanced educations and constitutes roughly 15% of the population. In 2005 the top 15% of income earners (age 25+) had incomes exceeding $62,500. The lower middle class (or middle-middle class for those who divide the middle class into three segments) consists of other mostly white collar employees with less autonomy in their work, lower educational attainment, lower personal income and less prestige than those of the upper middle class.

Sociologists such as Gilbert, Hickey, James Henslin, and William Thompson have brought forth class models in which the middle class is divided into two sections which combine to represent 47% to 49% of the population. Economist Michael Zweig defines class as power relationships among the members of a society, rather than as a lifestyle or by income. Zweig says that the middle class is only about 34% of the U.S. population, typically employed as managers, supervisors, small business owners and other professional people.

Class Structure in Various Societies

Although class can be discerned in any society, some cultures have published specific guidelines to rank. In some cases, the ideologies presented in these rankings may not concur with the mainstream power dialectic of social class as it is understood in modern English use.

Pre-capitalist Class Structures

Ancient Rome

Social class in ancient Rome played a major role in the lives of Romans. Ancient Roman society was hierarchical. Free-born adult male Roman citizens were divided into several classes, both by ancestry and by property. There were also several classes of non-citizens with different legal rights, along with married women, children, and slaves, who had no rights, and could be legally killed, ejected, or sold by the head of their household.

Renaissance Europe

The Mantegna Tarocchi, sets of cards made as an educational aid in Ferrara in the late 15th century, used the following hierarchy for the "Conditions of Man", largely ignoring the rural population:

1. Beggar
2. Servant (Famiglio)
3. Craftsman (Artigiano)
4. Merchant (Mercante)-presumably living mostly off income as a landlord
5. Gentleman (gentiluomo)
6. Knight (cavaliere)
7. Doge (doge)-i.e. a local ruler

8. King (Re)
9. Emperor (Imperatore)
10. Pope (Papa).

Aztec

Aztec society traditionally was divided into classes. The highest class were the *pîpiltin* or nobility. Originally this status was not hereditary, although the sons of *pillis* had access to better resources and education, so it was easier for them to become *pillis*. Later the class system took on hereditary aspects.

The second class were the *macehualtin* (people), originally peasants. Eduardo Noguera estimates that in later stages only 20% of the population was dedicated to agriculture and food production. The other 80% of society were warriors, artisans and traders.

Slaves or *tlacotin* also constituted an important class. Aztecs could become slaves because of debts, as a criminal punishment or as war captives. A slave could have possessions and even own other slaves.

Travelling merchants called *pochtecah* were a small, but important class as they not only facilitated commerce, but also communicated vital information across the empire and beyond its borders. They were often employed as spies.

Chinese

In pre-Confucian China, the feudal system divided the population into 6 classes. 4 noble classes with the king at the top, followed by the dukes, then the great men and finally the scholars.

Confucian doctrine later minimized the importance of the nobles (except the emperor), abolished great men and scholars as noble classes, and further divided commoner workers based on the perceived usefulness of their work. Scholars (now not exclusively nobles) ranked the highest because the opportunity to conceive clear ideas in a state of leisure would lead them to wise laws (an idea that has much in common with Plato's ideal of a philosopher king). The scholars were mainly from the gentry, who owned land, and may be educated and wealthy but had no aristocratic titles. Under them were the farmers, who produced necessary food, and the artisans who produced useful objects. Merchants ranked at the bottom because they did not actually produce anything, while soldiers were sometimes ranked even lower because of their perceived expendability. The Confucian model is notably different from the modern European view of social class, since merchants could attain great wealth without reaching the social status accorded to a poor farmer. In practice, a rich merchant might purchase land to reach farmer status, or even buy a good education for his heirs in the hopes that they would attain scholar status and go into the imperial civil service. The Chinese model was widely disseminated throughout east Asia.

Pre-revolutionary French

France was an monarchy with a king and other princes at the top of the class structure. The French States-General, established in 1302 was an assembly whose members were ranked according to hereditary class. The First Estate was the clergy, all Roman Catholic, and by this time with the bishops and higher roles dominated by sons of the nobility. The Second Estate consisted of lay members of the nobility, who constituted approximately two percent of the total population. The Third Estate consisted, technically, of everyone else, but was represented by representatives elected by a complicated system, in practice dominated by the bourgeois lawyers who held offices in the various regional Parlements. The peasantry had no official status in this system. This may be contrasted with the ideologically high status of farmers in Confucian China. The rigidity of the French hereditary system has been suggested as a major cause of the French Revolution.

Indian

Traditionally, the Indian caste system was one of the oldest and most important systems of social class. It differs from Varnashrama Dharma found in Hinduism, which allowed people born into a certain Varna to move upward or downwards depending on their qualification. It divided society based on skill and qualifications. Briefly, the Brahmin varna was idealized as a leisurely priest class devoted to religious ceremonies, while the Kshatriya defended them as military princes. The modern concept of the middle class was represented by the

Vaishya varna artisans, farmers, and merchants, and the lower varna were the Shudra labourers. Within this basic framework were arranged a huge number of jatis, or subcastes. It should be recognised not as a religious system (as Varnashrama Dharma prescribed in Hinduism), but a social system, which evolved from Varnashrama Dharma. After, the end of British occupation in 1947, the Constitution of India introduced various affirmative action plans to abolish the caste system. The people outside of the main Varnas were called Untouchables, because they were to not be touched by the "Twice Borns", or the higher three Varnas.

Iranian

Under the Qajar dynasty of Iran, the class structure was set up as follows:

- the permanent hereditary class of Qajar princes
- an upper class of "nobles and notables"
- religious leaders and students of theology
- merchants (note the difference from east Asian models)
- agricultural landowners
- master artisans and shopkeepers.

As in many official class structures, the labourers who made up the majority of the population but owned no land and relied on wages were not even considered part of the structure at all.

Japanese

The Japanese class structure, while influenced by the Chinese, was based on a much more feudal environment. The Emperor was not claimed to be a deity until pre-World War II military government did so but still was unquestionably at the pinnacle of the Japanese class structure (and still is, although no longer officially considered a god). However, for much of Japanese history the emperor was not allowed outside the palace grounds and his will was "interpreted" by a shogun, or military dictator. Beneath the shogun, daimyos or regional lords, administered the provinces through their samurai lieutenants. Perhaps through Chinese influence, and perhaps springing from a lack of arable land, the Japanese class structure also ranked farmers above merchants and other bourgeois. Classes changed after the Golden Age.

Korean

The Korean ruling class, or Korean power elite, is the relatively small number of Korean people who through similar schools, education, family clans, upbringing, or corporate chaebol wealth and urban power control decision making and policy within either of the partitioned Koreas.

This group is placed within the historical tradition of Confucianism and yangban scholars whose creation can be dated towards the end of the Goryeo dynasty; and that continues through the republican post-1945 and contemporary period; and which is represented by a controlling benevolent stewardship of the politics and economy of Korea by seniors or the older urban-dwelling elements of the population which crosses class, religious, party, and political lines.

Capitalist Class Structures

United Kingdom

The Parliament of the United Kingdom still contains a vestige of the pre-capitalist European class structure. The Queen maintains her status at the top of the social class structure, with the House of Lords up until very recently still representing the hereditary upper class, however due to the Life Peerage the vast majority of Lords in the House of Lords are of common birth and are not classified as Upper Class as they were not born into it, and the House of Commons technically representing everyone else. The House of Commons until the early 20th century represented the industrialist and landed classes. In the Victorian era of the United Kingdom, social class became a national obsession, with nouveau riche industrialists in the House of Commons trying to attain the status of House of Lords landowners through culture, marriage, title, and the construction of follies.

From a sociological point of view the class system in Britain changed substantially during the 'Thatcher Era'. Home ownership (on mortgage) was extended throughout the middle classes and below. With the loss of the majority of traditional working class industrial jobs from the market, a new 'underclass', below working class emerged. The 'underclass', defined as unemployed relying on state benefits, is the new bottom of the British class system.

In Britain people considered of lower social standing can earn high incomes, but an individual's social class is still largely assessed by their parent's mannerisms, education and the status.

Italy

Roman society is largely viewed as hierarchical, with slaves (*servi*) at the bottom, freedmen (*liberti*) above them, and free-born citizens (*cives*) at the top. Free citizens were themselves also divided by class. The broadest, and earliest, division was between the patricians, who could trace their ancestry to one of the 100 Patriarchs at the founding of the city, and the plebeians, who could not. This became less important in the later Republic, as some plebeian families became wealthy and entered politics, and some patrician families fell on hard times. Anyone, patrician or plebeian, who could count a consul as his ancestor was a noble (*nobilis*); a man who was the first of his family to hold the consulship, such as Marius or Cicero, was known as a *novus homo* ("new man") and ennobled his descendants. Patrician ancestry, however, still conferred considerable prestige, and many religious offices remained restricted to patricians.

A class division originally based on military service became more important. Membership of these classes was determined periodically by the Censors, according to property. The wealthiest were the Senatorial class, who dominated politics and command of the army. Next came the equestrians (*equites*, sometimes translated "knights"), originally those who could afford a warhorse, who formed a powerful mercantile class. Several further classes, originally based on what military equipment their members could afford, followed, with the *proletarii*, citizens who had no property at all, at the bottom. Before the reforms of Marius they were ineligible for military service and are often described as being just barely above freed slaves in terms of wealth and prestige.

Voting power in the Republic was dependent on class. Citizens were enrolled in voting "tribes", but the tribes of the richer classes had fewer members than the poorer ones, all the *proletarii* being enrolled in a single tribe. Voting was done in class order and stopped as soon as a majority of the tribes had been reached, so the poorer classes were often unable even to cast their votes.

Allied foreign cities were often given the Latin Right, an intermediary level between full citizens and foreigners (*peregrini*), which gave their citizens rights under Roman law and allowed their leading magistrates to become full Roman citizens. While there were varying degrees of Latin rights, the main division was between those *cum suffragio* ("with vote"; enrolled in a Roman tribe and able to take part in the *comitia tributa*) and *sine suffragio* ("without vote"; unable to take part in Roman politics). Some of Rome's Italian allies were given full citizenship after the Social War of 91–88 BC, and full Roman citizenship was extended to all free-born men in the Empire by Caracalla in 212. Women shared some basic rights with their male counterparts, but were not fully regarded as citizens and were thus not allowed to vote or participate in politics.

Today's Social Class Rank

A hierarchy of social class rank in Italy today, going from highest to lowest.

1. Bourgeoisie (10% of the working population) includes high-class entrepreneurs, managers, politicians, self-employed people, etc.
2. White-collar middle class (17% of the working population) includes middle class workers not employed in manual work.
3. Urban petit bourgeosie (14% of the working population), is mainly made up of shopkeepers, small-business entrepreneurs, self-employed artisians etc.
4. Rural petit bourgeosie (10% of the working population) consists of small entrepreneurs or estate owners who operate in the countryside, mainly in agriculture and forestry.
5. Urban working class (37% of the working population) refers to the people employed in manual work.

6. Rural working class (9% of the working population) consists of people operating in the primary industry, such as farmers, loggers, fishermen etc.

Latin American

In colonial Latin America access to positions of power and wealth were delineated by race. Accordingly, Peninsulars (Spaniards born in Spain and Portuguese born in Portugal) held the top ranks-including titles such as Viceroy, Captain General, etc. They were followed by Criollos (Those directly descended from Spaniards but born in America), who held considerable power and class but were barred from the highest decision-making posts. After these there was a system of castes, listed in order of rank, there were around a hundred castes, one of these were:

- Mestizo (Mixed Amerindian and Spaniard);
- Mulatto (Mixed Spaniard and African)
- Amerindian
- Zambo (Mixed Amerindian and African)
- Negro.

It is to be noted that even today there is a strong correlation between class and ethnicity.

New Zealand

Class in New Zealand is a product of both Maori and Western social structures. New Zealand was traditionally supposed to be a 'classless society' but this claim is problematic in a number of ways, and has been clearly untrue since at least the 1980s.

Maori Hierarchies

Maori society has traditionally been one based on rank, which derived from ancestry (whakapapa). Chiefs were invariably descended from other chiefs, although chieftainship was not the exclusive right of the first born son of the previous chief. If he did not show signs of leadership ability he would be passed over in favour of a brother or other relative. In some tribes women could take on leadership roles, although this was not usual. Women, lowly born men, and even people from other tribes were able to achieve positions of considerable influence. Such people have included Princess Te Puea Herangi and 'kingmaker' Wiremu Tamihana. Until the advent of Christianity it was normal for prisoners of war to be enslaved. Slaves had no rights and could be killed at the will of their master. However their children were free members of the tribe.

Present-day Maori society is far less hierarchical than it traditionally was, although it is still stratified by European standards. A disproportionate number of Maori MPs come from chiefly families, for example. However, a number of lowly-born Maori have achieved positions of considerable mana within their communities by virtue of their achievements or learning.

The 'Classless Society'

Until about the 1980s it was often claimed that New Zealand was a 'classless society'. Historian Keith Sinclair wrote in 1969 that although New Zealand was not a classless society, "it must be more nearly classless... than any advanced society in the world". From the nineteenth century many visitors also made this claim, for example British socialists Sidney and Beatrice Webb. The evidence for this was the relatively small range of wealth (that is, the wealthiest did not earn hugely more than the poorest earners), lack of deference to authority figures, high levels of class mobility, a high standard of working class living compared to Britain, progressive labour laws which protected workers and encouraged unionism, and a welfare state which was developed in New Zealand before most other countries.

Recently James Belich has argued that most of this is not evidence of an absence of class but rather of the relatively high status and standard of living of the working class in the nineteenth and early twentieth centuries. Unlike in Britain at this time, New Zealand working class people could regularly eat meat, own their own homes, and own horses (and later cars), while still being working class. Until the advent of compulsory secondary education in the 1930s, class mobility was limited, although much less so than in Britain.

It has also been argued that in New Zealand race takes the place of class, with Maori and other Polynesians earning less, having a lower standard of living and less education, and working in lower status jobs than people of European descent. They also face prejudice akin to that facing working class people in many European countries. Some argue that New Zealand only became a (white) 'workingman's paradise' because of the marginalisation of Maori and in particular the appropriation of Maori land.

New Zealanders' egalitarianism has been criticised as discouraging and denigrating ambition and individual achievement and success. New Zealanders tend to value modesty and distrust those who talk about their own merits. They especially dislike anyone who seems to consider themselves better than others even if the person in question is demonstrably more talented or successful than others. It is partly for this reason that mountaineer Sir Edmund Hillary is so admired in New Zealand; despite being the first person to climb Mount Everest he was always very modest. Extreme humility was arguably partly responsible for the early death of Prime Minister Norman Kirk, who may have survived his various health problems had he used his status to get preferential treatment from the public health system, or used private healthcare. This attitude can manifest itself in the tall poppy syndrome, which describes the 'cutting down' of anyone thought to have risen above the general mass of people.

New Zealand's claims to be a classless society were dealt a fatal blow in the 1980s and 1990s by the economic reforms of the fourth Labour government and its successor, the fourth National government. The reforms (sometimes called *Rogernomics*) made by these governments severely weakened the power of unions, removed a lot of protection from workers, cut social welfare benefits and made state housing less affordable. Over the period of these reforms, the gap between rich and poor New Zealanders has increased dramatically, with the incomes of the richest 10% of New Zealanders advancing while the other 90% stayed largely static. In addition the number of New Zealanders living in poverty is much higher than in the 1970s.. In an article entitled "Countries with the Biggest Gaps Between Rich and Poor", BusinessWeek ranked New Zealand at 6th in the world:

> *"The U.N. Development Program recently came out with a report looking, among other things, at income*

inequality worldwide... According to the OECD, New Zealand had the biggest rise in inequality among member nations in the two decades starting in the mid-1980s."

However although wealth is much more unevenly distributed than previously, New Zealand still lacks most of the overt signals of class which mark countries such as Britain. Most people do not care what others' parents do for a living, who a person is descended from, or where they went to school, and New Zealanders almost invariably have more respect for those who have earned their money through hard work than those who have inherited it or made it through investment.

The trend of greater social disparity has also seen a change in attitudes. Younger New Zealanders increasingly accept inequality as an unavoidable social reality, and egalitarian concerns are less popular.

Measures of Social Class

In 1972 Elley and Irving published *Socioeconomic Status in New Zealand*, which became one of the most cited papers in New Zealand social sciences. They outlined a socioeconomic index, now known as 'Elley-Irving (E-I)', based on 1966 Census data. E-I proposed six social strata based upon education and income, and grouped by occupation.

> *"The publication of the scale was welcomed by many researchers but regarded with suspicion by a number of lay critics who presumably clung to the belief that New Zealand was still a classless society. One newspaper headlined the production of a "snobbery scale". Such characterizations, and the numerous critics who misinterpreted its intentions, no doubt added to the frequency of its citing, but it is true that many researchers have made appropriate use of it for its original purpose. It is cited often because it is a useful tool."*
>
> —Warwick B. Elley, describing the impact of his paper

In the 1990s, P. Davis et al. published *New Zealand Socioeconomic Index of Occupational Status*, known as NZSEI. It was based on a 'returns to human capital' model of the stratification process and originally used data from the 1991 New Zealand Census (n=1,051,926) to generate scores for 97 occupational groups. It was later updated using 2006 Census data. NZSEI is a linear scale of ranked occupation, produced using an algorithm involving age, income and education, and aggregated to six discrete groupings (called *Socio-economic Status*, SES) to enable comparison with E-I and ISEI.

United States

The social structure of the United States is a vaguely defined concept which includes several commonly used terms that use educational attainment, income, wealth, and occupational prestige as the main determinants of class. While it is possible to create dozens of social classes within the confines of American society, most Americans employ a six or five class system.

The most commonly applied class concepts used in regards to contemporary American society are:

- Upper class: Those with great influence, wealth and prestige. Members of this group tend tc act as the grand-conceptualizers and have tremendous influence of the nation's institutions. This class makes up about 1% of the population and owns about a third of private wealth.
- Upper middle class: The upper middle class consists of white collar professionals with advanced post-secondary educational degrees and comfortable personal incomes. Upper middle class professionals have large amounts of autonomy in the workplace and therefore enjoy high job satisfaction. In terms of income and considering the 15% figure used by Thompson, Hickey and Gilber, upper middle class professionals earn roughly $62,500 (€41,000 or £31,500) or more and tend to reside in households with six figure incomes.
- (Lower) middle class: Semi-professionals, non-retail salespeople, and craftsmen who may have some college education. Out-sourcing tends to be a prominent problem among those in this class who often suffer from a lack of job security. Households in this class may need two income earners to make ends meet and therefore may

have household incomes rivaling the personal incomes of upper middle class professionals such as attorneys.

- Working class: According to some experts such as Michael Zweig, this class may constitute the majority of Americans and include those otherwise referred to as lower middle. It includes blue as well as white collar workers who have relatively low personal incomes and lack college degrees with many being among the 45% of Americans who have never attended college.
- Lower class: This class includes the poor, alienated and marginalized members of society. While most individuals in this class work, it is common for them to drift in and out of poverty.

Current Issues

There have been fierce debates in the area of sociology about whether or not social class has become relevant in terms of shaping identity. The arguments suggesting that it is no longer relevant are brought forward by supporters of postmodernism. One argument for class being unimportant follows:

Arguments against Relevance of Class

French sociologist Mattei Dogan has argued in his "From Social Class and Religious Identity to Status Incongruence in Post-Industrial Societies" that the relevance of social class has declined, giving way to a different form of social identification that is largely cultural and religious, and which raises identity conflicts called status incongruence. This can be observed, in particular, in the developing countries, but even in many post-industrial societies.

Arguments for Relevance of Class

Major areas of social science still rely on class based explanations of personal identity, for instance, the history from below school of Marxist history. Outside of Marxist influenced thought, there is still much evidence suggesting that class affects everyone. Some ideas from different sociologists follow:

- Jordan suggested that those in poverty had the same attitudes on work and family as those in other classes, this being backed up with surveys expressing that the poor/working class/lower class feel almost shame about their position in society.

- MacIntosh and Mooney noted that there was still an upper-class which seems to isolate itself from other classes. It is almost impossible to get into the upper-class. They (upper-class) kept their activities (marriage, education, peer groups) as a closed system.
- Marshall et al. noted that many manual class workers are still aware of many class issues. They believed in a possible conflict of interest, and saw themselves as working class. This counters the postmodern claims that it is consumption which defines an individual.
- Andrew Adonis and Stephen Pollard (1998) discovered a new super class, which consisted of elite professionals and managers, which held high salaries and share ownership.
- Chapman noted there was still an existence of a self-recruiting upper-class identity.
- Dennis Gilbert argues that class is bound to exist in any complex society as not all occupations are equal and that households do form pattern of interaction that give rise to social classes.

5

Raced Ways of Seeing

In the post-modern and multicultural worlds of criminology and criminal justice characterized by post-structuralism, post-Marxism, post-affirmative action, and post-feminism, the variables of class, race, and gender remain fundamental to both theory and practice. After all, the disciplines of criminology and the fields of criminal justice have always been about the real and imagined differences between "criminals" and "non-criminals." Theoretically, explanations of crime and crime control, regardless of perspective or school of thought, have sought to make sense out of these differences. In the process of trying to sort out these differences, virtually every theoretical framework has addressed class and race overtly, and gender at least covertly. Up until recently, the problem with this line of inquiry was not only that there had been very little, if any, agreement on the effects of these three critical variables, but worse yet, folks were still debating whether or not these variables matter.

By the turn of the 21st century, however, a growing number of criminologists from several orientations, including but not limited to critical, feminist, Marxist, positivist, and integrative, had come to appreciate, in different yet related ways, that class, race, and gender matter. Today, many inquiries are interested in finding out just how exactly class, race, and gender matter in the production of crime and criminal justice. Some inquiries focus on class, race, and gender as autonomous variables. Some inquiries focus on these three variables as inter-related. Of course, key questions on the complexities of these relations and on the means of exploring them still remain. And even though the ways of seeing difference or of approaching class, race, and gender vary, there is certainly an emerging consensus on the importance of these three variables, and increasingly, on the intersections between them or on their interactive or reciprocal relationships.

Discrimination

Discrimination is a sociological term referring to the treatment taken toward or against an individual of a certain group in consideration based solely on class or category. Discrimination is the *actual behaviour* towards another group. It involves excluding or restricting members of one group from opportunities that are available to other groups. The United Nations explains: "Discriminatory behaviours take many forms, but they all involve some form of exclusion or rejection." Discriminatory laws such as redlining have existed in many countries. In some countries, controversial attempts such as racial quotas have been used to redress negative effects of discrimination.

Race and Ethnicity Discrimination

Racial discrimination differentiates between individuals on the basis of real and perceived racial differences, and has been official government policy in several countries, such as South Africa in the apartheid era, and the USA.

In the United States, racial profiling of minorities by law enforcement officials has been called racial discrimination. As early as 1865, the Civil Rights Act provided a remedy for intentional race discrimination in employment by private employers and state and local public employers. The Civil Rights Act of 1871 applies to public employment or employment involving state action prohibiting deprivation of rights secured by the federal constitution or federal laws through action under colour of law. Title VII is the principal federal statute with regard to employment discrimination prohibiting unlawful employment discrimination by public and private employers, labor organizations, training programs and employment agencies based on race or colour, religion, gender, and national origin.

Title VII also prohibits retaliation against any person for opposing any practice forbidden by statute, or for making a charge, testifying, assisting, or participating in a proceeding under the statute. The Civil Rights Act of 1991 expanded the damages available in Title VII cases and granted Title VII plaintiffs the right to a jury trial. Title VII also provides that race and colour discrimination against every race and colour is prohibited.

In the UK the inquiry following the murder of Stephen Lawrence accused the police of institutional racism.

Weaver v NATFHE (now part of the UCU) Race/sex discrimination case. An Industrial (Employment) Tribunal in the UK in 1987 decided that a trade union was justified in not assisting a Black woman member, complaining of racist/sexist harassment, regardless of the merits of the case, because the accused male would lose his job. The Employment Appeal Tribunal upheld the decision, which still stands today as the definitive legal precedent in this field. Also known as the Bournville College Racial Harassment issue.

Within the criminal justice system in some Western countries, minorities are convicted and imprisoned disproportionately when compared with whites. In 1998, nearly one out of three black men between the ages of 20-29 were in prison or jail, on probation or parole on any given day in the United States. First Nations make up about 2% of Canada's population, but account for 18% of the federal prison population as of 2000. According to the Australian government's June 2006 publication of prison statistics, indigenous peoples make up 24% of the overall prison population in Australia. In 2004, Maori made up just 15% of the total population of New Zealand but 49.5% of prisoners. Maori were entering prison at 8 times the rate of non-Maori.

Age Discrimination

Age discrimination is discrimination on the grounds of age. Although theoretically the word can refer to the discrimination against any age group, age discrimination usually comes in one of three forms: discrimination against youth (also called adultism), discrimination against those 40 years old or older, and discrimination against elderly people.

In the United States, the Age Discrimination in Employment Act prohibits employment discrimination nationwide based on age with respect to employees 40 years of age or older. The Age Discrimination in Employment Act also addresses the difficulty older workers face in obtaining new employment after being displaced from their jobs, arbitrary age limits.

In many countries, companies more or less openly refuse to hire people above a certain age despite the increasing lifespans and average age of the population. The reasons for this range from vague feelings younger people are more "dynamic" and create a positive image for the company, to more concrete concerns about regulations granting older employees higher salaries or other benefits without these expenses being fully justified by an older employees' greater experience. Unions cite age as the most common form of discrimination in the workplace. Workers ages 45 and over form a disproportionate share of the long-term unemployed – those who have been out of work for six months or longer, according to the U.S. Bureau of Labor Statistics.

Some people consider that teenagers and youth (around 15–25 years old) are victims of adultism, age discrimination framed as a paternalistic form of protection. In seeking social justice, they feel that it is necessary to remove the use of a false moral agenda in order to achieve agency and empowerment.

This perspective is based on the grounds that youth should be treated more respectfully by adults and not as second-class citizens. Some suggest that social stratification in age groups causes outsiders to incorrectly stereotype and generalize the group, for instance that all adolescents are equally immature, violent or rebellious, listen to rock tunes, and do drugs. Some have organized groups against age discrimination.

Ageism is the causal effect of a continuum of fears related to age. This continuum includes:

- Ephebiphobia: the fear of youth.
- Gerontophobia: the fear of elderly people.
- Pediaphobia: the fear of infants or small children.

Related terms include:

- Adultism: Also called adultarchy, adult privilege, and adultcentrism/adultocentrism, this is the wielding of authority over young people and the preference of adults before children and youth.

- Jeunism: Also called "youthism" is the holding of beliefs or actions taken that preference 'younger' people before adults.

Sex and Gender Discrimination

Though gender discrimination and sexism refers to beliefs and attitudes in relation to the gender of a person, such beliefs and attitudes are of a social nature and do not, normally, carry any legal consequences. Sex discrimination, on the other hand, may have legal consequences.

Though what constitutes sex discrimination varies between countries, the essence is that it is an adverse action taken by one person against another person that would not have occurred had the person been of another sex. Discrimination of that nature in certain enumerated circumstances is illegal in many countries.

Currently, discrimination based on sex is defined as adverse action against another person, that would not have occurred had the person been of another sex. This is considered a form of prejudice and is illegal in certain enumerated circumstances in most countries.

Sexual discrimination can arise in different contexts. For instance an employee may be discriminated against by being asked discriminatory questions during a job interview, or because an employer did not hire, promote or wrongfully terminated an employee based on his or her gender, or employers pay unequally based on gender.

In an educational setting there could be claims that a student was excluded from an educational institution, program, opportunity, loan, student group, or scholarship due to his or her gender. In the housing setting there could be claims that a person was refused negotiations on seeking a house, contracting/leasing a house or getting a loan based on his or her gender. Another setting where there have been claims of gender discrimination is banking; for example if one is refused credit or is offered unequal loan terms based on one's gender. Another setting where there is usually gender discrimination is when one is refused to extend his or her credit, refused approval of credit/loan process, and if there is a burden of unequal loan terms based on one's gender.

Socially, sexual differences have been used to justify different roles for men and women, in some cases giving rise to claims of primary and secondary roles.

While there are alleged non-physical differences between men and women, major reviews of the academic literature on gender difference find only a tiny minority of characteristics where there are consistent psychological differences between men and women, and these relate directly to experiences grounded in biological difference. However, there are also some psychological differences in regard to how problems are dealt with and emotional perceptions and reactions which may relate to hormones and the successful characteristics of each gender during longstanding roles in past primitive lifestyles.

Unfair discrimination usually follows the gender stereotyping held by a society.

The United Nations had concluded that women often experience a "glass ceiling" and that there are no societies in which women enjoy the same opportunities as men. The term "glass ceiling" is used to describe a perceived barrier to advancement in employment based on discrimination, especially sex discrimination.

In the United States in 1995, the Glass Ceiling Commission, a government-funded group, stated: "Over half of all Master's degrees are now awarded to women, yet 95% of senior-level managers, of the top Fortune 1000 industrial and 500 service companies are men. Of them, 97% are white." In its report, it recommended affirmative action, which is the consideration of an employee's gender and race in hiring and promotion decisions, as a means to end this form of discrimination. In 2008, women accounted for 51% of all workers in the high-paying management, professional, and related occupations. They outnumbered men in such occupations as public relations managers; financial managers; and human resource managers.

The China's leading headhunter, Chinahr.com, reported in 2007 that the average salary for white-collar men was 44,000 yuan ($6,441), compared with 28,700 yuan ($4,201) for women.

The PwC research found that among FTSE 350 companies in the United Kingdom in 2002 almost 40% of senior management posts were occupied by women. When that research was repeated in 2007, the number of senior management posts held by women had fallen to 22%.

Transgender individuals, both male to female and female to male, often experience problems which often lead to dismissals, underachievement, difficulty in finding a job, social isolation, and, occasionally, violent attacks against them. Nevertheless, the problem of gender discrimination does not stop at trandgender individuals nor with women. Men are often the victim in certain areas of employment as men begin to seek work in office and childcare settings traditionally perceived as "women's jobs". One such situation seems to be evident in a recent case concerning alleged YMCA discrimination and a Federal Court Case in Texas.

The case actually involves alleged discrimination against both men and blacks in childcare, even when they pass the same strict background tests and other standards of employment. It is currently being contended in federal court, as of fall 2009, and sheds light on how a workplace dominated by a majority (-women in this case) sometimes will seemingly "justify" whatever they wish to do, regardless of the law. This may be done as an effort at self-protection, to uphold traditional societal roles, or some other faulty, unethical or illegal prejudicial reasoning.

Affirmative action also leads to white men being discriminated against for entry level and blue collar positions. An employer cannot hire a white man with the same "on paper" qualifications over a woman or minority worker or the employer will face prosecution.

Caste Discrimination

According to UNICEF and Human Rights Watch, caste discrimination affects an estimated 250 million people worldwide. Discrimination based on caste, as perceived by UNICEF, is prevalent mainly in parts of Asia (India, Sri Lanka, Bangladesh, Nepal, Japan) and Africa. Currently, there are an estimated 160 million Dalits or Scheduled Castes (formerly known as "untouchables") in India.. Dalit people face severe problems, such as segregation and violence against them An estimated 40 million people in India, most of them Dalits, are bonded workers, many working to pay off debts that were incurred generations ago.

There have been substantial improvements in the position of Dalits in post-independence India, consequent to the strict implementation of the rights and privileges enshrined in the Constitution of India, as implemented by the Protection of Civil rights Act, 1955. India has had a Dalit president, K.R. Narayanan, and the practise had disappeared in urban public life, though persist very strongly in rural areas, where modern ideas have not penetrated, and ancient ethnic divisions and hostilities against Dalits often dominate the discourse of inter-community relations, resulting in under represented Dalits facing discrimination and violence.

In modern times, Dalits, as well as tribal people and members of the lowest castes in India benefit from broad affirmative action programmes and are enjoying greater political power." The Constitution of India places special emphasis on outlawing caste discrimination, especially the practice of untouchability. In addition, the Indian penal code inflicts severe punishments on those who discriminate on the basis of caste. Anti-Dalit prejudice and discrimination exists primarily in rural areas, where small societies can track the caste lineage of individuals and discriminate accordingly.

Employment Discrimination

Employment discrimination refers to disabling certain people to apply and receive jobs based on their race, age, gender, religion, sexual orientation and disability. In relationship to Sociology, employment discrimination usually relates to what events are happening in society at the time. For example, it would seem ludicrous to hire an African American male, and absolutely unheard of to hire an African American woman over 50 years ago. However, in our society today, it is the absolute norm to hire any qualified person. Employment discrimination has decreased tremendously from previous years. This is due to laws that prohibit employment discrimination. In our society today, everyone is ordered to treat all different types of people equally and grant them the same opportunities. If a person hiring another breaks these rules, they can be sued for hate crimes.

Sexual Orientation Discrimination

In 2009, ILGA published a report based on research carried out by Daniel Ottosson at Södertörn University College, Stockholm, Sweden. This research found that of the 80 countries around the world that continue to consider homosexuality illegal, five carry the death penalty for homosexual activity, and two do in some regions of the country. In the report, this is described as “State sponsored homophobia”. This happens in Islamic states, or in two cases regions under Islamic authority.

On February 5, 2005 the IRIN issued a reported titled “Iraq: Male homosexuality still a taboo.” The article stated, among other things that honor killings by Iraqis against a gay family member are common and given some legal protection. In August 2009 Human Rights Watch published an extensive report detailing torture of men accused of being gay in Iraq, including the blocking of men’s anuses with glue and then giving the men laxatives.

South Africa has one of the world’s most progressive constitutions, but same-sex unions are often decried as “un-African.” Research shows 86% of black lesbians from the Western Cape live in fear of sexual assault.

Language Discrimination

Diversity of language is protected and respected by most nations who value cultural diversity. However, people are sometimes subjected to different treatment because their preferred language is associated with a particular group, class or category. Commonly, the preferred language is just another attribute of separate ethnic groups. Discrimination exists if there is prejudicial treatment against a person or a group of people who speak a particular language or dialect. Language discrimination is suggested to be labelled linguicism or logocism. Anti-discriminatory and inclusive efforts to accommodate persons who speak different languages or cannot have fluency in the country’s predominant or “official” language, is bilingualism such as official documents in two languages, and multiculturalism in more than two languages.

Reverse Discrimination

Some attempts at antidiscrimination have been criticized as reverse discrimination. In particular, minority quotas (e.g. affirmative action) discriminate against members of a dominant or majority group. In its opposition to race preferences, the American Civil Rights Institute's Ward Connerly stated, "There is nothing positive, affirmative, or equal about 'affirmative action' programs that give preference to some groups based on race."

Disability Discrimination

Discrimination against people with disabilities in favor of people who are not is called ableism or disablism. Disability discrimination, which treats non-disabled individuals as the standard of 'normal living', results in public and private places and services, education, and social work that are built to serve 'standard' people, thereby excluding those with various disabilities.

In the United States, the Americans with Disabilities Act provides guidelines for providing wheelchair access for public institutions.

Religious Discrimination

Religious discrimination is valuing or treating a person or group differently because of what they do or do not believe. A concept like that of 'religious discrimination' is necessary to take into account ambiguities of the term *religious persecution*. The infamous cases in which people have been executed for beliefs perceived to be heretic are generally recognisable as persecution. Other cases in which adherents of different religions (or denominations) are treated unequally before the law are sometimes difficult to assess. If behind laws, regulations or acts of authority perceived to be discriminating against a certain religion, there is the intention 'encourage' people to abandon their beliefs, the laws are religious persuction. Laws which only carry light punishments are described as *mild forms of religious persecution* or as *religious discrimination*.

Furthermore, even in societies where Freedom of Religion is a constitutional right, sometimes adherents of religious minorities voice concerns about religious discrimination against them. Insofar as legal policies are concerned, cases that are perceived as religious discrimination might be the result of an interference of the religious sphere with other spheres of the public that are regulated by law (and not aimed specifically against a religious minority.)

Generally people are free to have these issues clarified through the juridical system.

In a 1979 consultation on the issue, the United States commission on civil rights defined religious discrimination in relation to the civil rights guaranteed by the Fourteenth Amendment to the United States Constitution.

Whereas religious civil liberties, such as the right to hold or not to hold a religious belief, are essential for Freedom of Religion (in the United States secured by the First Amendment), religious discrimination occurs when someone is denied " the equal protection of the laws, equality of status under the law, equal treatment in the administration of justice, and equality of opportunity and access to employment, education, housing, public services and facilities, and public accommodation because of their exercise of their right to religious freedom."

Situation in Western Countries

However, cases of religious discrimination might also be the result of an interference of the religious sphere with other spheres of the public that are regulated by law. Although e.g. in the United States the Free Exercise Clause of the First Amendment states that *"Congress shall make no law respecting an establishment of religion, or prohibiting the free exercise thereof"*, in *Reynolds v. United States* the U.S. supreme court decided that religious duty was not a suitable defence to a criminal indictment. In this specific case a law against bigamy was not considered to be discriminating against Mormons, who, at that time sometimes practiced Polygyny.

Similar current issues in the United States are about the policy towards drugs or environmental policy. Practitioners of one branch of the native American religion perceive the regulations regarding the use of Peyote and the eagle feather law in the United States as discriminating. Similar cases can be found in many other western countries.

Further Examples

Charges of religious discrimination have been applied to governmental, social, and educational policies.

- The Eagle Feather Law, which governs the possession and religious use of eagle feathers, was officially written to protect then dwindling eagle populations while still protecting traditional Native American spiritual and religious customs, of which the use of eagles are central. The Eagle Feather Law later met charges of promoting racial and religious discrimination due to the law's provision authorizing the possession of eagle feathers to members of only one ethnic group, Native Americans, and forbidding Native Americans from including non-Native Americans in indigenous customs involving eagle feathers—a common modern practice dating back to the early 16th century.
- Charges of religious and racial discrimination have also been found in the education system. In a recent example, the dormitory policies at Boston University and The University of South Dakota were charged with racial and religious discrimination when they forbade a university dormitory resident from smudging while praying. The policy at The University of South Dakota was later changed to permit students to pray while living in the university dorms.
- The Seventh-day Adventist Church make it clear in their university catalog that they discriminate on the basis of religion. They discriminate against non-Adventists in hiring practices, disciplinary action, and promotions. The Seventh-day Adventist Church has made many anti-Catholic statements that the Bible identifies the Pope as the Anti-Christ. Today, the church has softened these statements, explaining that they interpret the biblical passages as referring to the papal institution and not to a specific person. Recently, they have also taken measures against church members who have publicly attacked the pope, especially those who claim that it is in the name of the church.
- During 1995-1998 Newfoundland had only Christian schools (four of them, Pentecostal, Roman Catholic,

Seventh-day Adventist, and inter-denominational (Anglican, Salvation Army and United Church)). The right to organize publicly supported religious schools was only given to certain Christian denominations, thus tax money used to support a selected group of Christian denominations. The denominational schools could also refuse admission of a student or the hiring of a qualified teacher on purely religious grounds. Quebec has used two school systems, one Protestant and the other Roman Catholic, but it seems this system will be replaced with two secular school systems: one French and the other English.

- In Greece since the independence from the Muslim Ottomans rule in the 19th century, the Greek Orthodox Church has been given privileged status and only the Greek Orthodox church, Roman Catholic, some Protestant churches, Judaism and Islam are recognized religions. The Muslim minority alleges that Greece persistently and systematically discriminates against Muslims.
- According to a *Human Rights Practices* report by the *U.S. State Department* on Mexico note that "some local officials infringe on religious freedom, especially in the south". There is conflict between Catholic/Mayan syncretists and Protestant evangelicals in the Chiapas region.
- In some U.S. jurisdictions legal restrictions exist which require a religious test as a qualification for holding public office, for instance in Texas an official may be "excluded from holding office" if he/she does not "acknowledge the existence of a Supreme Being." (i.e. God) thus atheists, agnostics, Buddhists, most Satanists, some Unitarian Universalists and New Age followers, who do not believe in a supreme being would be excluded from public office.
- In 2004, a case involving five Ohio prison inmates (two followers of Asatru, a minister of the Church of Jesus Christ Christian, a Wiccan witch and a Satanist) protesting denial of access to ceremonial items and opportunities for group worship was brought before the

Supreme Court. The Boston Globe reports on the 2005 decision of *Cutter v. Wilkinson* in favour of the claimants as a notable case. Among the denied objects was instructions for runic writing requested by an Asatruer. Inmates of the "Intensive Management Unit" at Washington State Penitentiary who are adherents of Asatru in 2001 were deprived of their Thor's Hammer medallions. In 2007, a federal judge confirmed that Asatru adherents in US prisons have the right to possess a Thor's Hammer pendant. An inmate sued the Virginia Department of Corrections after he was denied it while members of other religions were allowed their medallions.

- Religious discrimination has also been documented in employment, such as an Equal Employment Opportunity Commission (EEOC) law suit alleging discrimination against an Iranian-Muslim employee by the Merrill Lynch company in US.

Theories

Discrimination

Social theories such as Egalitarianism claim that social equality should prevail. In some societies, including most developed countries, each individual's civil rights include the right to be free from government sponsored social discrimination. Due to a belief in the capacity to perceive pain and/or suffering shared by all animals, 'abolitionist' or 'vegan' egalitarianism maintains that the interests of every individual (regardless its species), warrant equal consideration with the interests of humans, and that not doing so is "speciesist".

Conservative and Anarcho-Capitalist

In contrast, conservative writer and law professor Matthias Storme has claimed that the freedom of discrimination in human societies is a fundamental human right, or more precisely, the basis of all fundamental freedoms and therefore the most fundamental freedom. Author Hans-Hermann Hoppe, in an essay about his book Democracy: The God That Failed, asserts that a natural social order is characterized by increased discrimination.

Labelling Theory

Discrimination, in labelling theory, takes form as mental categorisation of minorities and the use of stereotype. This theory describes difference as deviance from the norm, which results in internal devaluation and social stigma that may be seen as discrimination. It is started by describing a 'natural' social order. It is distinguished between the fundamental principle of fascism and social democracy. The Nazis in 1930's-era Germany, the pre-1990 Apartheid government of South Africa used racial discriminatory agendas for their political ends. This practice continues with some present day governments.

Stereotypes and Scapegoats

Stereotyping is a type of discrimination. When a person is stereotyping they are thinking in terms of inflexible categories, and is linked to the psychological mechanism called displacement. Displacement is when one feels feelings of hostility or anger toward objects that are not the origin of those feelings. Many people blame scapegoats for problems that are not their fault. This is common when two deprived ethnic groups compete with one another for economic rewards. This is normally directed against groups that are relatively powerless, because they make an easy target. It frequently involves projection, which is the unconscious attribution to the others of ones own desires or characteristics.

6

Perspectives from Media Studies

The Role and Influence of Mass Media

Mass media is communication—whether written, broadcast, or spoken—that reaches a large audience. This includes television, radio, advertising, movies, the Internet, newspapers, magazines, and so forth.

Mass media is a significant force in modern culture, particularly in America. Sociologists refer to this as a mediated culture where media reflects and creates the culture. Communities and individuals are bombarded constantly with messages from a multitude of sources including TV, billboards, and magazines, to name a few. These messages promote not only products, but moods, attitudes, and a sense of what is and is not important. Mass media makes possible the concept of celebrity: without the ability of movies, magazines, and news media to reach across thousands of miles, people could not become famous. In fact, only political and business leaders, as well as the few notorious outlaws, were famous in the past. Only in recent times have actors, singers, and other social elites become celebrities or "stars."

The current level of media saturation has not always existed. As recently as the 1960s and 1970s, television, for example, consisted of primarily three networks, public broadcasting, and a few local independent stations. These channels aimed their programming primarily at two-parent, middle-class families. Even so, some middle-class households did not even own a television. Today, one can find a television in the poorest of homes, and multiple TVs in most middle-class homes. Not only has availability increased, but programming is increasingly diverse with shows aimed to please all ages, incomes, backgrounds, and attitudes. This widespread availability and exposure makes television the primary focus of most mass-media discussions. More recently, the Internet has increased its role exponentially as more businesses and households "sign on." Although TV and the Internet have dominated the mass media, movies and magazines—particularly those lining the aisles at grocery checkout stands—also play a powerful role in culture, as do other forms of media. What role does mass media play? Legislatures, media executives, local school officials, and sociologists have all debated this controversial question. While opinions vary as to the extent and type of influence the mass media wields, all sides agree that mass media is a permanent part of modern culture. Three main sociological perspectives on the role of media exist: the limited-effects theory, the class-dominant theory, and the culturalist theory.

Limited-effects Theory

The limited-effects theory argues that because people generally choose what to watch or read based on what they already believe, media exerts a negligible influence. This theory originated and was tested in the 1940s and 1950s. Studies that examined the ability of media to influence voting found that well-informed people relied more on personal experience, prior knowledge, and their own reasoning. However, media "experts" more likely swayed those who were less informed. Critics point to two problems with this perspective. First, they claim that limited-effects theory ignores the media's role in framing and limiting the discussion and debate of issues. How media frames the debate and what questions members of the media ask change the outcome of the discussion and the possible conclusions people may draw. Second, this theory came into existence when the availability and dominance of media was far less widespread.

Class-dominant Theory

The class-dominant theory argues that the media reflects and projects the view of a minority elite, which controls it.

Those people who own and control the corporations that produce media comprise this elite. Advocates of this view concern themselves particularly with massive corporate mergers of media organizations, which limit competition and put big business at the reins of media—especially news media. Their concern is that when ownership is restricted, a few people then have the ability to manipulate what people can see or hear. For example, owners can easily avoid or silence stories that expose unethical corporate behaviour or hold corporations responsible for their actions.

The issue of sponsorship adds to this problem. Advertising dollars fund most media. Networks aim programming at the largest possible audience because the broader the appeal, the greater the potential purchasing audience and the easier selling air time to advertisers becomes. Thus, news organizations may shy away from negative stories about corporations (especially parent corporations) that finance large advertising campaigns in their newspaper or on their stations. Television networks receiving millions of dollars in advertising from companies like Nike and other textile manufacturers were slow to run stories on their news shows about possible human-rights violations by these companies in foreign countries. Media watchers identify the same problem at the local level where city newspapers will not give new cars poor reviews or run stories on selling a home without an agent because the majority of their funding comes from auto and real estate advertising. This influence also extends to programming. In the 1990s a network cancelled a short-run drama with clear religious sentiments, *Christy,* because, although highly popular and beloved in rural America, the program did not rate well among young city dwellers that advertisers were targeting in ads.

Critics of this theory counter these arguments by saying that local control of news media largely lies beyond the reach of large corporate offices elsewhere, and that the quality of news depends upon good journalists. They contend that those less powerful and not in control of media have often received full media coverage and subsequent support. As examples they name numerous environmental causes, the anti-nuclear movement, the anti-Vietnam movement, and the pro-Gulf War movement.

While most people argue that a corporate elite controls media, a variation on this approach argues that a politically "liberal" elite controls media. They point to the fact that journalists, being more highly educated than the general population, hold more liberal political views, consider themselves "left of centre," and are more likely to register as Democrats. They further point to examples from the media itself and the statistical reality that the media more often labels conservative commentators or politicians as "conservative" than liberals as "liberal." Media language can be revealing, too. Media uses the terms "arch" or "ultra" conservative, but rarely or never the terms "arch" or "ultra" liberal. Those who argue that a political elite controls media also point out that the movements that have gained media attention—the environment, anti-nuclear, and anti-Vietnam—generally support liberal political issues. Predominantly conservative political issues have yet to gain prominent media attention, or have been opposed by the media. Advocates of this view point to the Strategic Arms Initiative of the 1980s Reagan administration. Media quickly characterized the defence program as "Star Wars," linking it to an expensive fantasy. The public failed to support it, and the program did not get funding or congressional support.

Culturalist Theory

The culturalist theory, developed in the 1980s and 1990s, combines the other two theories and claims that people interact with media to create their own meanings out of the images and messages they receive. This theory sees audiences as playing an active rather than passive role in relation to mass media. One strand of research focuses on the audiences and how they interact with media; the other strand of research focuses on those who produce the media, particularly the news.

Theorists emphasize that audiences choose what to watch among a wide range of options, choose how much to watch, and may choose the mute button or the VCR remote over the programming selected by the network or cable station. Studies of mass media done by sociologists parallel text-reading and interpretation research completed by linguists (people who study language). Both groups of researchers find that when people approach material, whether written text or media images and messages, they interpret that material based on their own knowledge and experience. Thus, when researchers ask different groups to explain the meaning of a particular song or video, the groups produce widely divergent interpretations based on age, gender, race, ethnicity, and religious background. Therefore, culturalist theorists claim that, while a few elite in large corporations may exert significant control over what information media produces and distributes, personal perspective plays a more powerful role in how the audience members interpret those messages.

Richard Peterson

Richard Peterson is a Professor of Sociology at Vanderbilt University. He has also served at the University of Wisconsin, the University of Leeds, and the National Endowment for the Arts. A participant in six professional societies, he was the founding Chair of the Culture Section of the American Sociological Association.

Dr. Peterson has authored or edited eight books, the most recent of which are Age and Arts Participation for the National Endowment for the Arts and Creating Country Music: Fabricating Authenticity for the University of Chicago Press. Both were widely reviewed by the national press and the latter has received several awards. Dr. Peterson's numerous articles have focused on the production and consumption of culture, patterns of leisure, and the working of the media industry.

With colleagues, Dr. Peterson is currently researching the impact of Internet transmission of music on the music industry and on the nature of popular music itself; the changing patterns of recreation among Internet users; long-standing fascination of whites with African-American music; and the Internet-driven coalescence of alternative country music.

Howard S Becker

Howard Saul Becker (born April 18, 1928, Chicago) is an American sociologist.

Biography

Howard Becker was born in Chicago, Illinois on April 18,1928. As an undergraduate and later a graduate student at the University of Chicago, he worked as a professional jazz pianist, and plays still. He earned his Ph.B., A.M., and Ph.D., all at the University of Chicago, 1946, 1949 and 1951, respectively.

His professor, Everett C. Hughes, whose primary interest was the sociology of work and professions, was an important influence on Becker. It was Hughes, Becker reports, who first encouraged him to undertake the study of jazz musicians as a professional group. This research led Becker to write extensively about drug use, and he put off publishing it for over a decade until 1963, when the political climate in the United States had improved. The resulting book, "Outsiders" was a critical work in the sociology of deviance and laid the foundation of labelling theory. In that book he "said everything I have to say about labelling theory."

For his doctoral dissertation, Becker studied Chicago schoolteachers. Generally speaking, his work reflects the prevailing thematic and theoretical preoccupations of Chicago sociology at that time, with its attention to symbolic interactions involving race, status, and power in the urban melting pot. Erving Goffman was a contemporary of Becker's at Chicago, and their research interests and writing styles both reflect a similar formative milieu. Since that time, Becker, Goffman and others such as Anselm Strauss have become known as the "Second Chicago School"

After receiving his Ph.D. in Sociology in 1951 he went on to teach in Sociology Departments at Northwestern University, the University of Washington, and the University of California at Santa Barbara. However, the majority of his research, writing and teaching was in other fields of sociology, including but not limited to the sociology of art, qualitative method, visual sociology and the practice of research and writing (composition theory) in social sciences.

Becker is acclaimed for the clarity of his prose, and is a staunch advocate of what has been termed the "Plain style" of writing. His stylistic predilections betray his academic pedigree: at the time he was a student, sociologists at the University of Chicago embraced European positivism and Midwestern pragmatism. They sought to communicate their ideas with scientific precision, on the one hand, while making them accessible to politicians and planners, on the other. He developed various aspects of a sociology of writing in his *Writing for Social Scientists: How to Start and Finish Your Thesis, Book, or Article*. It is considered to be one of the best books advising all academics how to write. The book reflects the conviction that clear prose and clear thinking are inseparable. He served on the advisory board for the 15th edition of the *Chicago Manual of Style*.

Becker is notable for coining the phrase "hierarchy of credibility" The Hierarchy of credibility is a concept according purportedly objective judgments of fact and evidence are necessarily tilted in favor of those at the top of a society because they will have had more resources to produce seemingly objective evidence that tends to favor the privileges they enjoy. Becker argues that it is the scholar's responsibility to find evidence that supports the claims of society's least privileged.

While he lives in San Francisco, Becker regularly sojourns in France, previously in the company of Alain Pessin, a sociologist at the University of Grenoble who wrote a book on Becker titled *Un sociologue en liberté. Lecture de Howard S. Becker* (A sociologist in liberty; a reading of Howard S. Becker). Pessin died in 2005.

Becker's students include Elijah Anderson and Mitchell Duneier.

7

Cultural Sociology of India

The culture of India has been shaped not only by its long history, unique geography and diverse demography, but also by its ancient heritages, which were formed during the Indus Valley Civilization and evolved further during the Vedic age, rise and decline of Buddhism, the Golden age, invasions from Central Asia, European colonization and the Indian independence movement.

India's languages, religions, dance, music, architecture and customs differ from place to place within the country, but nevertheless possess a commonality. The culture of India is an amalgamation of these diverse sub-cultures spread all over the Indian subcontinent and traditions that are several millennia old.

Regarded by some historians as the "oldest living civilization of Earth", the Indian tradition dates back to 8,000 BC and has a continuous recorded history for over 2,500 years. Several elements of India's diverse culture — such as Indian religions, yóga and Indian cuisine — have had a profound impact across the world.

Religions and Spirituality

India is the birth place of Hinduism, Buddhism, Jainism and Sikhism, collectively known as Indian religions. Indian religions, also known as Dharmic religions are a major form of world religions along with Abrahamic ones. Today, Hinduism and Buddhism are the world's third-and fourth-largest religions respectively, with over 2 billion followers altogether, and possibly as many as 2.5 or 2.6 billion followers. India is also the birthplace for the Sikh, Jain, Lingayat, and Ahmadiyya faiths.

India is one of the most religiously diverse nations in the world, with some of the most deeply religious societies and cultures. Religion still plays a central and definitive role in the life of most of its people.

The religion of 80% of the people is Hinduism. Islam is practiced by around 13% of all Indians. Sikhism, Jainism and especially Buddhism are influential not only in India but across the world. Christianity, Zoroastrianism, Judaism and the Baha'í Faith are also influential but their numbers are smaller. Despite the strong role of religion in Indian life, atheism and agnostics also have visible influence along with a self-ascribed tolerance to other people.

Society

Overview

According to Eugene M. Makar, traditional Indian culture is defined by relatively strict social hierarchy. He also mentions that from an early age, children are reminded of their roles and places in society. This is reinforced by the fact that many believe gods and spirits have an integral and functional role in determining their life. Several differences such as religion divide the culture. However, a far more powerful division is the traditional Hindu bifurcation into non-polluting and polluting occupations. Strict social taboos have governed these groups for thousands of years. In recent years, particularly in cities, some of these lines have blurred and sometimes even disappeared. Important family relations extend as far as gotra, the mainly patrilinear lineage or clan assigned to a Hindu at birth. In rural areas & sometimes in urban areas as well, it is common that three or four generations of the family live under the same roof. The patriarch often resolves family issues.

Family

Family plays a significant role in the Indian culture. For generations, India has had a prevailing tradition of the joint family system. It is a system under which extended members of a family – parents, children, the children's spouses and their offspring, etc. – live together. Usually, the eldest male member is the head in the joint Indian family system. He makes all important decisions and rules, and other family members abide by them. Even today, the vast majority of Indians have their marriages planned by their parents and other respected family-members, with the consent of the bride and groom. Arranged matches are made after taking into account factors such as age, height, personal values and tastes, the backgrounds of their families (wealth, social standing), their castes and the astrological compatibility of the couples' horoscopes.

In India, the marriage is thought to be for life, and the divorce rate is extremely low — 1.1% compared with about 50% in the United States. The arranged marriages generally have a much lower divorce rate. The divorce rates have risen significantly in recent years:

> *"Opinion is divided over what the phenomenon means: for traditionalists the rising numbers portend the breakdown of society while, for some modernists, they speak of a healthy new empowerment for women."*

Animals

The varied and rich wildlife of India has had a profound impact on the region's popular culture. Common name for wilderness in India is Jungle which was adopted by the British colonialists to the English language. The word has been also made famous in *The Jungle Book* by Rudyard Kipling. India's wildlife has been the subject of numerous other tales and fables such as the *Panchatantra* and the *Jataka tales.*

In Hinduism, the cow is regarded as a symbol of *ahimsa* (non-violence), mother goddess and bringer of good fortune and wealth. For this reason, cows are revered in Hindu culture and feeding a cow is seen as an act of worship.

Namaste

Namaste, *Namaskar* or *Namaskara* or *Namaskaram*, *Vanakkam* or *Sat Shri Akal* is a common spoken greeting or salutation in the Indian subcontinent. Namaskar is considered a slightly more formal version than namaste but both express deep respect. It is commonly used in India and Nepal by Hindus, Jains, Buddhists and Sikhs, and many continue to use this outside the Indian subcontinent. In Indian and Nepali culture, the word is spoken at the beginning of written or verbal communication. However, the same hands folded gesture is made usually wordlessly upon departure. Taken literally, it means "I bow to you". The word is derived from Sanskrit (namah): to bow, obeisance, reverential salutation, and respect, and (te): "to you". As explained by an Indian scholar, in literal terms Namaste refers to 'That which is of God in me bows to that which is of God in you'.

Festivals

India, being a multi-cultural and multi-religious society, celebrates holidays and festivals of various religions. The three national holidays in India, the Independence Day, the Republic Day and the Gandhi Jayanti, are celebrated with zeal and enthusiasm across India. In addition, many states and regions have local festivals depending on prevalent religious and linguistic demographics. Popular religious festivals include the Hindu festivals of *Navratri Diwali*, *Ganesh Chaturthi*, *Durga puja*, *Holi*, *Rakshabandhan* and *Dussehra*. Several harvest festivals, such as *Sankranthi*, *Pongal* and *Onam*, "Nuakhai" are also fairly popular.

Certain festivals in India are celebrated by multiple religions. Notable examples include Diwali, which is celebrated by Hindus, Sikhs and Jains, and *Buddh Purnima*, celebrated by Buddhists and Hindus. Islamic festivals, such *Eid ul-Fitr*, *Eid al-Adha* and *Ramadan*, are celebrated by Muslims across India. Sikh Festivals, such as *Guru Nanak Jayanti*, *Baiskhi* are celebrated with full fanfare by Sikhs and Hindu. Adding colors to the culture of India, the Dree Festival is one of the tribal festivals of India celebrated by the Apatanis of the Zirs of death hai.

Cuisine

The multiple varieties of Indian cuisine are characterized by their sophisticated and subtle use of many spices and herbs. Each family of this cuisine is characterized by a wide assortment of dishes and cooking techniques. Though a significant portion of Indian food is vegetarian, many traditional Indian dishes also include chicken, goat, lamb, fish, and other meats.

Food is an important part of Indian culture, playing a role in everyday life as well as in festivals. Indian cuisine varies from region to region, reflecting the varied demographics of the country. Generally, Indian cuisine can be split into five categories— northern, southern, eastern, western and north-eastern. India is known for its love for food and spices. India has some of the best restaurants and cafes which can be easily explored at Foodiebay.com.

Despite this diversity, some unifying threads emerge. Varied uses of spices are an integral part of food preparation, and are used to enhance the flavour of a dish and create unique flavors and aromas. Cuisine across India has also been influenced by various cultural groups that entered India throughout history, such as the Persians, Mughals, and European colonists. Though the *tandoor* originated in Central Asia, Indian tandoori dishes, such as *chicken tikka* made with Indian ingredients, enjoy widespread popularity.

Indian cuisine is one of the most popular cuisines across the globe. Historically, Indian spices and herbs were one of the most sought after trade commodities. The spice trade between India and Europe led to the rise and dominance of Arab traders to such an extent that European explorers, such as Vasco da Gama and Christopher Columbus, set out to find new trade routes with India leading to the *Age of Discovery*. The popularity of *curry*, which originated in India, across Asia has often led to the dish being labelled as the "pan-Asian" dish.

Clothing

Traditional clothing in India greatly varies across different parts of the country and is influenced immensely by local culture, geography and climate. Popular styles of dress include draped garments such as sari for women and dhoti or lungi for men; in addition, stitched clothes such as salwar kameez for women and kurta-pyjama and European-style trousers and shirts for men, are also popular.

In India, a person's social status is perceived to be symbolized by his or her attire. Indian dress etiquette discourages exposure of skin and wearing transparent or tight clothes. Most Indian clothes are made from cotton which is ideal for the region's hot weather. Since India's weather is mostly hot and rainy, majority of Indians wear sandals. Worn by women on their forehead, the *bindi* is considered to be a highly auspicious mark in Hindu religion. Traditionally, the red bindi (or *sindoor*) was worn only by the married Hindu women, but now it has become a part of women's fashion. Some Indian traditions consider the *bindi* to be representative of the third eye.

India's clothing styles have continuously evolved over the course of the country's history. Ancient Vedic texts mention clothes made from barks and leaves (known as *phataka*). The 11th century BC *Rig-veda* mentions dyed and embroidered garments (known as *paridhan* and *pesas* respectively) and thus highlights the development of sophisticated garment manufacturing techniques during the Vedic age.

In 5th century BC, Greek historian Herodotus describes the richness of the quality of Indian cotton clothes. By 2nd century AD, muslins manufactured in southern India were imported by the Roman Empire and silk cloth was one of the major exports of ancient India along with Indian spices. Stitched clothing in India was developed before 10th century AD and was further popularized in 15th century by Muslim empires in India. Draped clothing styles remained popular with India's Hindu population while the Muslims increasingly adopted tailored garments.

During the British Raj, India's large clothing and handicrafts industry was left paralyzed so as to make place for British industrial cloth.

Consequently, Indian independence movement leader Mahatma Gandhi successfully advocated for what he termed as *khadi clothing* — light colored hand-woven clothes — so as to decrease reliance of the Indian people on British industrial goods.

The 1980s was marked by a widespread modification to Indian clothing fashions which was characterized by a large-scale growth of fashion schools in India, increasing involvement of women in the fashion industry and changing Indian attitudes towards multiculturalism. These developments played a pivotal role in the fusion of Indian and Western clothing styles.

Languages and Literature

History

With its oldest core dating back to as early as 1500 BC, the Rigvedic Sanskrit is one of the oldest attestations of any Indo-Iranian language, and one of the earliest attested members of the Indo-European language family, the family which includes English and most European languages. Sanskrit has had a profound impact on the languages and literature of India. Hindi, India's most spoken language, is a "Sanskritized register" of the Khariboli dialect.

In addition, all modern Indo-Aryan languages, Munda languages and Dravidian languages, have borrowed many words either directly from Sanskrit (*tatsama* words), or indirectly via middle Indo-Aryan languages (*tadbhava* words). Words originating in Sanskrit are estimated to constitute roughly fifty percent of the vocabulary of modern Indo-Aryan languages, and the literary forms of (Dravidian) Telugu, Malayalam and Kannada. Part of the Eastern Indo-Aryan languages, the Bengali language arose from the eastern Middle Indic languages and its roots are traced to the 5th century BC Ardhamagadhi language.

Tamil, one of India's major classical languages, descends from Proto-Dravidian languages which was spoken around the third millennium BC in peninsular India. Tamil literature has existed for over two thousand years and the earliest epigraphic records found date from around the third century BC. Another major Dravidian language, Kannada is attested epigraphically from the mid-1st millennium AD, and literary Old Kannada flourished in the 9th to 10th century Rashtrakuta Dynasty. Pre-old Kannada (or *Purava HaleGannada*) was the language of Banavasi in the early Common Era, the Satavahana and Kadamba periods and hence has a history of over 2000 years. The Ashoka rock edict found at Brahmagiri (dated to 230 BC) has been suggested to contain a word in identifiable Kannada.

According to 2001 India census, Hindi is the most spoken language in India, followed by Bengali, Telugu, Marathi and Tamil. In contemporary Indian literature, there are two major literary awards; these are the Sahitya Akademi Fellowship and the Jnanpith Award. Seven Jnanpith awards each have been awarded in Tamil, Kannada, six in Hindi, five in Bengali, four in Malayalam, three each in Marathi, Gujarati, Urdu and Oriya.

Poetry

India has strong traditions of poetry ever since the ancient Rigveda (*[gveda*), as well as prose compositions dating back to the Vedic civilization. Poetry is often closely related to musical traditions, and much of poetry can be attributed to religious movements. Writers and philosophers were often also skilled poets.

Throughout India's history, poetry has not only served spirituality and social reform goals, but has also served as a non-violent tool of nationalism and freedom. These traditions can be traced back to influential medieval Indian poets such as Basaveshwara (*vachanas*), Kabîra and Purandara Dasa (*padas* and *devaranamas*). Examples of influential poets during the modern era include Rabindranath Tagore, Kuvempu and K. S. Narasimhaswamy.

Epics

The Ramayana and the Mahabharata are the oldest preserved and well-known epics of India. Versions have been adopted as the epics of Southeast Asian countries like Thailand, Malaysia and Indonesia. The Ramayana consists of 24,000 verses in seven books (*kanas*) and 500 cantos (*sargas*), and tells the story of Rama (an incarnation of the Hindu preserver-god Vishnu), whose wife Sita is abducted by the demon king of Lanka, Ravana.

This epic played a pivotal role in establishing the role of dharma as a principal ideal guiding force for Hindu way of life. The earliest parts of the Mahabharata text date to 400 BC and is estimated to have reached its final form by the early Gupta period (ca. 4th c. AD).

Other regional variations of these, as well as unrelated epics include the Tamil Ramavataram, Kannada *Pampa Bharata*, Hindi *Ramacharitamanasa*, and Malayalam *Adhyathmaramayanam*. In addition to these two great Indian epics, there are five major epics in the classical Tamil language—*Silappatikaram*, *Manimekalai*, *Civaka-cintamani*, Valayapathi and *Kundalakesi*.

Performing Arts

Dance

Indian dance too has diverse *folk* and *classical* forms. Among the well-known folk dances are the *bhangra* of the Punjab, the *bihu* of Assam, the *chhau* of Jharkhand and Orissa, the *ghoomar* of Rajasthan, the *dandiya* and *garba* of Gujarat, the *Yakshagana* of Karnataka and *lavani* of Maharashtra and *Dekhnni* of Goa. Eight dance forms, many with narrative forms and mythological elements, have been accorded classical dance status by India's *National Academy of Music, Dance, and Drama*. These are: *bharatanatyam* of the state of Tamil Nadu, *kathak* of Uttar Pradesh, *kathakali* and *mohiniattam* of Kerala, *kuchipudi* of Andhra Pradesh, *manipuri* of Manipur, *odissi* of the state of Odisha and the *sattriya* of Assam.

Drama and Theatre

Indian drama and theatre has a long history alongside its music and dance. Kalidasa's plays like Shakuntala and Meghadoota are some of the older plays, following those of Bhasa. One of the oldest surviving theatre traditions of the world is the 2,000 year old Kutiyattam of Kerala. It strictly follows the Natya Shastra. Natyacharya Mani Madhava Chakyar is credited for reviving the age old drama tradition from extinction. He was known for mastery of Rasa Abhinaya. He started to perform the Kalidasa plays like *Abhijñanaúakuntala*, *Vikramorvaúîya* and *Malavikagnimitra*; Bhasa's *Swapnavasavadatta* and *Pancharatra*; Harsha's *Nagananda*.

Music

The music of India includes multiple varieties of religious, folk, popular, pop, and classical music. The oldest preserved examples of Indian music are the melodies of the *Samaveda* that are still sung in certain Vedic Shrauta sacrifices. India's classical music tradition is heavily influenced by Hindu texts. It includes two distinct styles: Carnatic and Hindustani music.

The earliest account of Indian musical hymns is found in the 1000 BC Samaveda. It proposed a tonal structure consisting of seven notes, which were named, in descending order, as

Krusht, *Pratham*, *Dwitiya*, *Tritiya*, *Chaturth*, *Mandra* and *Atiswar*. These refer to the notes of a flute, which was the only fixed frequency instrument. Both the Hindustani classical music and the Carnatic classical music systems are based on the melodic mode (known as Raga), sung to a rhythmic cycle or tala. These principles were refined in the natyaúastra (200 BC) and the dattilam (300 AD).

Purandaradasa is considered the "father of carnatic music" (*Karnataka sangeeta pitamaha*). He concluded his songs with a salutation to Lord Purandara Vittala and is believed to have composed as many as 475,000 songs in the Kannada language. However, only about 1000 are known today.

Prominent contemporary Indian musical forms include filmi and Indipop. Filmi refers to the wide range of music written and performed for mainstream Indian cinema, primarily Bollywood, and accounts for more than 70 percent of all music sales in the country. Indipop is one of the most popular contemporary styles of Indian music which is either a fusion of Indian folk, classical or Sufi music with Western musical traditions.

Visual Arts

Painting

The earliest Indian paintings were the rock paintings of pre-historic times, the petroglyphs as found in places like Bhimbetka, some of which go back to the Stone Age. Ancient texts outline theories of darragh and anecdotal accounts suggnkkkkk was common for households to paint their doorways or indoor rooms where guests resided.

Cave paintings from Ajanta, Bagh, Ellora and Sittanavasal and temple paintings testify to a love of naturalism. Most early and medieval art in India is Hindu, Buddhist or Jain. A freshly made coloured flour design (Rangoli) is still a common sight outside the doorstep of many (mostly South Indian) Indian homes. Raja Ravi Varma is one the classical painters from medieval India.

Madhubani painting, Mysore painting, Rajput painting, Tanjore painting, Mughal painting are some notable Genres of Indian Art; while Nandalal Bose, M. F. Husain, S. H. Raza,

Geeta Vadhera, Jamini Roy and B.Venkatappa are some modern painters. Among the present day artists, Atul Dodiya, Bose Krishnamacnahri, Devajyoti Ray and Shibu Natesan represent a new era of Indian art where global art shows direct amalgamation with Indian classical styles. These recent artists have acquired international recognition. Jehangir Art Gallery, Mumbai, Mysore Palace has on display a few good Indian paintings.

Sculpture

The first sculptures in India date back to the Indus Valley civilization, where stone and bronze figures have been discovered. Later, as Hinduism, Buddhism, and Jainism developed further, India produced some extremely intricate bronzes as well as temple carvings. Some huge shrines, such as the one at Ellora were not constructed by using blocks but carved out of solid rock.

Sculptures produced in the northwest, in stucco, schist, or clay, display a very strong blend of Indian and Classical Hellenistic or possibly even Greco-Roman influence. The pink sandstone sculptures of Mathura evolved almost simultaneously. During the Gupta period (4th to 6th century) sculpture reached a very high standard in execution and delicacy in modelling. These styles and others elsewhere in India evolved leading to classical Indian art that contributed to Buddhist and Hindu sculpture throughout Southeast Central and East Asia.

Architecture

Indian architecture encompasses a multitude of expressions over space and time, constantly absorbing new ideas. The result is an evolving range of architectural production that nonetheless retains a certain amount of continuity across history. Some of its earliest production are found in the Indus Valley Civilization (2600–1900 BC) which is characterised by well planned cities and houses. Religion and kingship do not seem to have played an important role in the planning and layout of these towns.

During the period of the Mauryan and Gupta empires and their successors, several Buddhist architectural complexes, such as the caves of Ajanta and Ellora and the monumental Sanchi Stupa were built. Later on, South India produced several Hindu temples like Chennakesava Temple at Belur, the Hoysaleswara Temple at Halebidu, and the Kesava Temple at Somanathapura, Brihadeeswara Temple, Thanjavur, the Sun Temple, Konark, Sri Ranganathaswamy Temple at Srirangam, and the Buddha stupa (Chinna Lanja dibba and Vikramarka kota dibba) at Bhattiprolu. Angkor Wat, Borobudur and other Buddhist and Hindu temples indicate strong Indian influence on South East Asian architecture, as they are built in styles almost identical to traditional Indian religious buildings.

The traditional system of Vaastu Shastra serves as India's version of Feng Shui, influencing town planning, architecture, and ergonomics. It is unclear which system is older, but they contain certain similarities. Feng Shui is more commonly used throughout the world. Though Vastu is conceptually similar to Feng Shui in that it also tries to harmonize the flow of energy, (also called life-force or Prana in Sanskrit and Chi/Ki in Chinese/ Japanese), through the house, it differs in the details, such as the exact directions in which various objects, rooms, materials, etc. are to be placed.

With the advent of Islamic influence from the west, Indian architecture was adapted to allow the traditions of the new religion. Fatehpur Sikri, Taj Mahal, Gol Gumbaz, Qutub Minar, Red Fort of Delhi are creations of this era, and are often used as the stereotypical symbols of India. The colonial rule of the British Empire saw the development of Indo-Saracenic style, and mixing of several other styles, such as European Gothic. The Victoria Memorial or the Chhatrapati Shivaji Terminus are notable examples.

Indian architecture has influenced eastern and southeastern Asia, due to the spread of Buddhism. A number of Indian architectural features such as the temple mound or stupa, temple spire or sikhara, temple tower or pagoda and temple gate or torana, have become famous symbols of Asian culture, used extensively in East Asia and South East Asia. The central spire is also sometimes called a vimanam. The southern temple gate, or gopuram is noted for its intricacy and majesty.

Contemporary Indian architecture is more cosmopolitan. Cities are extremely compact and densely populated. Mumbai's Nariman Point is famous for its Art Deco buildings. Recent creations such as the Lotus Temple, and the various modern urban developments of India like Chandigarh, are notable.

Sports and Martial Arts

Field hockey is India's official national Sport; and the Indian field hockey team won the 1975 Men's Hockey World Cup and 8 gold, 1 silver and 2 bronze medals at the Olympic games. However, Cricket is the most popular Sport in India; the India national cricket team won the 1983 Cricket World Cup and the 2007 ICC World Twenty20, and shared the 2002 ICC Champions Trophy with Sri Lanka. Domestic competitions include the Ranji Trophy, the Duleep Trophy, the Deodhar Trophy, the Irani Trophy and the Challenger Series. In addition, BCCI conducts the Indian Premier League, a Twenty20 competition.

India is the host of 2010 Commonwealth Games, played in New Delhi. It hosted a spectacular display of Indian culture and heritage to the entire world during the opening ceremony of the games.

Chess is commonly believed to have originated in northwestern India during the Gupta empire, where its early form in the 6th century was known as *chaturanga*. Other games which originated in India and continue to remain popular in wide parts of northern India include kabaddi, gilli-danda, and kho kho. Traditional southern Indian games include snake boat race and kuttiyum kolum.

Indian Martial Arts

One of the best known forms of ancient Indian martial arts is the *Kalarippayattu* from Kerala. This ancient fighting style originated in southern India in 12th century BC and is regarded as one of the oldest surviving martial arts. In this form martial arts, various stages of physical training include ayurvedic massage with sesame oil so as to impart suppleness to the body (*uzichil*), a series of sharp body movements so as to gain control over various parts of the body (*miapayattu*) and complex sword fighting techniques (*paliyankam*). Silambam, which was developed around 200 AD, traces its roots to the Sangam period in southern India. Silambam is unique among Indian martial arts because it uses complex footwork techniques (*kaaladi*) including a variety of spinning styles and a bamboo staff is used as the main weapon. The ancient Tamil Sangam literature mentions that between 400 BC and 600 AD, soldiers from southern India received special martial arts training which revolved primarily around the use of spear (*vel*), sword (*val*) and shield (*kedaham*).

In northern India, the *musti yuddha* evolved in 1100 AD and focused on mental, physical and even spiritual training. In addition, the *Dhanur Veda* tradition was an influential fighting arts style which considered the bow and the arrow to be the supreme weapons. The *Dhanur Veda* was first described in the 5th century BC VicGu PuraGa and is also mentioned in both of the major ancient Indian epics, *Ramayana* and *Mahabharata*. A distinctive factor of Indian martial arts is the heavy emphasis laid on meditation (*dhyana*) as a tool to remove fear, doubt and anxiety.

Indian martial arts techniques have had a profound impact on other martial arts styles across Asia. The 3rd century BC *Yoga Sutras of Patanjali* taught how to meditate single-mindedly on points located inside one's body, which was later used in martial arts, while various mudra finger movements were taught in Yogacara Buddhism. These elements of yoga, as well as finger movements in the *nata* dances, were later incorporated into various martial arts. According to some historical accounts, Indian Buddhist monk Bodhidharma was one of the main founders of the Shaolin Kungfu.

Popular Media

Television

Indian television started off in 1959 in New Delhi with tests for educational telecasts. Indian small screen programming started off in the mid 1970s. At that time there was only one national channel Doordarshan, which was government owned. 1982 saw revolution in TV programming in India, with the New Delhi Asian games, India saw the colour version of TV, that year. The Ramayana and Mahabharat were some among the popular television series produced. By the late 1980s more and more people started to own television sets. Though there was a single channel, television programming had reached saturation. Hence the government opened up another channel which had part national programming and part regional. This channel was known as DD 2 later DD Metro. Both channels were broadcasted terrestrially.

In 1991, the government liberated its markets, opening them up to cable television. Since then, there has been a spurt in the number of channels available. Today, Indian silver screen is a huge industry by itself, and has thousands of programmes in all the states of India. The small screen has produced numerous celebrities of their own kind some even attaining national fame for themselves. TV soaps are extremely popular with housewives as well as working women, and even men of all kinds. Some lesser known actors have found success in Bollywood. Indian TV now has many of the same channels as Western TV, including stations such as Cartoon Network, Nickelodeon, HBO, FX, and MTV India.

Cinema

Bollywood is the informal name given to the popular Mumbai-based film industry in India. Bollywood and the other major cinematic hubs (in Bengali, Kannada, Malayalam, Marathi, Tamil, Punjabi and Telugu) constitute the broader Indian film industry, whose output is considered to be the largest in the world in terms of number of films produced and number of tickets sold.

India has produced many critically acclaimed cinema-makers like K.Vishwanath, Bapu, Jagdaman Grewal, Satyajit Ray, Ritwik Ghatak, Guru Dutt, K. Vishwanath, Adoor Gopalakrishnan, Girish Kasaravalli, Shekhar Kapoor, Hrishikesh Mukherjee, Shankar Nag, Girish Karnad, G. V. Iyer,etc. With the opening up of the economy in the recent years and consequent exposure to world cinema, audience tastes have been changing. In addition, multiplexes have mushroomed in most cities, changing the revenue patterns.

8

Theory of Civilization in the Sociology of Culture

The word culture has completely different meanings in the social sciences and in current language. In the latter, the meaning of the term has for long been mainly influenced by the humanistic conception of culture, which derives from the Roman cultura animi a term that Cicero seems to have invented in order to translate the Greek concept oipaideia. This is the classical sense of the word, based upon high productions of mind and art. Referring to the intellectual, esthetic, and ethical aspects of human beings (for which the German language uses the term Bildung), culture thus involves the legitimacy of value judgments and of the idea of a hierarchy between societies as much as inside them.

In the social sciences, on the contrary, the term has generally a widely inclusive meaning, which is actually aimed against the humanistic normative conception of culture, since almost anything may be considered as culture. This conception, which opens an almost unlimited field to the term culture, has been the basis of the ensemble of theories which may be termed culturalist trend. It is characterized by a systematical relativism, strongly backed up by the fact that the overall conception of culture is in itself a powerful relativistic tool. The popularization of the relativistic use of the term culture in postmodern societies since the late 1900s poses a serious danger for culture.

The Term Culture in the Social Sciences

This term has received, first in anthropology and afterwards in sociology, a very specific meaning, that prevailed despite the reluctance of very important authors, such as Morgan, Durkheim, and Radcliffe Brown to use it in this way.

The Tylorian Everything is Culture Conception

At the basis of the concept of culture as it is mostly used in the social sciences stands the well known founding definition of the English ethnologist Edward Barrett Tylor (1832 1917), in his book Primitive Culture (1871). He borrowed much of the sense he gave to the term from Bismarckian Germany, whose conception of Kultur included any kind of expression of the national character. According to the German usage, Tylor takes culture to be synonymous with civilization, and therefore gives to that word what he calls a wide ethnographic sense. For him, culture is that complex whole produced by people's historical experience, of which he gives several examples: knowledge, belief, art, morals, law, custom. But this enumeration is not a closed one. Tylorian culture also includes ... any other capabilities and habits acquired by man as a member of society. This definition is characterized by the huge breadth of its application.

Derived from the German term Kultur, the idea of a broad ethnographic sense of the word culture perfectly suited Anglo Saxon ethnologists from German or Austrian origin. The German born US anthropologist Franz Boas (1858 1942) and the British anthropologist Bronislaw Malinowski (1884 1942), who was born in Poland as an Austrian subject, both took an outstanding part in the victorious settlement of the term culture in the very core of the social sciences.

Although since Tylor many other definitions of culture have been formulated, his everything is culture conception remained a basic creed for nearly all anthropologists during the twentieth century, and it still prevails. In its anthropological sense, culture includes religion, law, art, and literature, as well as all of everyday life in its often prosaic and even trivial aspects, such as cooking, sexual habits, or sanitary practices.

In the early 1900s, Emile Durkheim, Marcel Mauss and other French sociologists were reluctant to use the term culture in its Tylorian sense, and preferred to go on using the word civilization. Yet, the anthropologists broad use of the term culture has progressively spread to sociology. Nevertheless, during the 1950s, many American intellectuals, like Hannah Arendt, did resist the idea of mass culture, which they deemed to be no culture at all, but a deadly threat to it. In the early 1960s, American sociologists still regarded mass culture as a subject of debate, and the mass media as a most important field for sociological studies. Meanwhile, it was a French sociologist, Edgar Morin (1962) who took mass culture as an essential sociological field of study.

Radcliffe Brown's Attempt to Resist Tylorian Culture

The founder of social anthropology, the British anthropologist Alfred Reginald Radcliffe Brown (1881 1955) based his theory upon the study of' social structures, along the lines of Durkheim's sociological concept of function.

In order to keep social anthropology completely separated from cultural anthropology, for some 20 years Radcliffe Brown and his followers avoided using the word culture as much as possible. Then, in 1952, he defined culture as the process by which a person acquires, from contact with other persons or from such things as books or works of art, knowledge, skill, ideas, beliefs, tastes, sentiments. So culture is for him the process of intellectual, esthetic, and ethical human development. Culture is the process by which one becomes a cultured person.

Though an anthropologist, and although his functionalist theory is as much relativistic and holistic as culturalism is, Radcliffe Brown has a classical and humanistic conception of culture. This is because the term has no part in his system, not being his own relativistic tool.

He states (1952) that the total social structure of a society together with the totality of social usages in which that structure appears and on which it depends for its continued existence are constituent of a social system, whereas most anthropologists would have regarded all that as culture. Since he had decided to take as basic the social structure instead of the culture patterns of cultural anthropology, Radcliffe Brown had no need of the Tylorian sense of culture. In fact he had even every reason to refuse that use of the word, which was the basis of a powerful rival theory. Hence his humanistic formulation.

Furthermore, Radcliffe Brown's functionalism derived from Morgan, Durkheim and the whole French sociological school. As they had not admitted the Tylorian use of the term culture, Radcliffe Brown was naturally induced to follow their example.

However, Malinowski, the other great name of anthropological functionalism, regarded a broad conception of culture as natural. Posthumously published in 1944, his most important book is entitled: A Scientific Theory of Culture and Other Essays. Thus, in the 1930s and 1940s, anthropological functionalism was divided into two rival schools: social structure against culture, Radcliffe Brown's school versus Malinowski's school, one of their motives of disagreement being opposing ideas about the concept of culture. In the UK, this quarrel was considered as opposing social anthropology to cultural anthropology. But, at the same time, nearly all US anthropologists were adherents of cultural anthropology since studying cultures.'

As a result of that, in the USA, since the end of the 1940s, the functionalist theory has been taken over, in an somewhat attenuated way, by sociologists, chiefly Robert King Merton and Talcott Parsons, who adhered to the social anthropologists point of view.

Accordingly, they stressed society and not culture as the subject of their research. US sociologists thus stood opposed to US cultural anthropologists. So that the past rivalry of the functionalists schools of Malinowski and Radcliffe Brown had become a professional quarrel opposing US anthropologists and sociologists, since the former claimed to deal solely with culture, and the latter with society.'

Yet, in the early 1950s, some of Radcliffe Brown's followers began to use the term culture with a very broad meaning: for Raymond W. Firth, it included both the way of life and the content of social relations (1951), and for Meyer Fortes, both social structure and organization (1953). Afterwards, in 1958, American anthropologists and sociologists made an end to their quarrel by means of a peace treaty signed by A. L. Kroeber and Parsons, who mutually acknowledged the validity of one another's field of study: society as well as culture. The everything is culture conception had won.

The Culturalist Trend

The Tylorian omnibus conception of culture (Singer 1968) has been the basis of the set of theories known as culturalism, and it remains the basis of the culturalist way of thought which still reigns over anthropology and a large part of sociology.

In the first half of the twentieth century, US cultural anthropology has been principally influenced by Tylor, Boas, and through him by the German diffusionists, like Fritz Graebner, who had introduced the idea of Kulturkreis (culture area). In the 1930s, US cultural anthropologists began to develop the idea that each culture was an individual unity, well organized and functioning as a system. This holistic and systemic conception was clearly formulated by Malinowski in the article on culture that he wrote for the Encyclopedia of the Social Sciences (1931). A few years after, Margaret Mead (1935), Ralph Linton (1936) and Abram Kardiner (1939) emphasized the idea of a culture being an integrated totality. The aim of ethnologists and anthropologists became to show the inner coherence of each culture functioning as an organized whole, in which any component element is linked to all the others.

For the ethnology and cultural anthropology of the 1930s 1950s, the organization of culture systems consisted of a complex architecture of patterns of culture, which Ruth Benedict had endeavored to describe and classify. Hence the definition formulated in 1952 by Alfred L. Kroeber and Clyde Kluckhohn: 'Culture consists of patterns, explicit and implicit, of and for behaviour, acquired and transmitted by symbols, constituting the distinctive achievement of human groups Each society is regarded as a distinctive cultural whole, characterized by its peculiar system of values. The beliefs existing in a given society are thought to be a product of culture. Following Linton, several culturalist authors even affirmed that the personality structure of the individuals in a particular group was determined by the group's culture. The most extreme advocate of this opinion was Kardiner, with his idea that each sociocultural system shaped a basic personality, the T just being a cultural precipitate. Therefore, culturalists deem socialization, the social process through which the main values of a society are transmitted from one generation to the next, to be of the utmost importance, and they believe it to be a very deterministic process. On the whole, those theories led to an extremely mechanic conception, which attributes to culture the production of beliefs, and to inculcation and conditioning the power to put them into people's minds and to determine their behaviours. So the US anthropologist Leslie A. White, the leader of the culturalist school called culturology, went so far as writing (1968) that man is, and remains, a puppet of his culture.'

Culturalism has rightly been reproached for its belief in the ability of social systems to work in such a mechanical way that people so much believe what they have to believe that they feel the need to do what they have to do. It has also been established that the culturalists holistic conception of a system of values common to a whole society was generally untrue, except perhaps in the very simplest ones.

Hence the notion of subculture used by culturalists for their study of complex modern societies. As for the culturalist principle of an inner coherence of culture systems, which comes from a counterhistorical method, it maybe partly exist in the most simple societies, but certainly not in complex ones. Against this assumed idea of a whole inside linkage of each culture', the French sociologists Raymond Boudon and Frangois Bourricaud also observed (1982) that the everything is culture conception was based upon an erroneous obviousness, so that it would be more adequate to use the term culture only when speaking of artifacts and mental products.

A few anthropologists have dared to criticize the mechanical conditioning model of culturalism. It is chiefly the English anthropologist Robin Horton (1973) and the American anthropologist Melford E. Spiro (1987) who disputed the creed according to which belief and behaviour did not result from reasons but were just the product of cultural conditioning. Nevertheless, since Boas the culturalist point of view does represent the mainstream in anthropology. And it has also influenced a great deal of sociology, and even philosophy. For instance, Richard Rorty asserts in a perfectly culturalist way that the idea prevailing in democracies of totalitarianism being evil is just the result of cultural conditioning (1989). The culturalist trend always works for the benefit of relativism, and the mere use of the term culture in an everything is culture sense does just the same.

The Comprehensive Sense of Culture: A Relativistic Tool

As an evolutionist, Tylor naturally regarded nineteeth century England as the pinnacle of civilization. But since he intended to treat mankind as homogeneous in nature, he felt the need of a concept synonymous with civilization, but more applicable to everybody and every society, past as well as present. Hence his widely inclusive definition of culture, which permitted him to find evidences of culture among all societies and human groups, though placed in different grades of civilization. Since everything was asserted to be culture, it became possible to find culture everywhere. The Tylor revolution granted a culture even to the most primitive peoples.

Yet, the most famous ethnologist in the 1870s and 1880s, the American evolutionist Lewis H. Morgan (1818 81), did not adopt the Tylorian meaning of the term culture. In his book Ancient Society (1877), he went on using the notion of society'. Instead of Tylor's stages of culture', he prefered to delineate ethnical periods, which he considered to be developmental stages leading, through barbarism, from savagery to civilization. But Morgan died and Tylor prevailed, and in the USA, at the end of the 1800s, Boas, being of German origin, naturally used the Tylorian sense of culture.

It was also Boas who threw out of anthropology the very idea of grades of civilization determining a hierarchy of societies and human groups. Rejecting the evolutionist theory, he declared the total relativity of cultures. The Boas revolution closely followed the Tylorian one. However, through Boas, cultural relativism actually proceeded from Nietzsche, who had brought all traditional values to trial, and announced that they were now delusive, since deprived of basis by the decline of dogmatic creeds. As it is well known, Nietzsche sought to destroy the very idea of objective reality, so that he is the father of modern relativism. The influence of Nietzschean ideas accounts for Boas's basic postulate of the relativity of values in the different cultures and his complete rejection of the value judgments of nineteenth century evolutionism.

In the 1940s, cultural relativism received, through the American anthropologist Melville J. Herskovits's Cultural

Anthropology (1948), the support of Ernest Cassirer's German historical idealism (1942). According to Herskovits, exactly following Cassirer, human beings are living in a symbolic universe built by them: the universe of culture, and so know no reality but the symbolic, that is, cultural. Herskovits asserts that all human experience of the physical world as well as of society are determined by enculturation, and accordingly culturally mediated. In this theory, all perceptions, evaluations, and judgments are a function of the cultural system to which one belongs, and are relative to it. Since Herskovits as well as Cassirer consider that all reality is perceived through the screen of culture, this one is deemed to be the measure of all things.

The Tylorian sense of culture has been very useful for cultural relativists, as it permitted them to dispense with the word civilization in order to avoid the closely related ideas of hierarchy and comparative judgment. Being based upon the determinist assumption that values are a function or product of each culture, cultural relativism does infer that all value judgments are necessarily culturally conditioned or determined. Therefore they are deemed to have no validity outside the cultural context from which they proceed. Value judgments concerning alien cultures are therefore strictly forbiden by cultural relativism, which reproaches those judgments with being the product of a preference for one's own culture and a prejudice against the other ones: namely ethnocentrism, which twentieth century relativistic anthropology has regarded as the supreme offence, as much as evolutionism itself. Since the relativistic postulate of comparative judgment having no validity is asserted to be accurate, the corollary cannot but be the principle of an equivalent validity of all value systems. So that the American anthropologist David Bidney could observe (1968):' Reverence for cultural values, rather than reverence for life, becomes the absolute virtue advocated by the cultural relativist.'

The term culture used in a comprehensive sense has been the main vector of the egalitarianist assumption ensuing from cultural relativism, according to which all value systems must be considered to be equally legitimate units. If the meaning of the word culture is taken to include ways of life as well as social relations, there is culture everywhere. Whereas the humanistic idea of culture stands opposite to the absence of culture, or even the barbarity, of certain individuals, groups, or societies, the very fact of absence of culture or barbarity is denied by using the term culture about these individuals, groups, or societies. Since everybody belongs to a social structure and a value system, everybody is regarded as belonging to a culture or a subculture. Sociologists as well as anthropologists consider each society and each social group to have its culture, and they usually strictly obey the relativistic prohibition of comparative evaluations of values, which would lead to classifications showing the factual existence of various grades of civilization. The widely inclusive conception of culture of the social sciences is used with the purpose of eliminating the very idea of uncultured groups. It allows indeed the social scientist to report the presence of culture in the working class or in a primitive tribe as well as in the most learned circles. The everything is culture use of the word culture works just like an optical illusion. It brings about that fallacious value of equality of all societies and groups which is imperatively ordered by cultural relativism. The term culture taken in a comprehensive sense is a necessity of cultural relativism, of which it is the most indispensable tool as well as the very basis.

The theory according to which all reality is symbolic is in no way cogent. As has been noticed by Raymond Boudon and Frangois Bourricaud (1982), if that means that all human experience is mediated by a symbolic system like articulate speech or science, it is merely a commonplace statement. And if symbolic is taken as synonymous with ficticious, it is an erroneous idea. Likewise, the rejection of value judgments actually lacks logical validity. As a matter of fact, the assumption of an equivalent value of all cultures is itself nothing but a value judgment, hidden behind the virtuous looking facade of cultural relativism. The prohibition of value judgments thus results from a value judgment. As emphasized by Allan Bloom (1987), the assertion of values and cultures being relative is by no means proved: it is just a philosophical postulate, which stems from a political intention. And when cultural relativism disclaims freedom of judgment and rational analysis in order to prevent the development of any prejudice against alterity, it is just a way to avoid subjecting our own prejudices to logical criticism. Hence, the social sciences have the utmost need, as

David Bidney (1968) had already stressed, to transcend the limitations of both cultural relativism and ethnocentrism through the pursuit of scientific truths concerning facts and values.'

However, the relativistic trend prevails, particularly in anthropology. Since nearly all twentieth century anthropologists have repudiated evolutionism, Leslie A. White (1968) and his school being the main exception, anthropology has been, through the twentieth century and at the present time, essentially relativistic. Despite the endeavors of some authors like Melford E. Spiro (1987) and Robin Horton (1973), or like the British anthropologist Robin Fox (1989) who has turned to sociobiology, anthropology and cultural relativism may almost be taken as synonyms. The US social anthropologist Clifford Geertz did affirm (1984) that cultural relativism was justified by the factual obviousness that value systems are of course disparate. According to Geertz (1984), relativism has such an obvious validity that it is impossible to resist it. Yet, what is most obvious is that relativism is the core and basis of culturalism, and that twentieth century anthropology works as a relativistic machine. Accordingly, the relativists fancy for anthropology is in no way surprising. They have often stated anthropology to be the queen of sciences. The cognitive relativist Feyerabend even asserted (1975) that it was the sole genuine science.

The use of a broad sense of the word culture as a relativistic tool is also present in the other social sciences, especially in sociology. Such is the case in the neomarxist functionalist theory of the French sociologist Pierre Bourdieu (1979). In the 1960s and 1970s, Bourdieu emphasized the statement that culture (in the classical and humanistic sense of the term) was nothing but a culture expressing the beliefs and behaviour of the dominant class. According to him, this culture is just a culture amongst many others, but it is imposed as the only legitimate one by school, universities, and other cultural institutions, in order to bring about what he terms social reproduction. Since they have been brought up in other cultures, working class children are considered by Bourdieu to be handicapped when facing at school a culture which is not their own one, while children from the dominant class have all the means to be successful with it. So, stresses Bourdieu, the domination of the same upper class can be reproduced from generation to generation. Bourdieu deems culture to have in itself no real superiority, but just to be useful for the members of the dominant class in order to distinguish themselves from the rest of the society. He regards artistic or literary value, which he believes to have no actual existence in itself, as merely resulting from the preferences of the dominant class, and hence as being an illusion. Therefore, the combination of Bourdieu's Marxist ideology with his perfect relativism leads to an absolute cultural nihilism.

In sociology, the culturalist holistic idea of values being the product of closed wholes has probably been taken in the most absolute way by ethnomethodol ogists. According to them, cultures', subcultures, and any other groups are so much closed units that their values have solely an inside meaning. And they even assert that observers can understand nothing of the cultural products of a group in which they are not immersed. So ethnomethodologists deny the validity of outside observers studies, affirming that their supposed understanding would be distorted by the fallacy of sociocentrism. Although ethnomethodologists do not consider, as most culturalists do, social actors to be puppets of their culture, ethnomethodology is certainly an extremely relativistic sociclogical theory, based upon an everything is culture conception.

Several streams of sociology explain beliefs and behaviour by the mechanical model of inculcation and conditioning, just as does cultural anthropology. So does the neomarxist functionalism of Bourdieu (1979), with the theory or habitus thought as a class conditioned behaviour. But the idea of inculcation and conditioning by means of socialization is also present in the whole Durkheimian trend, and even to a certain extent in Parsons functionalism', since it particularly stresses social integration. And, of course, behaviourists following B. F. Skinner's positivistic line regard moral instincts as a product of social conditioning.

As they have to study the diversity of cultures, and as this term has long been linked to the idea of relativism, anthropologists have a professional slant to take cultural relativism as granted. But the prevailing of relativism in the social sciences is very much strengthened by the general relativistic atmosphere which characterizes postmodern societies. Relativism has invaded literary criticism, with the deconstructionistic theory of the French Heideggerians Roland Barthes and Jacques Derrida, and the French Heideggerian Michel Foucault has initiated a relativistic interpretation of history. As Allan Bloom (1987) and Raymond Boudon (1990) have pointed out, all those theories mainly derive from the Nietzschean assertion that there are no facts, but only interpretations: a famous phrase that Barthes, Derrida, Foucault and their followers wrongly separated from its context, so that they unduly took it literally. These same authors theories have been used as a justification by the relativistic movement known as political correctness, which since the 1980s has dominated US universities. Relativism has even been epistemologicaly theorized, chiefly by Thomas S. Kuhn (1962) and Paul K. Feyerabend (1975). Feyerabend's anarchist cognitive theory, which does not differentiate science from archaic myths or from magic, is clearly a counter epistemology. With Feyerabend's well known saying, anything goes, relativism leads to nihilism.

The lack of validity of these theories has been pointed out by Raymond Boudon (1990, 1995), who demonstrated that cognitive relativism was based upon an epistemological archaism. He also observed, about the assertion of an obvious legitimacy of relativim, that since Geertz (1984) considered all conceptions of the world to emanate from cultures, relativism itself was one of these conception. Therefore, in a culturalist perspective, relativism in no way can be a methodological rule that is above suspicion, but just a plain cultural product of postmodern societies. In fact, it is because relativism does fit in with them that it is at the present time so fashionable. Here lies its strength, which is extremely dangerous for culture.

Cultures Versus Culture

The everything is culture conception is no longer confined to anthropological and sociological books and journals, but has spread beyond, so that the broad sense of culture now belongs to everyday language. It is daily used by the media, and has become popularized.

There is even in several countries a ministerial department entrusted with culture an idea proceeding from the USSR.

Such a department was created in France as early as 1958, and departments were established in the 1980s and 1990s in some other Western democracies, such as Belgium, Spain, Italy, and Germany. The French Culture Ministry has adopted since the 1970s, and still more since 1981, a comprehensive sense of culture. In the sociological research ordered by this department, the different ways of filling spare time, and all kinds of fun and entertainment, are called cultural habits. In a political purpose, the wide ethnographic sense of culture is officially acknowledged by the French government.

The term culture as it is used in postmodern societies, particularly in the media, has mostly nothing to do with genuine culture, but is more frequently used in order to refer to beliefs, behaviours, ways of life, customs, habits, and even the whole of society: culture is now often used instead of the term identity.'

Having a relativistic effect, a broad use of the term culture puts everything on the same level, so that fun and entertainment are regarded as equal to genuine culture. As pointed out by Allan Bloom (1987), the failure of culture becomes a culture. Though the present democratic societies formally worship culture', the popularization of the relativistic use of the term actually destroys in the whole society the very idea of the eminent value of culture. Here is indeed the main danger for culture.

9

Creativity and Human History

Creativity refers to the phenomenon whereby something new is created which has some kind of value. What counts as "new" may be in reference to the individual creator, or to the society or domain within which the novelty occurs. What counts as "valuable" is similarly defined in a variety of ways.

Scholarly interest in creativity ranges widely: the mental and neurological processes associated with creative activity; the relationship between personality type and creative ability; the relationship between creativity and intelligence, learning and mental health; and ways of fostering creativity through training and technology.

Creativity and creative acts are therefore studied across several discplines-psychology, cognitive science, education, philosophy (particularly philosophy of science), theology, sociology, linguistics, business studies, and economics. As a result there is a multitude of definitions and approaches.

Etymology

The English word creativity and its lexeme come from the Latin term *creo* "to create, make". The word "create" appears in English as early as the 14th century, notably in Chaucer (in The Parson's Tale). However, its modern meaning as an act of human creation did not emerge until after the Enlightenment.

Definition

In a summary of scientific research into creativity Michael Mumford suggested: ""Over the course of the last decade, however, we seem to have reached a general agreement that creativity involves the production of novel, useful products". Beyond this general commonality, authors have diverged dramatically in their precise definitions, with Peter Meusburger claiming that over a hundred different versions can be found in the literature.

Novel: Historical and Personal Creativity

Some writers, such as Mihaly Csíkszentmihalyi, have defined creativity in terms of rare individuals. Others, such as Ken Robinson, while focussing on creativity in a general population, include "originality" as part of the definition. However, others still have made a distinction between originality in historic terms, and novelty with regard to the creator. Margaret Boden distinguishes between h-creativity (historical) and p-creativity (personal), and Anna Craft makes a similar distinction between "high" and "little c" creativity.

History of the Term and the Concept

A shift occurred in modern times. Renaissance men had a sense of their own independence, freedom and creativity, and sought to give voice to this sense. The first to actually apply the word "creativity" was the Polish poet Maciej Kazimierz Sarbiewski, who applied it exclusively to poetry. For over a century and a half, the idea of *human* creativity met with resistance, due to the fact that the term "creation" was reserved for creation "from nothing." Baltasar Gracian (1601–58) would only venture to write: "Art is the completion of nature, as if it were *a second Creator...*"

The ancient Greek concept of art, with the exception of poetry, involved not freedom of action but subjection to *rules*. In Rome, this Greek concept was partly shaken, and visual artists were viewed as sharing, with poets, imagination and inspiration.

Although neither the Greeks nor the Romans had a word that directly corresponded to the word "creativity," their art, architecture, music (although no music from this time has been documented), inventions and discoveries provide numerous examples of what today would be described as creative works. The Greek scientist of Syracuse, Archimedes experienced the creative moment in his Eureka experience, finding the answer to a problem he had been wrestling with for a long time. At the time, the concept of an external creative "daemon" (Greek) or "genius" (Latin), linked to the sacred or the divine, probably came closest to describing the creative talents that brought forth such works.

By the 18th century and the Age of Enlightenment, the concept of creativity was appearing more often in art theory, and was linked with the concept of imagination.

The Western view of creativity can be contrasted with the Eastern view. For Hindus, Confucianists, Taoists and Buddhists, creation was at most a kind of discovery or mimicry, and the idea of creation "from nothing" had no place in these philosophies and religions.

In the West, by the 19th century, not only had art come to be regarded as creativity, but *it alone* was so regarded. When later, at the turn of the 20th century, there began to be discussion of creativity in the sciences and in nature (e.g., Henri Bergson), this was generally taken as the transference, to the sciences, of concepts that were proper to art. In the late 19th and early 20th centuries, leading mathematicians and scientists such as Hermann von Helmholtz (1896) and Henri Poincaré (1908) began to reflect on and publicly discuss their creative processes, and these insights were built on in early accounts of the creative process by pioneering theorists such as Graham Wallas (1926) and Max Wertheimer (1945).

However, the formal starting point to the scientific study of creativity, from the standpoint of orthodox psychological literature, is generally considered to have been J.P. Guilford's 1950 address to the American Psychological Association, which helped popularize the topic and focus attention on a scientific approach to conceptualizing creativity and measuring it psychometrically. However, the London School of Psychology had instigated psychometric studies of creativity as early as 1927 with the work of H. L. Hargreaves into the Faculty of Imagination.

In parallel with these developments, other investigators have taken a more pragmatic approach, teaching practical creativity techniques. Three of the best-known are:

- Alex Osborn's "brainstorming" (1950s to present),
- Genrikh Altshuller's Theory of Inventive Problem Solving (TRIZ, 1950s to present),
- and Edward de Bono's "lateral thinking" (1960s to present).

Distinguishing between Creativity and Innovation

It is often useful to explicitly distinguish between *creativity* and *innovation.*

Creativity is typically used to refer to the act of producing new ideas, approaches or actions, while innovation is the process of both generating *and applying* such creative ideas in some specific context.

In the context of an organization, therefore, the term *innovation* is often used to refer to the entire process by which an organization generates creative new ideas and converts them into novel, useful and viable commercial products, services, and business practices, while the term *creativity* is reserved to apply specifically to the generation of novel ideas by individuals or groups, as a necessary step within the innovation process.

For example, Amabile et al. (1996) suggest that while innovation "begins with creative ideas,"

> *"...creativity by individuals and teams* is a starting point for innovation; *the first is a necessary* but not sufficient *condition for the second."*

Although the two words are novel, they go hand in hand. In order to be innovative, employees have to be creative to stay competitive.

Creativity in Psychology and Cognitive Science

The study of the mental representations and processes underlying creative thought belongs to the domains of psychology and cognitive science.

A psychodynamic approach to understanding creativity was proposed by Sigmund Freud, who suggested that creativity arises as a result of frustrated desires for fame, fortune, and love, with the energy that was previously tied up in frustration and emotional tension in the neurosis being sublimated into creative activity. Freud later retracted this view.

Graham Wallas

Graham Wallas, in his work *Art of Thought*, published in 1926, presented one of the first models of the creative process. In the Wallas stage model, creative insights and illuminations may be explained by a process consisting of 5 stages:

(i) *preparation* (preparatory work on a problem that focuses the individual's mind on the problem and explores the problem's dimensions),

(ii) *incubation* (where the problem is internalized into the unconscious mind and nothing appears externally to be happening),

(iii) *intimation* (the creative person gets a "feeling" that a solution is on its way),

(iv) *illumination* or insight (where the creative idea bursts forth from its preconscious processing into conscious awareness); and

(v) *verification* (where the idea is consciously verified, elaborated, and then applied).

In numerous publications, Wallas' model is just treated as four stages, with "intimation" seen as a sub-stage. There has been some empirical research looking at whether, as the concept of "incubation" in Wallas' model implies, a period of interruption or rest from a problem may aid creative problem-solving. Ward lists various hypotheses that have been advanced to explain why incubation may aid creative problem-solving, and notes how some empirical evidence is consistent with the hypothesis that incubation aids creative problem-solving in that it enables "forgetting" of misleading clues. Absence of incubation may lead the problem solver to become fixated on inappropriate strategies of solving the problem. This work disputes the earlier hypothesis that creative solutions to problems arise mysteriously from the unconscious mind while the conscious mind is occupied on other tasks.

Wallas considered creativity to be a legacy of the evolutionary process, which allowed humans to quickly adapt to rapidly changing environments. Simonton provides an updated perspective on this view in his book, *Origins of genius: Darwinian perspectives on creativity*.

J.P. Guilford

Guilford performed important work in the field of creativity, drawing a distinction between convergent and divergent production (commonly renamed convergent and divergent thinking). Convergent thinking involves aiming for a single, correct solution to a problem, whereas divergent thinking involves creative generation of multiple answers to a set problem. Divergent thinking is sometimes used as a synonym for creativity in psychology literature. Other researchers have occasionally used the terms *flexible* thinking or fluid intelligence, which are roughly similar to (but not synonymous with) creativity.

Arthur Koestler

In *The Act of Creation*, Arthur Koestler lists three types of creative individual-the *Artist*, the *Sage* and the *Jester*.

Believers in this trinity hold all three elements necessary in business and can identify them all in "truly creative" companies as well. Koestler introduced the concept of *bisociation*—that creativity arises as a result of the intersection of two quite different frames of reference.

Geneplore Model

In 1992, Finke et al. proposed the "Geneplore" model, in which creativity takes place in two phases: a generative phase, where an individual constructs mental representations called preinventive structures, and an exploratory phase where those structures are used to come up with creative ideas. Weisberg argued, by contrast, that creativity only involves ordinary cognitive processes yielding extraordinary results.

Conceptual Blending

In the '90s, various approaches in cognitive science that dealt with metaphor, analogy and structure mapping have been converging, and a new integrative approach to the study of creativity in science, art and humour has emerged under the label conceptual blending.

> "Creativity is the ability to illustrate what is outside the box from within the box."
>
> —The Ride

Creativity and Everyday Imaginative Thought

In everyday thought, people often spontaneously imagine alternatives to reality when they think "if only...". Their counterfactual thinking is viewed as an example of everyday creative processes. It has been proposed that the creation of counterfactual alternatives to reality depends on similar cognitive processes to rational thought.

Psychological Examples from Science and Mathematics

Jacques Hadamard

Jacques Hadamard, in his book *Psychology of Invention in the Mathematical Field*, uses introspection to describe mathematical thought processes.

In contrast to authors who identify language and cognition, he describes his own mathematical thinking as largely wordless, often accompanied by mental images that represent the entire solution to a problem.

He surveyed 100 of the leading physicists of his day (ca. 1900), asking them how they did their work. Many of the responses mirrored his own.

Hadamard described the experiences of the mathematicians/ theoretical physicists Carl Friedrich Gauss, Hermann von Helmholtz, Henri Poincaré and others as viewing entire solutions with "sudden spontaneity."

The same has been reported in literature by many others, such as Denis Brian, G.H. Hardy, Walter Heitler, B.L. van der Waerden, and Harold Ruegg.

To elaborate on one example, Einstein, after years of fruitless calculations, suddenly had the solution to the general theory of relativity revealed in a dream "like a giant die making an indelible impress, a huge map of the universe outlined itself in one clear vision."

Hadamard described the process as having steps (i) preparation, (ii) incubation, (iv) illumination, and (v) verification of the five-step Graham Wallas creative-process model, leaving out (iii) intimation, with the first three cited by Hadamard as also having been put forth by Helmholtz:

Marie-Louise Von Franz

Marie-Louise von Franz, a colleague of the eminent psychiatrist Carl Jung, noted that in these unconscious scientific discoveries the "always recurring and important factor... is the simultaneity with which the complete solution is intuitively perceived and which can be checked later by discursive reasoning."

She attributes the solution presented "as an archetypal pattern or image." As cited by von Franz, according to Jung, "Archetypes... manifest themselves only through their ability to *organize* images and ideas, and this is always an unconscious process which cannot be detected until afterwards."

Creativity and Affect

Some theories suggest that creativity may be particularly susceptible to affective influence.

Creativity and Positive affect Relations

According to Isen, positive affect has three primary effects on cognitive activity:

1. Positive affect makes additional cognitive material available for processing, increasing the number of cognitive elements available for association;
2. Positive affect leads to defocused attention and a more complex cognitive context, increasing the breadth of those elements that are treated as relevant to the problem;
3. Positive affect increases cognitive flexibility, increasing the probability that diverse cognitive elements will in fact become associated. Together, these processes lead positive affect to have a positive influence on creativity.

Fredrickson in her Broaden and Build Model suggests that positive emotions such as joy and love broaden a person's available repertoire of cognitions and actions, thus enhancing creativity.

According to these researchers, positive emotions increase the number of cognitive elements available for association (attention scope) and the number of elements that are relevant to the problem (cognitive scope).

Creativity and Negative affect Relations

On the other hand, some theorists have suggested that negative affect leads to greater creativity. A cornerstone of this perspective is empirical evidence of a relationship between affective illness and creativity. In a study of 1,005 prominent 20th century individuals from over 45 different professions, the University of Kentucky's Arnold Ludwig found a slight but significant correlation between depression and level of creative achievement. In addition, several systematic studies of highly creative individuals and their relatives have uncovered a higher incidence of affective disorders (primarily bipolar disorder and depression) than that found in the general population.

Creativity and affect at Work

Three patterns may exist between affect and creativity at work: positive (or negative) mood, or change in mood, predictably precedes creativity; creativity predictably precedes mood; and whether affect and creativity occur simultaneously.

It was found that not only might affect precede creativity, but creative outcomes might provoke affect as well. At its simplest level, the experience of creativity is itself a work event, and like other events in the organizational context, it could evoke emotion. Qualitative research and anecdotal accounts of creative achievement in the arts and sciences suggest that creative insight is often followed by feelings of elation. For example, Albert Einstein called his 1907 general theory of relativity "the happiest thought of my life." Empirical evidence on this matter is still very tentative.

In contrast to the possible incubation effects of affective state on subsequent creativity, the affective consequences of creativity are likely to be more direct and immediate. In general, affective events provoke immediate and relatively-fleeting emotional reactions. Thus, if creative performance at work is an affective event for the individual doing the creative work, such an effect would likely be evident only in same-day data.

Another longitudinal research found several insights regarding the relations between creativity and emotion at work. First, a positive relationship between positive affect and creativity, and no evidence of a negative relationship. The more positive a person's affect on a given day, the more creative thinking they evidenced that day and the next day—even controlling for that next day's mood. There was even some evidence of an effect two days later.

In addition, the researchers found no evidence that people were more creative when they experienced both positive and negative affect on the same day. The weight of evidence supports a purely linear form of the affect-creativity relationship, at least over the range of affect and creativity covered in our study: the more positive a person's affect, the higher their creativity in a work setting.

Finally, they found four patterns of affect and creativity affect can operate as an antecedent to creativity; as a direct consequence of creativity; as an indirect consequence of creativity; and affect can occur simultaneously with creative activity. Thus, it appears that people's feelings and creative cognitions are interwoven in several distinct ways within the complex fabric of their daily work lives.

Creativity and Intelligence

There has been debate in the psychological literature about whether intelligence and creativity are part of the same process (the conjoint hypothesis) or represent distinct mental processes (the disjoint hypothesis). Evidence from attempts to look at correlations between intelligence and creativity from the 1950s onwards, by authors such as Barron, Guilford or Wallach and Kogan, regularly suggested that correlations between these concepts were low enough to justify treating them as distinct concepts.

Some researchers believe that creativity is the outcome of the same cognitive processes as intelligence, and is only judged as creativity in terms of its consequences, i.e. when the outcome of cognitive processes happens to produce something novel, a view which Perkins has termed the "nothing special" hypothesis.

A very popular model is what has come to be known as "the threshold hypothesis," proposed by Ellis Paul Torrance, which holds that a high degree of intelligence appears to be a necessary but not sufficient condition for high creativity. This implies that, in a general sample, there will be a positive correlation between creativity and intelligence, but this correlation will not be found if only a sample of the most highly intelligent people are assessed. Research into the threshold hypothesis, however, has produced mixed results ranging from enthusiastic support to refutation and rejection.

An alternative perspective, Renzulli's three-rings hypothesis, sees giftedness as based on both intelligence and creativity. More on both the threshold hypothesis and Renzulli's work can be found in O'Hara and Sternberg.

Neurobiology of Creativity

The neurobiology of creativity has been addressed in the article "Creative Innovation: Possible Brain Mechanisms." The authors write that "creative innovation might require coactivation and communication between regions of the brain that ordinarily are not strongly connected." Highly creative people who excel at creative innovation tend to differ from others in three ways:

- they have a high level of specialized knowledge,
- they are capable of divergent thinking mediated by the frontal lobe.
- and they are able to modulate neurotransmitters such as norepinephrine in their frontal lobe.

Thus, the frontal lobe appears to be the part of the cortex that is most important for creativity.

This article also explored the links between creativity and sleep, mood and addiction disorders, and depression.

In 2005, Alice Flaherty presented a three-factor model of the creative drive. Drawing from evidence in brain imaging, drug studies and lesion analysis, she described the creative drive as resulting from an interaction of the frontal lobes, the temporal lobes, and dopamine from the limbic system. The frontal lobes can be seen as responsible for idea generation, and the temporal lobes for idea editing and evaluation. Abnormalities in the frontal lobe (such as depression or anxiety) generally decrease creativity, while abnormalities in the temporal lobe often increase creativity. High activity in the temporal lobe typically inhibits activity in the frontal lobe, and vice versa. High dopamine levels increase general arousal and goal directed behaviours and reduce latent inhibition, and all three effects increase the drive to generate ideas.

Working Memory and the Cerebellum

Vandervert described how the brain's frontal lobes and the cognitive functions of the cerebellum collaborate to produce creativity and innovation. Vandervert's explanation rests on considerable evidence that all processes of working memory (responsible for processing all thought) are adaptively modeled by the cerebellum. The cerebellum (consisting of 100 billion neurons, which is more than the entirety of the rest of the brain) is also widely known to adaptively model all bodily movement. The cerebellum's adaptive models of working memory processing are then fed back to especially frontal lobe working memory control processes where creative and innovative thoughts arise. (Apparently, creative insight or the "aha" experience is then triggered in the temporal lobe.) According to Vandervert, the details of creative adaptation begin in "forward" cerebellar models which are anticipatory/exploratory controls for movement and thought. These cerebellar processing and control architectures have been termed Hierarchical Modular Selection and Identification for Control (HMOSAIC). New, hierarchically arranged levels of the cerebellar control architecture (HMOSAIC) develop as mental mulling in working memory is extended over time. These new levels of the control architecture are fed forward to the frontal lobes. Since the cerebellum adaptively models all movement and all levels of thought and emotion, Vandervert's approach helps explain creativity and innovation in sports, art, music, the design of video games, technology, mathematics, the child prodigy, and thought in general.

REM Sleep

Creativity involves the forming of associative elements into new combinations that are useful or meet some requirement. Sleep aids this process. REM rather than NREM sleep appears to be responsible. This has been suggested to be due to changes in cholinergic and noradrenergic neuromodulation that occurs during REM sleep. During this period of sleep, high levels of acetylcholine in the hippocampus suppress feedback from the hippocampus to the neocortex, and lower levels of acetylcholine and norepinephrine in the neocortex encourage the spread of associational activity within neocortical areas without control from the hippocampus.

This is in contrast to waking consciousness, where higher levels of norepinephrine and acetylcholine inhibit recurrent connections in the neocortex. It is proposed that REM sleep would add creativity by allowing "neocortical structures to reorganize associative hierarchies, in which information from the hippocampus would be reinterpreted in relation to previous semantic representations or nodes."

Creativity and Mental Health

A study by psychologist J. Philippe Rushton found creativity to correlate with intelligence and psychoticism. Another study found creativity to be greater in schizotypal than in either normal or schizophrenic individuals. While divergent thinking was associated with bilateral activation of the prefrontal cortex, schizotypal individuals were found to have much greater activation of their *right* prefrontal cortex. This study hypothesizes that such individuals are better at accessing both hemispheres, allowing them to make novel associations at a faster rate. In agreement with this hypothesis, ambidexterity is also associated with schizotypal and schizophrenic individuals. Three recent studies by Mark Batey and Adrian Furnham have demonstrated the relationships between schizotypal and hypomanic personality and several different measures of creativity.

Particularly strong links have been identified between creativity and mood disorders, particularly manic-depressive disorder (a.k.a. bipolar disorder) and depressive disorder (a.k.a. unipolar disorder). In *Touched with Fire: Manic-Depressive Illness and the Artistic Temperament*, Kay Redfield Jamison summarizes studies of mood-disorder rates in writers, poets and artists. She also explores research that identifies mood disorders in such famous writers and artists as Ernest Hemingway (who shot himself after electroconvulsive treatment), Virginia Woolf (who drowned herself when she felt a depressive episode coming on), composer Robert Schumann (who died in a mental institution), and even the famed visual artist Michelangelo.

Measuring Creativity

Creativity Quotient

Several attempts have been made to develop a *creativity quotient* of an individual similar to the intelligence quotient (IQ), however these have been unsuccessful. Most measures of creativity are dependent on the personal judgement of the tester, so a standardized measure is difficult, if not impossible, to develop.

Psychometric Approach

J.P. Guilford's group, which pioneered the modern psychometric study of creativity, constructed several tests to measure creativity in 1967:

- Plot Titles, where participants are given the plot of a story and asked to write original titles.
- Quick Responses is a word-association test scored for uncommonness.
- Figure Concepts, where participants were given simple drawings of objects and individuals and asked to find qualities or features that are common by two or more drawings; these were scored for uncommonness.
- Unusual Uses is finding unusual uses for common everyday objects such as bricks.
- Remote Associations, where participants are asked to find a word between two given words (e.g. Hand _____ Call)
- Remote Consequences, where participants are asked to generate a list of consequences of unexpected events (e.g. loss of gravity).

Building on Guilford's work, Torrance developed the Torrance Tests of Creative Thinking in 1966. They involved simple tests of divergent thinking and other problem-solving skills, which were scored on:

- Fluency – The total number of interpretable, meaningful, and relevant ideas generated in response to the stimulus.
- Originality – The statistical rarity of the responses among the test subjects.

- Elaboration – The amount of detail in the responses.

The Creativity Achievement Questionnaire, a self-report test that measures creative achievement across 10 domains, was described in 2005 and shown to be reliable and valid when compared to other measures of creativity and to independent evaluation of creative output. The psychometric approach has been criticized by Robert Sternberg for falling "short of distinguishing imagination from fantasy, relevant from irrelevant material, and contextually valid from rambling associations".

Social-personality Approach

Some researchers have taken a social-personality approach to the measurement of creativity. In these studies, personality traits such as independence of judgement, self-confidence, attraction to complexity, aesthetic orientation and risk-taking are used as measures of the creativity of individuals. Other researchers have related creativity to the trait, *openness to experience*.

As the research into the relationship between personality traits and creativity continues to grow, a more complete picture has developed. Within the framework of the Big Five model of personality some consistent traits have emerged. Openness to experience has been shown to be consistently related to a whole host of different assessments of creativity.

However, research has shown there to be subtle differences between different domains (e.g. Art v Science). The meta-analysis by Gregory Feist has shown that Artists tend to report elevated Neuroticism and higher levels of Introversion. While Scientists generally show higher level of Conscientiousness

Other Approaches to Measurement

Genrich Altshuller in the 1950s introduced approaching creativity as an *exact science* with TRIZ and a Level-of-Invention measure.

The creativity of thousands of Japanese, expressed in terms of their problem-solving and problem-recognizing capabilities, has been measured in Japanese firms. Howard Gruber insisted on a case-study approach that expresses the existential and unique quality of the creator. Creativity to Gruber was the product of purposeful work and this work could be described only as a confluence of forces in the specifics of the case.

Creativity in Various Contexts

Creativity has been studied from a variety of perspectives and is important in numerous contexts. Most of these approaches are undisciplinary, and it is therefore difficult to form a coherent overall view. The following sections examine some of the areas in which creativity is seen as being important.

Creativity Profiles

Creativity comes in different forms. A number of different theorists have suggested models of the creative person. One model suggests that there are kinds to produce growth, innovation, speed, etc. These are referred to as the four "Creativity Profiles" that can help achieve such goals.

(i) *Incubate* (Long-term Development)

(ii) *Imagine* (Breakthrough Ideas)

(iii) *Improve* (Incremental Adjustments)

(iv) *Invest* (Short-term Goals).

Research by Dr Mark Batey of the Psychometrics at Work Research Group at Manchester Business School has suggested that the creative profile can be explained by four primary creativity traits with narrow facets within each

(i) "Idea Generation" (Fluency, Originality, Incubation and Illumination)

(ii) "Personality" (Curiosity and Tolerance for Ambiguity)

(iii) "Motivation" (Intrinsic, Extrinsic and Achievement)

(iv) "Confidence" (Producing, Sharing and Implementing).

This model was developed in a sample of 1000 working adults using the statistical techniques of Exploratory Factor Analysis followed by Confirmatory Factor Analysis by Structural Equation Modelling.

An important aspect of the creativity profiling approach is to account for the tension between predicting the creative profile of an individual, as characterised by the psychometric approach, and the evidence that team creativity is founded on diversity and difference.

Creativity in Diverse Cultures

Francois Jullien in "Process and Creation, 1989" is inviting us to look at that concept from a Chinese cultural point of view. Fangqi Xu has reported creativity courses in a range of countries. Todd Lubart has studied extensively the cultural aspects of creativity and innovation.

Creativity in Art and Literature

Most people associate creativity with the fields of art and literature. In these fields, *originality* is considered to be a sufficient condition for creativity, unlike other fields where both *originality* and *appropriateness* are necessary.

Within the different modes of artistic expression, one can postulate a continuum extending from "interpretation" to "innovation".

Established artistic movements and genres pull practitioners to the "interpretation" end of the scale, whereas original thinkers strive towards the "innovation" pole. Note that we conventionally expect some "creative" people (dancers, actors, orchestral members, etc.) to perform (interpret) while allowing others (writers, painters, composers, etc.) more freedom to express the new and the different.

Contrast alternative theories, for example:

- artistic inspiration, which provides the transmission of visions from divine sources such as the Muses; a taste of the Divine. Compare with invention.
- artistic evolution, which stresses obeying established ("classical") rules and imitating or appropriating to produce subtly different but unshockingly understandable work. Compare with crafts.
- artistic conversation, as in Surrealism, which stresses the depth of communication when the creative product is the language.

In the art practice and theory of Davor Dzalto, human creativity is taken as a basic feature of both the personal existence of human being and art production. For this thinker, creativity is a basic cultural and anthropological category, since it enables human manifestation in the world as a "real presence" in contrast to the progressive "virtualization" of the world.

Creative Industries and Services

Today, creativity forms the core activity of a growing section of the global economy—the so-called "creative industries"—capitalistically generating (generally non-tangible) wealth through the creation and exploitation of intellectual property or through the provision of creative services. The Creative Industries Mapping Document 2001 provides an overview of the creative industries in the UK. The creative professional workforce is becoming a more integral part of industrialized nations' economies.

Creative professions include writing, art, design, theatre, television, radio, motion pictures, related crafts, as well as marketing, strategy, some aspects of scientific research and development, product development, some types of teaching and curriculum design, and more. Since many creative professionals (actors and writers, for example) are also employed in secondary professions, estimates of creative professionals are often inaccurate. By some estimates, approximately 10 million US workers are creative professionals; depending upon the depth and breadth of the definition, this estimate may be double.

Creativity in other Professions

Creativity is also seen as being increasingly important in a variety of other professions. Architecture and industrial design are the fields most often associated with creativity, and more generally the fields of design and design research. These fields explicitly value creativity, and journals such as *Design Studies* have published many studies on creativity and creative problem solving.

Fields such as science and engineering have, by contrast, experienced a less explicit (but arguably no less important) relation to creativity. Simonton shows how some of the major scientific advances of the 20th century can be attributed to the creativity of individuals. This ability will also be seen as increasingly important for engineers in years to come.

Accounting has also been associated with creativity with the popular euphemism *creative accounting*. Although this term often implies unethical practices, Amabile has suggested that even this profession can benefit from the (ethical) application of creative thinking.

In a recent global survey of approximately 1600 CEO's, the leadership trait that was considered to be most crucial for success was creativity. This suggests that the world of business is beginning to accept that creativity is essential for all employees in all industries, rather than being simply the preserve of the creative industries.

Creativity in Organizations

Amabile argued that to enhance creativity in business, three components were needed:

- Expertise (technical, procedural and intellectual knowledge),
- Creative thinking skills (how flexibly and imaginatively people approach problems),
- and Motivation (especially intrinsic motivation).

There are two types of motivation:

- extrinsic motivation – external factors, for example threats of being fired or money as a reward,
- intrinsic motivation – comes from inside an individual, satisfaction, enjoyment of work etc.

Six managerial practices to encourage motivation are:

- Challenge – matching people with the right assignments;
- Freedom – giving people autonomy choosing means to achieve goals;
- Resources – such as time, money, space etc. There must be balance fit among resources and people;
- Work group features – diverse, supportive teams, where members share the excitement, willingness to help and recognize each other's talents;
- Supervisory encouragement – recognitions, cheering, praising;
- Organizational support – value emphasis, information sharing, collaboration.

Nonaka, who examined several successful Japanese companies, similarly saw creativity and knowledge creation as being important to the success of organizations. In particular, he emphasized the role that tacit knowledge has to play in the creative process. In business, originality is not enough. The idea must also be appropriate—useful and actionable.

Economic Views of Creativity

In the early 20th century, Joseph Schumpeter introduced the economic theory of *creative destruction*, to describe the way in which old ways of doing things are endogenously destroyed and replaced by the new.

Creativity is also seen by economists such as Paul Romer as an important element in the recombination of elements to produce new technologies and products and, consequently, economic growth. Creativity leads to capital, and creative products are protected by intellectual property laws.

The *creative class* is seen by some to be an important driver of modern economies. In his 2002 book, *The Rise of the Creative Class*, economist Richard Florida popularized the notion that regions with "3 T's of economic development: Technology, Talent and Tolerance" also have high concentrations of creative professionals and tend to have a higher level of economic development.

Fostering Creativity

Daniel Pink, in his 2005 book *A Whole New Mind*, repeating arguments posed throughout the 20th century, argues that we are entering a new age where creativity is becoming increasingly important. In this *conceptual age*, we will need to foster and encourage *right-directed thinking* (representing creativity and emotion) over *left-directed thinking* (representing logical, analytical thought). However, this simplification of 'right' versus 'left' brain thinking is not supported by the research data.

Nickerson provides a summary of the various creativity techniques that have been proposed. These include approaches that have been developed by both academia and industry:

1. Establishing purpose and intention
2. Building basic skills
3. Encouraging acquisitions of domain-specific knowledge
4. Stimulating and rewarding curiosity and exploration
5. Building motivation, especially internal motivation
6. Encouraging confidence and a willingness to take risks

7. Focusing on mastery and self-competition
8. Promoting supportable beliefs about creativity
9. Providing opportunities for choice and discovery
10. Developing self-management (metacognitive skills)
11. Teaching techniques and strategies for facilitating creative performance
12. Providing balance.

Some see the conventional system of schooling as "stifling" of creativity and attempt (particularly in the pre-school/kindergarten and early school years) to provide a creativity-friendly, rich, imagination-fostering environment for young children. Compare Waldorf School.

A growing number of psychologists are supporting the idea that there are methods of increasing the creativity of an individual. Several different researchers have proposed approaches to prop up this idea, ranging from psychological-cognitive, such as:

- Osborn-Parnes Creative Problem Solving Process
- Synectics;
- Science-based creative thinking;
- Purdue Creative Thinking Program; and
- lateral thinking (courtesy of Edward de Bono), to the highly-structured, such as:
- TRIZ (the Theory of Inventive Problem-Solving);
- ARIZ (the Algorithm of Inventive Problem-Solving), both developed by the Russian scientist Genrich Altshuller; and
- Computer-Aided Morphological analysis.

Understanding and Enhancing the Creative Process with New Technologies

A simple but accurate review on this new Human-Computer Interactions (HCI) angle for promoting creativity has been written by Todd Lubart, an invitation full of creative ideas to develop further this new field.

Groupware and other Computer Supported Collaborative Work (CSCW) platforms are now the stage of Network Creativity on the web or on other private networks. These tools have made more obvious the existence of a more connective, cooperative and collective nature of creativity rather than the prevailing individual one. Creativity Research on Global Virtual Teams is showing that the creative process is affected by the national identities, cognitive and conative profiles, anonymous interactions at times and many other factors affecting the teams members, depending on the early or later stages of the cooperative creative process. They are also showing how NGO's cross-cultural virtual team's innovation in Africa would also benefit from the pooling of best global practices online. Such tools enhancing cooperative creativity may have a great impact on society and as such should be tested while they are built following the Motto: "Build the Camera while shooting the film". Some European FP7 scientific programs like Paradiso are answering a need for advanced experimentally-driven research including large scale experimentation test-beds to discover the technical, societal, and economic implications of such groupware and collaborative tools to the Internet.

On the other hand, creativity research may one day be pooled with a computable metalanguage like IEML from the University of Ottawa Collective Intelligence Chair, Pierre Levy. It might be a good tool to provide an interdisciplinary definition and a rather unified theory of creativity. The creative processes being highly fuzzy, the programming of cooperative tools for creativity and innovation should be adaptive and flexible. Empirical Modelling seems to be a good choice for Humanities Computing.

If all the activity of the universe could be traced with appropriate captors, it is likely that one could see the creative nature of the universe to which humans are active contributors. After the web of documents, the Web of Things might shed some light on such a universal creative phenomenon which should not be restricted to humans. In order to trace and enhance cooperative and collective creativity, Metis Reflexive Global Virtual Team has worked for the last few years on the development of a Trace Composer at the intersection of personal experience and social knowledge.

Metis Reflexive Team has also identified a paradigm for the study of creativity to bridge European theory of "useless" and non-instrumentalized creativity, North American more pragmatic creativity and Chinese culture stressing more creativity as a holistic process of continuity rather than radical change and originality. This paradigm is mostly based on the work of the German philosopher Hans Joas, one that emphasizes the creative character of human action. This model allows also for a more comprehensive theory of action. Joas elaborates some implications of his model for theories of social movements and social change. The connection between concepts like creation, innovation, production and expression is facilitated by the creativity of action as a metaphore but also as a scientific concept.

The Creativity and Cognition conference series, sponsored by the ACM and running since 1993, has been an important venue for publishing research on the intersection between technology and creativity. The conference now runs biennially, next taking place in 2011.

Social Attitudes to Creativity

Although the benefits of creativity to society as a whole have been noted, social attitudes about this topic remain divided. The wealth of literature regarding the development of creativity and the profusion of creativity techniques indicate wide acceptance, at least among academics, that creativity is desirable.

There is, however, a dark side to creativity, in that it represents a *"quest for a radical autonomy apart from the constraints of social responsibility"*. In other words, by encouraging creativity we are encouraging a departure from society's existing norms and values. Expectation of conformity runs contrary to the spirit of creativity. Sir Ken Robinson argues that the current education system is "educating people out of their creativity".

Nevertheless, employers are increasingly valuing creative skills. A report by the Business Council of Australia, for example, has called for a higher level of creativity in graduates. The ability to "think outside the box" is highly sought after. However, the above-mentioned paradox may well imply that firms pay lip service to thinking outside the box while maintaining traditional, hierarchical organization structures in which individual creativity is not rewarded. The ways in which societies have perceived the concept of creativity have changed throughout history, as has the term itself. The ancient Greek concept of art (in Greek, "*techne*" — the root of "technique" and "technology"), with the exception of poetry, involved not freedom of action but subjection to *rules*. In Rome, the Greek concept was partly shaken, and visual artists were viewed as sharing, with poets, imagination and inspiration.

Under medieval Christianity, the Latin "*creatio*" came to designate God's act of "*creatio ex nihilo*" ("creation from nothing"); thus "*creatio*" ceased to apply to human activities. The Middle Ages, however, went even further than antiquity, when they revoked poetry's exceptional status: it, too, was an art and therefore craft and not creativity.

Renaissance men sought to give voice to their sense of their freedom and creativity. The first to apply the word "creativity," however, was the 17th-century Polish poet Maciej Kazimierz Sarbiewski — but he applied it only to poetry. For over a century and a half, the idea of *human* creativity met with resistance, due to the fact that the term "creation" was reserved for creation "from nothing."

In the 19th century, art took its revenge: now not only was art recognized as creativity, but *it alone* was. When later, at the turn of the 20th century, there began to be discussion as well of creativity in the sciences and in nature, this was taken as the transference, to the sciences and to nature, of concepts that were proper to art.

Term and Concept

The ancient Greeks had no terms corresponding to "to create" or "creator." The expression "*poiein*" ("to make") sufficed. And even that was not extended to art in general, but only to *poiesis* (poetry) and to the *poietes* (poet, or "maker") who *made* it. Plato asks in *The Republic*, "Will we say, of a painter, that he makes something?" and answers, "Certainly not, he merely imitates." To the ancient Greeks, the concept of a creator and of creativity implied freedom of action, whereas the Greeks' concept of art involved subjection to laws and rules. Art (in Greek, "*techne*") was "the making of things, according to rules." It contained no creativity, and it would have been — in the

Greeks' view — a bad state of affairs if it *had*. This understanding of art had a distinct premise: Nature is perfect and is subject to laws, therefore man ought to discover its laws and submit to them, and not seek freedom, which will deflect him from that *optimum* which he can attain. The artist was a discoverer, not an inventor.

The sole exception to this Greek view — a *great* exception— was poetry. The poet made new things — brought to life a new world — while the artist merely *imitated*. And the poet, unlike the artist, was *not* bound by laws. There were no terms corresponding to "creativity" or "creator," but in reality the poet was understood to be one who creates. And only he was so understood. In music, there was no freedom: melodies were prescribed, particularly for ceremonies and entertainments, and were known tellingly as "*nomoi*" ("laws"). In the visual arts, freedom was limited by the proportions that Polyclitus had established for the human frame, and which he called "the canon" (meaning, "measure"). Plato argued in *Timaeus* that, to execute a good work, one must contemplate an eternal model. Later the Roman, Cicero, would write that art embraces those things "of which we have knowledge" ("*quae sciuntur*").

Poets saw things differently. Book I of the *Odyssey* asks, "Why forbid the singer to please us with singing *as he himself will?*" Aristotle had doubts as to whether poetry was imitation of reality, and as to whether it required adherence to truth: it was, rather, the realm of that "which is neither true nor false."

In Rome, these Greek concepts were partly shaken. Horace wrote that not only poets but painters as well were entitled to the privilege of daring whatever they wished to ("*quod libet audendi*"). In the declining period of antiquity, Philostratus wrote that "one can discover a similarity between poetry and art and find that they have imagination in common."

Callistratos averred that "Not only is the art of the poets and prosaists inspired, but likewise the hands of sculptors are gifted with the blessing of divine inspiration." This was something new: classical Greeks had not applied the concepts of imagination and inspiration to the visual arts but had restricted them to poetry. Latin was richer than Greek: it had a term for "creating" ("*creatio*") and for "*creator*," and had *two* expressions — *"facere"* and *"creare"* — where Greek had but one, *"poiein."* Still, the two Latin terms meant much the same thing.

A fundamental change, however, came in the Christian period: *"creatio"* came to designate God's act of "creation from nothing" (*"creatio ex nihilo"*). *"Creatio"* thus took on a different meaning than *"facere"* ("to make"), and ceased to apply to human functions. As the 6th-century Roman official and literary figure Cassiodorus wrote, "things made and created differ, for we can make, who cannot create."

Alongside this new, religious interpretation of the expression, there persisted the ancient view that art is not a domain of creativity. This is seen in two early and influential Christian writers, Pseudo-Dionysius and St. Augustine. Later medieval men such as Hraban the Moor, and Robert Grosseteste in the 13th century, thought much the same way. The Middle Ages here went even further than antiquity; they made no exception of poetry: it too had its rules, was an art, and was therefore craft and not creativity.

All this changed in modern times. Renaissance men had a sense of their own independence, freedom and creativity, and sought to give voice to this sense of independence and creativity.

The philosopher Marsilio Ficino wrote that the artist "thinks up" (*"excogitatio"*) his works; the theoretician of architecture and painting, Leon Battista Alberti, that he "preordains" (*"preordinazione"*); Raphael, that he shapes a painting according to his idea; Leonardo da Vinci, that he employs "shapes that do not exist in nature"; Michelangelo, that the artist realizes his vision rather than imitating nature; Giorgio Vasari, that "nature is conquered by art"; the Venetian art theoretician, Paolo Pino, that painting is "inventing what is not"; Paolo Veronese, that painters avail themselves of the same liberties as do poets and madmen; Federico Zuccari (1542–1609), that the artist shapes "a new world, new paradises"; Cesare Cesariano (1483–1541), that architects are "demi-gods."

Among musicians, the Dutch composer and musicologist Jan Tinctoris (1446–1511) demanded novelty in what a composer did, and defined a composer as "one who produces *new* songs." Still more emphatic were those who wrote about poetry: G.P.

Capriano held (1555) that the poet's invention springs "from nothing." Francesco Patrizi (1586) saw poetry as "fiction," "shaping," "transformation."

Finally, at long last, someone ventured to use the word, "creation." He was the 17th-century Polish poet and theoretician of poetry, Maciej Kazimierz Sarbiewski (1595–1640), known as "the last Latin poet." In his treatise, *De perfecta poesi*, he not only wrote that a poet "invents," "after a fashion builds," but also that the poet *"creates anew"* (*"de novo creat"*). Sarbiewski even added: "in the manner of God" (*"instar Dei"*).

Sarbiewski, however, regarded creativity as the exclusive privilege of poetry; creativity was not open to visual artists. "Other arts merely imitate and copy but do not create, because they assume the existence of the material from which they create or of the subject." As late as the end of the 17th century, André Félibien (1619–75) would write that the painter is "so to speak [a] creator." The Spanish Jesuit Baltasar Gracian (1601–58) wrote similarly as Sarbiewski: "Art is the completion of nature, as it were *a second Creator...*"

By the 18th century, the concept of creativity was appearing more often in art theory. It was linked with the concept of imagination, which was on all lips. Joseph Addison wrote that the imagination "has something in it like creation." Voltaire declared (1740) that "the true poet is creative." With both these authors, however, this was rather only a *comparison* of poet with creator.

Other writers took a different view. Denis Diderot felt that imagination is merely "the memory of forms and contents," and "creates nothing" but only combines, magnifies or diminishes. It was precisely in 18th-century France, indeed, that the idea of man's creativity met with resistance. Charles Batteux wrote that "The human mind *cannot create*, strictly speaking; all its products bear the stigmata of their model; even monsters invented by an imagination unhampered by laws can only be composed of parts taken from nature." Luc de Clapiers, marquis de Vauvenargues (1715–47), and Étienne Bonnot de Condillac (1715–80) spoke to a similar effect.

Their resistance to the idea of human creativity had a triple source. The expression, "creation," was then reserved for creation *ex nihilo* (Latin: *from nothing*), which was inaccessible to man. Second, creation is a mysterious act, and Enlightenment psychology did not admit of mysteries. Third, artists of the age were attached to their rules, and creativity seemed irreconcilable with rules. The latter objection was the weakest, as it was already beginning to be realized (e.g., by Houdar de la Motte, 1715) that rules ultimately are a *human invention*.

In the 19th century, art took its compensation for the resistance of preceding centuries against recognizing it as creativity. Now not only was art regarded as creativity, but *it alone* was so regarded. When later, at the turn of the 20th century, there began to be discussion as well of creativity in the sciences and in nature (e.g., Henri Bergson), this was generally taken as the transference, to the sciences and to nature, of concepts proper to art.

The start of the *scientific* study of creativity is sometimes taken as J. P. Guilford's 1950 address to the American Psychological Association, which helped popularize the subject.

Other students of creativity have taken a more pragmatic approach, teaching practical creativity techniques. Three of the best-known are Alex Osborn's "brainstorming" (1950s to present), Genrikh Altshuller's Theory of Inventive Problem-Solving (TRIZ, 1950s to present), and Edward de Bono's "lateral thinking" (1960s to present).

10

Philosophy and Civilization

Philosophy is the study of general and fundamental problems concerning matters such as existence, knowledge, values, reason, mind, and language. It is distinguished from other ways of addressing such problems by its critical, generally systematic approach and its reliance on rational argument.

The word "philosophy" comes from the Greek *philosophia*, which literally means "love of wisdom", and was originally a word referring to the special way of life of early Greek philosophers.

Branches of Philosophy

The following branches are the main areas of study:

- Metaphysics is the study of the nature of being and the world. Traditional branches are cosmology and ontology.
- Epistemology is concerned with the nature and scope of knowledge, and whether knowledge is possible. Among its central concerns has been the challenge posed by skepticism and the relationships between truth, belief, and justification.
- Ethics, or "moral philosophy", is concerned with questions of how persons ought to act or if such questions are answerable. The main branches of ethics are meta-ethics, normative ethics, and applied ethics. Meta-ethics concerns the nature of ethical thought, comparison of various ethical systems, whether there are absolute ethical truths, and how such truths could be known. Ethics is also associated with the idea of morality.

Plato's early dialogues include a search for definitions of virtue.

- Political philosophy is the study of government and the relationship of individuals and communities to the state. It includes questions about justice, the good, law, property, and the rights and obligations of the citizen.
- Aesthetics deals with beauty, art, enjoyment, sensory-emotional values, perception, and matters of taste and sentiment.
- Logic is the study of valid argument forms. Beginning in the late 19th century, mathematicians such as Frege focused on a mathematical treatment of logic, and today the subject of logic has two broad divisions: mathematical logic (formal symbolic logic) and what is now called philosophical logic.
- Philosophy of mind deals with the nature of the mind and its relationship to the body, and is typified by disputes between dualism and materialism. In recent years there has been increasing similarity between this branch of philosophy and cognitive science.
- Philosophy of language is inquiry into the nature, origins, and usage of language.
- Philosophy of religion is a branch of philosophy that asks questions about religion.

Most academic subjects have a philosophy, for example the philosophy of science, the philosophy of mathematics, the philosophy of logic, the philosophy of law, and the philosophy of history. In addition, a range of academic subjects have emerged to deal with areas that historically were the subject of philosophy. These include psychology, anthropology and science.

Western Philosophy

The introduction of the terms "philosopher" and "philosophy" has been ascribed to the Greek thinker Pythagoras. The ascription is based on a passage in a lost work of Herakleides Pontikos, a disciple of Aristotle. It is considered to be part of the widespread legends of Pythagoras of this time. "Philosopher" replaced the word "sophist" (from *sophoi*), which meant "wise men", teachers of rhetoric, who were important in Athenian democracy.

The history of philosophy is customarily divided into six periods: Ancient philosophy, Medieval philosophy, Renaissance philosophy, Early and Late Modern philosophy and Contemporary philosophy.

Ancient Philosophy (c. 600 BC–c. AD 500)

Ancient philosophy is the philosophy of the Graeco-Roman world from the 6th century [circa 585] BC to the 6th century AD. It is usually divided into three periods: the pre-Socratic period, the period of Plato and Aristotle, and the post-Aristotelian (or Hellenistic) period. A fourth period that is sometimes added includes the Neoplatonic and Christian philosophers of Late Antiquity. The most important of the ancient philosophers (in terms of subsequent influence) are Plato and Aristotle.

The main subjects of ancient philosophy are: understanding the fundamental causes and principles of the universe; explaining it in an economical way; the epistemological problem of reconciling the diversity and change of the natural universe, with the possibility of obtaining fixed and certain knowledge about it; questions about things that cannot be perceived by the senses, such as numbers, elements, universals, and gods; the analysis of patterns of reasoning and argument; the nature of the good life and the importance of understanding and knowledge in order to pursue it; the explication of the concept of justice, and its relation to various political systems.

In this period the crucial features of the philosophical method were established: a critical approach to received or established views, and the appeal to reason and argumentation.

Medieval Philosophy (c. 500–c. 1350)

Medieval philosophy is the philosophy of Western Europe and the Middle East during the Middle Ages, roughly extending from the Christianization of the Roman Empire until the Renaissance. Medieval philosophy is defined partly by the rediscovery and further development of classical Greek and Hellenistic philosophy, and partly by the need to address theological problems and to integrate sacred doctrine (in Islam,

Judaism, and Christianity) with secular learning. The history of European medieval philosophy is traditionally divided into three main periods: the period in the Latin West following the Early Middle Ages until the 12th century, when the works of Aristotle and Plato were preserved and cultivated; and the "golden age" of the 12th, 13th and 14th centuries in the Latin West, which witnessed the culmination of the recovery of ancient philosophy, and significant developments in the field of Philosophy of religion, Logic and Metaphysics.

The medieval era was disparagingly treated by the Renaissance humanists, who saw it as a barbaric "middle" period between the classical age of Greek and Roman culture, and the "rebirth" or *renaissance* of classical culture. Yet this period of nearly a thousand years was the longest period of philosophical development in Europe, and possibly the richest. Jorge Gracia has argued that "in intensity, sophistication, and achievement, the philosophical flowering in the thirteenth century could be rightly said to rival the golden age of Greek philosophy in the fourth century B.C."

Some problems discussed throughout this period are the relation of faith to reason, the existence and unity of God, the object of theology and metaphysics, the problems of knowledge, of universals, and of individuation.

Philosophers from the Middle Ages include the Muslim philosophers Alkindus, Alfarabi, Alhazen, Avicenna, Algazel, Avempace, Abubacer and Averroes; the Jewish philosophers Maimonides and Gersonides; and the Christian philosophers Augustine of Hippo, Boethius, Anselm, Gilbert of Poitiers, Peter Abelard, Roger Bacon, Bonaventure, Thomas Aquinas, Duns Scotus, William of Ockham and Jean Buridan. The medieval tradition of scholasticism continued to flourish as late as the 17th century, in figures such as Francisco Suarez and John of St. Thomas.

Aquinas, father of Thomism, was immensely influential, placed a greater emphasis on reason and argumentation, and was one of the first to use the new translation of Aristotle's metaphysical and epistemological writing. His work was a significant departure from the Neoplatonic and Augustinian thinking that had dominated much of early Scholasticism.

Many modern ethicists both within and outside the Catholic Church (notably Philippa Foot and Alasdair MacIntyre) have recently commented on Aquinas's virtue ethics as a way of avoiding utilitarianism or Kantian "sense of duty" (deontology). Through the work of 20th-century philosophers such as Elizabeth Anscombe, his principle of double effect and his theory of intentional activity generally have been influential. Cognitive neuroscientist and philosopher Walter Freeman proposes that Thomism is the system explaining cognition that is most compatible with neurodynamics, in a 2008 article in the journal *Mind and Matter* entitled "Nonlinear Brain Dynamics and Intention According to Aquinas." The influence of Aquinas's aesthetics also can be found in the works of the Italian semiotician Umberto Eco.

Renaissance Philosophy (c. 1350–c. 1600)

The Renaissance ("rebirth") was a period of transition between the Middle Ages and modern thought, in which the recovery of classical texts shifted philosophical interests away from technical studies in logic, metaphysics, and theology towards eclectic inquiries into morality, philology, and mysticism. The study of classics, particularly the newly rediscovered works of Plato and the Neoplatonists, and of the humane arts more generally (such as history and literature) enjoyed a popularity hitherto unknown in Christendom. The concept of man displaced God as the central object of philosophical reflection.

The Renaissance also renewed interest in nature considered as an organic whole comprehensible independently of theology, as in the work of Nicholas of Kues, Giordano Bruno, Galileo Galilei, and Telesius. Such movements in natural philosophy dovetailed with a revival of interest in magic, hermeticism, and astrology, which were thought to yield hidden ways of knowing and mastering nature (e.g., in Marsilio Ficino and Giovanni Pico della Mirandola).

These new movements in philosophy developed contemporaneously with larger political and religious transformations in Europe: the decline of feudalism and the Reformation. The rise of the monarchic nation-state found voice in increasingly secular political philosophies, as in the work of Niccolò Machiavelli, Thomas More, Jean Bodin, Tommaso Campanella, and Hugo Grotius. And while the Reformers showed little direct interest in philosophy, their destruction of the traditional foundations of theological and intellectual authority harmonized with the revival of fideism and skepticism in thinkers such as Erasmus, Montaigne and Francisco Sanches.

Early Modern Philosophy (c. 1600–c. 1800)

Modern philosophy begins with the response to skepticism and the rise of modern physical science. Philosophy in this period centres on the relation between experience and reality, the ultimate origin of knowledge, the nature of the mind and its relation to the body, the implications of the new natural sciences for free will and God, and the emergence of a secular basis for moral and political philosophy. Canonical figures include Hobbes, Descartes, Locke, Spinoza, Leibniz, Berkeley, Rousseau, Hume, and Kant. Chronologically, this era spans the 17th and 18th centuries, and is generally considered to end with Kant's systematic attempt to reconcile Newtonian physics with traditional metaphysical topics.

Late Modern Philosophy (c. 1800–c. 1900)

Later modern philosophy is usually considered to begin after the philosophy of Immanuel Kant at the beginning of the 19th century. German idealists, such as Fichte, Hegel, and Schelling, transformed the work of Kant by maintaining that the world is constituted by a rational or mind-like process, and as such is entirely knowable. Schopenhauer's identification of this world-constituting process as an irrational will to live influenced later 19th-and early 20th-century thinking, such as the work of Nietzsche and Freud.

Rejecting idealism, other philosophers, many working from outside the university, initiated lines of thought that occupied academic philosophy in the early and mid-20th century:

- Frege's work in logic and Sidgwick's work in ethics provided the tools for early analytic philosophy.
- Husserl initiated the school of phenomenology.
- Peirce and William James initiated the school of pragmatism.

- Kierkegaard and Nietzsche laid the groundwork for existentialism and post-structuralism.
- Karl Marx began the study of social materialist philosophy.

Contemporary Philosophy (c. 1900–present)

Within the last century, philosophy has increasingly become an activity practiced within the university, and accordingly it has grown more specialized and more distinct from the natural sciences. Much of philosophy in this period concerns itself with explaining the relation between the theories of the natural sciences and the ideas of the humanities or common sense.

In the Anglophone world, analytic philosophy became the dominant school. In the first half of the century, it was a cohesive school, more or less identical to logical positivism, united by the notion that philosophical problems could and should be solved by attention to logic and language.

In the latter half of the 20th century, analytic philosophy diffused into a wide variety of disparate philosophical views, only loosely united by historical lines of influence and a self-identified commitment to clarity and rigor. Recently, the experimental philosophy movement has reappraised philosophical problems through the techniques of social science research.

On continental Europe, no single school or temperament enjoyed dominance. The flight of the logical positivists from central Europe during the 1930s and 1940s, however, diminished philosophical interest in natural science, and an emphasis on the humanities, broadly construed, figures prominently in what is usually called "continental philosophy". 20th-century movements such as phenomenology, existentialism, hermeneutics, critical theory, structuralism, and poststructuralism are included within this loose category.

Major philosophers of the 20th century include:

- Ludwig Wittgenstein, who profoundly shaped both logical positivism and ordinary language philosophy.
- Bertrand Russell, whose pioneering work in logic was a model for the early development of analytic philosophy.

- Martin Heidegger, who drew on the ideas of Kierkegaard, Nietzsche, and Husserl to propose an existential approach to ontology.
- Karl R. Popper, whose work on falsifiability is seen as a major development in the Philosophy of Science.
- W.V.O. Quine, whose work in logic and the philosophy of language underpinned a highly influential form of naturalism.
- Saul Kripke, whose work in modal logic and the philosophy of language led to a revival of metaphysics in English-speaking philosophy.
- John Rawls, whose seminal work Theory of Justice revitalized the area of liberal political philosophy, and moved away from a traditional analytic approach with his Contractarian argument.

Eastern Philosophy

Many societies have considered philosophical questions and built philosophical traditions based upon each other's works. Eastern and Middle Eastern philosophical traditions have influenced Western philosophers. Russian (which, often arbitrarily, is referred to as both Eastern and Western), Jewish, Islamic, and the greatly varied African philosophical traditions have contributed to, or been influenced by, Western philosophy: yet each has retained a distinctive identity. The differences between traditions are often well captured by consideration of their favoured historical philosophers, and varying stress on ideas, procedural styles, or written language. The subject matter and dialogues of each can be studied using methods derived from the others, and there are significant commonalities and exchanges between them. *Eastern philosophy* refers to the broad traditions that originated or were popular in India, Persia, China, Korea, Japan, and to an extent, the Middle East (which overlaps with Western philosophy due to the spread of the Abrahamic religions and the continuing intellectual traffic between these societies and Europe.)

Babylonian Philosophy

The origins of Babylonian philosophy can be traced back to the wisdom of early Mesopotamia, which embodied certain philosophies of life, particularly ethics, in the forms of dialectic, dialogues, epic poetry, folklore, hymns, lyrics, prose, and proverbs. The reasoning and rationality of the Babylonians developed beyond empirical observation. The Babylonian text *Dialog of Pessimism* contains similarities to the agonistic thought of the sophists, the Heraclitean doctrine of contrasts, and the dialogues of Plato, as well as a precursor to the maieutic Socratic method of Socrates and Plato. The Milesian philosopher Thales is also traditionally said to have studied philosophy in Mesopotamia.

Chinese Philosophy

Philosophy has had a tremendous effect on Chinese civilization, and East Asia as a whole. Many of the great philosophical schools were formulated during the Spring and Autumn Period and Warring States Period, and came to be known as the Hundred Schools of Thought. The four most influential of these were Confucianism, Taoism, Mohism, and Legalism. Later on, during the Tang Dynasty, Buddhism from Nepal also became a prominent philosophical and religious discipline. (It should be noted that philosophy and religion were clearly distinguished in the West, whilst these concepts were more continuous in the East due to, for example, the philosophical concepts of Buddhism.) Similarly to Western philosophy, Chinese philosophy also covers a broad and complex range of thought, possessing a multitude of schools that address every branch and subject area of philosophy.

Indian Philosophy

The term Indian philosophy (Sanskrit: *Darshanas*), may refer to any of several traditions of philosophical thought that originated in the Indian subcontinent, including Hindu philosophy, Buddhist philosophy, and Jain philosophy. Having the same or rather intertwined origins, all of these philosophies have a common underlying theme of Dharma, and similarly attempt to explain the attainment of emancipation. They have been formalized and promulgated chiefly between 1000 BC to a few centuries AD, with residual commentaries and reformations continuing up to as late as the 20th century by Aurobindo and ISKCON among others, who provided stylized interpretations.

In the history of the Indian subcontinent, following the establishment of a Vedic culture, the development of philosophical and religious thought over a period of two millennia gave rise to what came to be called the six schools of *astika*, or orthodox, Indian or Hindu philosophy. These schools have come to be synonymous with the greater religion of Hinduism, which was a development of the early Vedic religion.

Hindu philosophy constitutes an integral part of the culture of South Asia, and is the first of the Dharmic philosophies that were influential throughout the Far East. The great diversity in thought and practice of Hinduism is nurtured by its liberal universalism.

Persian Philosophy

Persian philosophy can be traced back as far as Old Iranian philosophical traditions and thoughts, with their ancient Indo-Iranian roots. These were considerably influenced by Zarathustra's teachings. Throughout Iranian history and due to remarkable political and social influences such as the Macedonian, the Arab, and the Mongol invasions of Persia, a wide spectrum of schools of thought arose. These espoused a variety of views on philosophical questions, extending from Old Iranian and mainly Zoroastrianism-influenced traditions to schools appearing in the late pre-Islamic era, such as Manicheism and Mazdakism, as well as various post-Islamic schools. Iranian philosophy after Arab invasion of Persia is characterized by different interactions with the Old Iranian philosophy, the Greek philosophy and with the development of Islamic philosophy. The Illumination school and the Transcendent theosophy are regarded as two of the main philosophical traditions of that era in Persia. Zoroastrianism has been identified as one of the key early events in the development of philosophy.

Main Theories

Realism and Nominalism

Realism sometimes means the position opposed to the 18th-century idealism, namely that some things have real existence outside the mind. Its standard meaning is the doctrine that abstract entities corresponding to universal terms like "man" or "table" or "red" actually exist (e.g. for Plato in a separate realm of ideas). It is opposed to nominalism, the view that abstract or universal terms are words only, or denote mental states such as ideas, beliefs, or intentions. The latter position, developed by Peter Abelard and famously held by William of Ockham, is called conceptualism.

Rationalism and Empiricism

Rationalism is any view emphasizing the role or importance of human reason. Extreme rationalism tries to base all knowledge on reason alone. Rationalism typically starts from premises that cannot coherently be denied, then attempts by logical steps to deduce every possible object of knowledge.

The first rationalist, in this broad sense, is often held to be Parmenides (fl. 500 BC), who argued that it is impossible to doubt that thinking actually occurs.

But thinking must have an object, therefore something *beyond* thinking really exists. Parmenides deduced that what really exists must have certain properties – for example, that it cannot come into existence or cease to exist, that it is a coherent whole, that it remains the same eternally (in fact, exists altogether outside time). This is known as the third man argument. Zeno of Elea (born c. 489 BC) was a disciple of Parmenides, and argued that motion is impossible, since the assertion that it exists implies a contradiction.

Plato (427–347 BC) was also influenced by Parmenides, but combined rationalism with a form of realism. The philosopher's work is to consider being, and the essence (ousia) of things. But the characteristic of essences is that they are universal. The nature of a man, a triangle, a tree, applies to all men, all triangles, all trees. Plato argued that these essences are mind-independent "forms", that humans (but particularly philosophers) can come to know by reason, and by ignoring the distractions of sense-perception.

Modern rationalism begins with Descartes. Reflection on the nature of perceptual experience, as well as scientific discoveries in physiology and optics, led Descartes (and also Locke) to the view that we are directly aware of ideas, rather than objects. This view gave rise to three questions:

1. Is an idea a true copy of the real thing that it represents? Sensation is not a direct interaction between bodily objects and our sense, but is a physiological process involving representation (for example, an image on the retina). Locke thought that a "secondary quality" such as a sensation of green could in no way resemble the arrangement of particles in matter that go to produce this sensation, although he thought that "primary qualities" such as shape, size, number, were really in objects.
2. How can physical objects such as chairs and tables, or even physiological processes in the brain, give rise to mental items such as ideas? This is part of what became known as the mind-body problem.
3. If all the contents of awareness are ideas, how can we know that anything exists apart from ideas?

Descartes tried to address the last problem by reason. He began, echoing Parmenides, with a principle that he thought could not coherently be denied: I *think*, therefore I *am* (often given in his original Latin: *Cogito ergo sum*). From this principle, Descartes went on to construct a complete system of knowledge (which involves proving the existence of God, using, among other means, a version of the ontological argument). His view that reason alone could yield substantial truths about reality strongly influenced those philosophers usually considered modern rationalists (such as Baruch Spinoza, Gottfried Leibniz, and Christian Wolff), while provoking criticism from other philosophers who have retrospectively come to be grouped together as empiricists.

Empiricism, in contrast to rationalism, downplays or dismisses the ability of reason alone to yield knowledge of the world, preferring to base any knowledge we have on our senses. This dates back to the concept of *tabula rasa* (unscribed tablet) implicit in Aristotle's *On the Soul*, described more explicitly in Avicenna's *The Book of Healing*, and demonstrated in Ibn Tufail's *Hayy ibn Yaqdhan* as a thought experiment. John Locke propounded the classic empiricist view in *An Essay Concerning Human Understanding* in 1689, developing a form of naturalism and empiricism on roughly scientific (and Newtonian) principles.

During this era, religious ideas played a mixed role in the struggles that preoccupied secular philosophy. Bishop Berkeley's famous idealist refutation of key tenets of Isaac Newton is a case of an Enlightenment philosopher who drew substantially from religious ideas. Other influential religious thinkers of the time include Blaise Pascal, Joseph Butler, Thomas Reid, and Jonathan Edwards. Other major writers, such as Jean-Jacques Rousseau and Edmund Burke, took a rather different path. The restricted interests of many of the philosophers of the time foreshadow the separation and specialization of different areas of philosophy that occurred in the 20th century.

Skepticism

Skepticism is a philosophical attitude that, in its most extreme form, questions the possibility of obtaining *any* sort of knowledge. It was first articulated by Pyrrho, who believed that everything could be doubted except *appearances*. Sextus Empiricus (2nd century AD), skepticism's most prominent advocate, describes it as an "ability to place in antithesis, in any manner whatever, appearances and judgments, and thus ... to come first of all to a suspension of judgment and then to mental tranquility."

Skepticism so conceived is not merely the use of doubt, but is the use of doubt for a particular end: a calmness of the soul, or *ataraxia*. Skepticism poses itself as a challenge to dogmatism, whose adherents think they have found the truth.

Sextus noted that the reliability of perception may always be questioned, because it is idiosyncratic to the perceiver. The appearance of individual things changes depending on whether they are in a group: for example, the shavings of a goat's horn are white when taken alone, yet the intact horn is black. A pencil, when viewed lengthwise, looks like a stick; but when examined at the tip, it looks merely like a circle.

Skepticism was revived in the early modern period by Michel de Montaigne and Blaise Pascal. Its most extreme exponent, however, was David Hume. Hume argued that there are only two kinds of reasoning: what he called *probable* and *demonstrative*. Neither of these two forms of reasoning can lead us to a reasonable belief in the continued existence of an external world. Demonstrative reasoning cannot do this, because demonstration (that is, deductive reasoning from well-founded premises) alone cannot establish the uniformity of nature (as captured by scientific laws and principles, for example). Such reason alone cannot establish that the future will resemble the past. We have certain beliefs about the world (that the sun will rise tomorrow, for example), but these beliefs are the product of habit and custom, and do not depend on any sort of logical inferences from what is already given *certain*. But *probable* reasoning (inductive reasoning), which aims to take us from the observed to the unobserved, cannot do this either: it *also* depends on the uniformity of nature, and this supposed uniformity cannot be proved, without circularity, by any appeal to uniformity. The best that either sort of reasoning can accomplish is conditional truth: *if* certain assumptions are true, *then* certain conclusions follow. So nothing about the world can be established with certainty. Hume concludes that there is no solution to the skeptical argument – except, in effect, to ignore it.

Even if these matters were resolved in every case, we would have in turn to justify our standard of justification, leading to an infinite regress (hence the term *regress skepticism*).

Many philosophers have questioned the value of such skeptical arguments. The question of whether we can achieve knowledge of the external world is based on how high a standard we set for the justification of such knowledge. If our standard is absolute certainty, then we cannot progress beyond the existence of mental sensations. We cannot even deduce the existence of a coherent or continuing "I" that experiences these sensations, much less the existence of an external world. On the other hand, if our standard is too low, then we admit follies and illusions into our body of knowledge. This argument against absolute skepticism asserts that the practical philosopher must move beyond solipsism, and accept a standard for knowledge that is high but not absolute.

Idealism

Idealism is the epistemological doctrine that nothing can be directly known outside of the minds of thinking beings. Or in an alternative stronger form, it is the metaphysical doctrine that nothing exists apart from minds and the "contents" of minds. In modern Western philosophy, the epistemological doctrine begins as a core tenet of Descartes – that what is in the mind is known more reliably than what is known through the senses. The first prominent modern Western idealist in the metaphysical sense was George Berkeley. Berkeley argued that there is no deep distinction between mental states, such as feeling pain, and the ideas about so-called "external" things, that appear to us through the senses. There is no real distinction, in this view, between certain sensations of heat and light that we experience, which lead us to believe in the external existence of a fire, and the fire itself. Those sensations are all there is to fire. Berkeley expressed this with the Latin formula *esse est percipi*: "to be is to be perceived". In this view the opinion, "strangely prevailing upon men", that houses, mountains, and rivers have an existence independent of their perception by a thinking being is false.

Forms of idealism were prevalent in philosophy from the 18th century to the early 20th century. Transcendental idealism, advocated by Immanuel Kant, is the view that there are limits on what can be understood, since there is much that cannot be brought under the conditions of objective judgment. Kant wrote his *Critique of Pure Reason* (1781–1787) in an attempt to reconcile the conflicting approaches of rationalism and empiricism, and to establish a new groundwork for studying metaphysics. Kant's intention with this work was to look at what we know and then consider what must be true about it, as a logical consequence of the *way* we know it. One major theme was that there are fundamental features of reality that escape our direct knowledge because of the natural limits of the human faculties. Although Kant held that objective knowledge of the world required the mind to impose a conceptual or categorical framework on the stream of pure sensory data – a framework including space and time themselves – he maintained that *things-in-themselves* existed independently of our perceptions and judgments; he was therefore not an idealist in any simple sense. Indeed, Kant's account of *things-in-themselves* is both controversial and highly complex. Continuing his work, Johann Gottlieb Fichte and Friedrich Schelling dispensed with belief in the independent existence of the world, and created a thoroughgoing idealist philosophy.

The most notable work of this German idealism was G. W. F. Hegel's *Phenomenology of Spirit*, of 1807. Hegel admitted his ideas weren't new, but that all the previous philosophies had been incomplete. His goal was to correctly finish their job. Hegel asserts that the twin aims of philosophy are to account for the contradictions apparent in human experience (which arise, for instance, out of the supposed contradictions between "being" and "not being"), and also simultaneously to resolve and preserve these contradictions by showing their compatibility at a higher level of examination ("being" and "not being" are resolved with "becoming"). This program of acceptance and reconciliation of contradictions is known as the "Hegelian dialectic". Philosophers in the Hegelian tradition include Ludwig Andreas Feuerbach, who coined the term projection as pertaining to our inability to recognize anything in the external world without projecting qualities of ourselves upon those things; Karl Marx; Friedrich Engels; and the British idealists, notably T.H. Green, J.M.E. McTaggart, and F.H. Bradley.

Few 20th century philosophers have embraced idealism. However, quite a few have embraced Hegelian dialectic. Immanuel Kant's "Copernican Turn" also remains an important philosophical concept today.

Pragmatism

Pragmatism was founded in the spirit of finding a scientific concept of truth that does not depend on personal insight (revelation) or reference to some metaphysical realm. The truth of a statement should be judged by the effect it has on our actions, and truth should be seen as what the whole of scientific enquiry ultimately agrees on. This should probably be seen as a guiding principle more than a definition of what it means for something to be true, though the details of how this principle should be interpreted have been subject to discussion since Charles S. Peirce first conceived it. Peirce's maxim of pragmatism is as follows: "Consider what effects, which might conceivably have practical bearings, we conceive the object of our conception to have. Then, our conception of these effects is the whole of our conceptions of the object." Like postmodern neo-pragmatist Richard Rorty, many are convinced that pragmatism asserts that the truth of beliefs does not consist in their correspondence with reality, but in their usefulness and efficacy.

The late 19th-century American philosophers Charles Sanders Peirce and William James were its co-founders, and it was later developed by John Dewey as instrumentalism. Since the usefulness of any belief at any time might be contingent on circumstance, Peirce and James conceptualised final truth as something only established by the future, final settlement of all opinion. Critics have accused pragmatism of falling victim to a simple fallacy: because something that is true proves useful, that usefulness is the basis for its truth. Thinkers in the pragmatist tradition have included John Dewey, George Santayana, W.V.O. Quine and C.I. Lewis. Pragmatism has more recently been taken in new directions by Richard Rorty, John Lachs, Donald Davidson, Susan Haack, and Hilary Putnam.

Phenomenology

Edmund Husserl's phenomenology was an ambitious attempt to lay the foundations for an account of the structure of conscious experience in general. An important part of Husserl's phenomenological project was to show that all conscious acts are directed at or about objective content, a feature that Husserl called *intentionality*.

In the first part of his two-volume work, the *Logical Investigations* (1901), he launched an extended attack on psychologism. In the second part, he began to develop the technique of *descriptive phenomenology*, with the aim of showing how objective judgments are indeed grounded in conscious experience – not, however, in the first-person experience of particular individuals, but in the properties essential to any experiences of the kind in question.

He also attempted to identify the essential properties of any act of meaning. He developed the method further in *Ideas* (1913) as *transcendental phenomenology*, proposing to ground actual experience, and thus all fields of human knowledge, in the structure of consciousness of an ideal, or transcendental, ego. Later, he attempted to reconcile his transcendental standpoint with an acknowledgement of the intersubjective life-world in which real individual subjects interact. Husserl published only a few works in his lifetime, which treat phenomenology mainly in abstract methodological terms; but he left an enormous quantity of unpublished concrete analyses.

Husserl's work was immediately influential in Germany, with the foundation of phenomenological schools in Munich and Göttingen. Phenomenology later achieved international fame through the work of such philosophers as Martin Heidegger (formerly Husserl's research assistant), Maurice Merleau-Ponty, and Jean-Paul Sartre. Indeed, through the work of Heidegger and Sartre, Husserl's focus on subjective experience influenced aspects of existentialism.

Existentialism

Existentialism is a term applied to the work of a number of late 19th-and 20th-century philosophers who, despite profound doctrinal differences, shared the belief that philosophical thinking begins with the human subject – not merely the thinking subject, but the acting, feeling, living human individual. In existentialism, the individual's starting point is characterized by what has been called "the existential attitude", or a sense of disorientation and confusion in the face of an apparently meaningless or absurd world. Many existentialists have also regarded traditional systematic or academic philosophy, in both style and content, as too abstract and remote from concrete human experience.

Although they didn't use the term, the 19th-century philosophers Søren Kierkegaard and Friedrich Nietzsche are widely regarded as the fathers of existentialism. Their influence, however, has extended beyond existentialist thought.

The main target of Kierkegaard's writings was the idealist philosophical system of Hegel which, he thought, ignored or excluded the inner subjective life of living human beings. Kierkegaard, conversely, held that "truth is subjectivity", arguing that what is most important to an actual human being are questions dealing with an individual's inner relationship to existence. In particular, Kierkegaard, a Christian, believed that the truth of religious faith was a subjective question, and one to be wrestled with passionately.

Although Kierkegaard and Nietzsche were among his influences, the extent to which the German philosopher Martin

Heidegger should be considered an existentialist is debatable. In *Being and Time* he presented a method of rooting philosophical explanations in human existence (*Dasein*) to be analysed in terms of existential categories (*existentiale*); and this has led many commentators to treat him as an important figure in the existentialist movement. However, in *The Letter on Humanism*, Heidegger explicitly rejected the existentialism of Jean-Paul Sartre.

Sartre became the best-known proponent of existentialism, exploring it not only in theoretical works such as *Being and Nothingness*, but also in plays and novels. Sartre, along with Simone de Beauvoir, represented an avowedly atheistic branch of existentialism, which is now more closely associated with their ideas of nausea, contingency, bad faith, and the absurd than with Kierkegaard's spiritual angst. Nevertheless, the focus on the individual human being, responsible before the universe for the authenticity of his or her existence, is common to all these thinkers.

Structuralism and Post-structuralism

Inaugurated by the linguist Ferdinand de Saussure, structuralism sought to clarify systems of signs through analyzing the discourses they both limit and make possible. Saussure conceived of the sign as being delimited by all the other signs in the system, and ideas as being incapable of existence prior to linguistic structure, which articulates thought. This led continental thought away from humanism, and toward what was termed the decentering of man: language is no longer spoken by man to express a true inner self, but language speaks man.

Structuralism sought the province of a hard science, but its positivism soon came under fire by poststructuralism, a wide field of thinkers, some of whom were once themselves structuralists, but later came to criticize it. Structuralists believed they could analyse systems from an external, objective standing, for example, but the poststructuralists argued that this is incorrect, that one cannot transcend structures and thus analysis is itself determined by what it examines, while the distinction between the signifier and signified was treated as crystalline by structuralists, poststructuralists asserted that every attempt to grasp the signified results in more signifies, so meaning is always in a state of being deferred, making an ultimate interpretation impossible.

Structuralism came to dominate continental philosophy throughout the 1960s and early '70s, encompassing thinkers as diverse as Claude Lévi-Strauss, Roland Barthes and Jacques Lacan. Post-structuralism came to predominate over the 1970s onwards, including thinkers such as Michel Foucault, Jacques Derrida, Gilles Deleuze and even Roland Barthes; it incorporated a critique of structuralism's limitations.

The Analytic Tradition

The term *analytic philosophy* roughly designates a group of philosophical methods that stress detailed argumentation, attention to semantics, use of classical logic and non-classical logics and clarity of meaning above all other criteria. Michael Dummett in his *Origins of Analytical Philosophy* makes the case for counting Gottlob Frege *The Foundations of Arithmetic* as the first analytic work, on the grounds that in that book Frege took the linguistic turn, analyzing philosophical problems through language. Bertrand Russell and G.E. Moore are also often counted as founders of analytic philosophy, beginning with their rejection of British idealism, their defence of realism and the emphasis they laid on the legitimacy of analysis. Russell's classic works *The Principles of Mathematics*, *On Denoting* and *Principia Mathematica*, aside from greatly promoting the use of classical first order logic in philosophy, set the ground for much of the research program in the early stages of the analytic tradition, emphasizing such problems as: the reference of proper names, whether existence is a property, the meaning of propositions, the analysis of definite descriptions, the discussions on the foundations of mathematics; as well as exploring issues of metaphysical commitment and even metaphysical problems regarding time, the nature of matter, mind, persistence and change, which Russell tackled often with the aid of mathematical logic. The philosophy developed as a critique of Hegel and his followers in particular, and of grand systems of speculative philosophy in general, though by no means all analytic philosophers reject the philosophy of Hegel nor speculative philosophy. Some schools in the group include logical atomism, logical positivism, and ordinary language. The motivation behind the work of analytic philosophers has been varied. Some have held that philosophical problems arise through misuse of language or because of misunderstandings of the logic of our language, while some maintain that there are genuine philosophical problems and that philosophy is continuous with science.

In 1921, Ludwig Wittgenstein published his *Tractatus Logico-Philosophicus*, which gave a rigidly "logical" account of linguistic and philosophical issues. At the time, he understood most of the problems of philosophy as mere puzzles of language, which could be solved by investigating and then minding the logical structure of language. Years later, he reversed a number of the positions he set out in the *Tractatus*, in for example his second major work, *Philosophical Investigations* (1953). *Investigations* was influential in the development of "ordinary language philosophy," which was promoted by Gilbert Ryle, J.L. Austin, and a few others. In the United States, meanwhile, the philosophy of W.V.O. Quine was having a major influence, with such classics as Two Dogmas of Empiricism. In that paper Quine criticizes the distinction between analytic and synthetic statements, arguing that a clear conception of analyticity is unattainable. He argued for holism, the thesis that language, including scientific language, is a set of interconnected sentences, none of which can be verified on its own, rather, the sentences in the language depend on each other for their meaning and truth conditions. A consequence of Quine's approach is that language as a whole has only a thin relation to experience. Some sentences that refer directly to experience might be modified by sense impressions, but as the whole of language is theory-laden, for the whole language to be modified, more than this is required. However, most of the linguistic structure can in principle be revised, even logic, in order to better model the world. Notable students of Quine include Donald Davidson and Daniel Dennett. The former devised a program for giving a semantics to natural language and thereby answer the philosophical conundrum "what is meaning?". A crucial part of the program was the use of Alfred Tarski's semantic theory of truth. Dummett, among others, argued that truth conditions should be dispensed within the theory of meaning, and replaced by assertibility conditions. Some propositions, on this view, are neither true nor false, and thus such a theory of meaning entails a rejection of the law of the excluded middle. This, for Dummett, entails antirealism, as Russell himself pointed out in *An Inquiry into Meaning and Truth*.

By the 1970s there was a renewed interest in many traditional philosophical problems by the younger generations of analytic philosophers. David Lewis, Saul Kripke, Derek Parfit and others took an interest in traditional metaphysical problems, which they began exploring by the use of logic and philosophy of language. Among those problems some distinguished ones were: free will, essentialism, the nature of personal identity, identity over time, the nature of the mind, the nature of causal laws, space-time, the properties of material beings, modality, etc. In those universities where analytic philosophy has spread, these problems are still being discussed passionately. Analytic philosophers are also interested in the methodology of analytic philosophy itself, with Timothy Williamson, Wykeham Professor of Logic at Oxford, publishing recently a book entitled *The Philosophy of Philosophy*. Some notable figures in contemporary analytic philosophy are: Timothy Williamson, John Searle, Thomas Nagel, Hilary Putnam, Michael Dummett, and Saul Kripke. Analytic philosophy has sometimes been accused of not contributing to the political debate or to traditional questions in aesthetics. However, with the appearance of *A Theory of Justice* by John Rawls and *Anarchy, State and Utopia* by Robert Nozick, analytic political philosophy acquired respectability. Analytic philosophers have also shown depth in their investigations of aesthetics, with Roger Scruton, Richard Wollheim, Jerrold Levinson and others developing the subject to its current shape.

Moral and Political Philosophy

Human Nature and Political Legitimacy

From ancient times, and well beyond them, the roots of justification for political authority were inescapably tied to outlooks on human nature. In *The Republic*, Plato declared that the ideal society would be run by a council of philosopher-kings, since those best at philosophy are best able to realize the good. Even Plato, however, required philosophers to make their way in the world for many years before beginning their rule at the age of fifty. For Aristotle, humans are political animals (i.e. social animals), and governments are set up to pursue good for the community. Aristotle reasoned that, since the state (*polis*) was the highest form of community, it has the purpose of pursuing the highest good. Aristotle viewed political power as the result of natural inequalities in skill and virtue. Because of these differences, he favoured an aristocracy of the able and virtuous. For Aristotle, the person cannot be complete unless he or she lives in a community. His *The Nicomachean Ethics* and *The Politics* are meant to be read in that order. The first book addresses virtues (or "excellences") in the person as a citizen; the second addresses the proper form of government to ensure that citizens will be virtuous, and therefore complete. Both books deal with the essential role of justice in civic life.

Nicolas of Cusa rekindled Platonic thought in the early 15th century. He promoted democracy in Medieval Europe, both in his writings and in his organization of the Council of Florence. Unlike Aristotle and the Hobbesian tradition to follow, Cusa saw human beings as equal and divine (that is, made in God's image), so democracy would be the only just form of government. Cusa's views are credited by some as sparking the Italian Renaissance, which gave rise to the notion of "Nation-States".

Later, Niccolò Machiavelli rejected the views of Aristotle and Thomas Aquinas as unrealistic. The ideal sovereign is not the embodiment of the moral virtues; rather the sovereign does whatever is successful and necessary, rather than what is morally praiseworthy. Thomas Hobbes also contested many elements of Aristotle's views. For Hobbes, human nature is essentially anti-social: people are essentially egoistic, and this egoism makes life difficult in the natural state of things. Moreover, Hobbes argued, though people may have natural inequalities, these are trivial, since no particular talents or virtues that people may have will make them safe from harm inflicted by others. For these reasons, Hobbes concluded that the state arises from a common agreement to raise the community out of the state of nature. This can only be done by the establishment of a sovereign, in which (or whom) is vested complete control over the community, and is able to inspire awe and terror in its subjects.

Many in the Enlightenment were unsatisfied with existing doctrines in political philosophy, which seemed to marginalize or neglect the possibility of a democratic state. Jean-Jacques Rousseau was among those who attempted to overturn these doctrines: he responded to Hobbes by claiming that a human is by nature a kind of "noble savage", and that society and social contracts corrupt this nature. Another critic was John Locke. In *Second Treatise on Government* he agreed with Hobbes that the nation-state was an efficient tool for raising humanity out of a deplorable state, but he argued that the sovereign might become an abominable institution compared to the relatively benign unmodulated state of nature.

Following the doctrine of the fact-value distinction, due in part to the influence of David Hume and his student Adam Smith, appeals to human nature for political justification were weakened. Nevertheless, many political philosophers, especially moral realists, still make use of some essential human nature as a basis for their arguments.

Marxism is derived from the work of Karl Marx and Friedrich Engels. Their idea that capitalism is based on exploitation of workers and causes alienation of people from their human nature, the historical materialism, their view of social classes, etc., have influenced many fields of study, such as sociology, economics, and politics. Marxism inspired the Marxist school of communism, which brought a huge impact on the history of the 20th century.

Consequentialism, Deontology, and the Aretaic Turn

One debate that has commanded the attention of ethicists in the modern era has been between consequentialism (actions are to be morally evaluated solely by their *consequences*) and deontology (actions are to be morally evaluated solely by consideration of agents' *duties*, the *rights* of those whom the action concerns, or both).

Jeremy Bentham and John Stuart Mill are famous for propagating utilitarianism, which is the idea that the fundamental moral rule is to strive toward the "greatest happiness for the greatest number". However, in promoting this idea they also necessarily promoted the broader doctrine of consequentialism.

Adopting a position opposed to consequentialism, Immanuel Kant argued that moral principles were simply products of reason. Kant believed that the incorporation of consequences into moral deliberation was a deep mistake, since it denies the necessity of practical maxims in governing the working of the will. According to Kant, reason requires that we conform our actions to the categorical imperative, which is an absolute duty. An important 20th-century deontologist, W.D. Ross, argued for weaker forms of duties called *prima facie* duties.

More recent works have emphasized the role of character in ethics, a movement known as the *aretaic turn* (that is, the *turn towards virtues*). One strain of this movement followed the work of Bernard Williams. Williams noted that rigid forms of consequentialism and deontology demanded that people behave impartially. This, Williams argued, requires that people abandon their personal projects, and hence their personal integrity, in order to be considered moral.

G.E.M. Anscombe, in an influential paper, "Modern Moral Philosophy" (1958), revived virtue ethics as an alternative to what was seen as the entrenched positions of Kantianism and consequentialism. Aretaic perspectives have been inspired in part by research of ancient conceptions of virtue. For example, Aristotle's ethics demands that people follow the *Aristotelian mean*, or balance between two vices; and Confucian ethics argues that virtue consists largely in striving for harmony with other people. Virtue ethics in general has since gained many adherents, and has been defended by such philosophers as Philippa Foot, Alasdair MacIntyre, and Rosalind Hursthouse.

Applied Philosophy

The ideas conceived by a society have profound repercussions on what actions the society performs. The applied study of philosophy yields applications such as those in ethics – applied ethics in particular – and political philosophy. The political and economic philosophies of Confucius, Sun Zi, Chanakya, Ibn Khaldun, Ibn Rushd, Ibn Taimiyyah, Niccolò Machiavelli, Gottfried Leibniz, John Locke, Jean-Jacques

Rousseau, Karl Marx, John Stuart Mill, Mahatma Gandhi, Martin Luther King Jr. and others – all of these have been used to shape and justify governments and their actions.

In the field of philosophy of education, progressive education as championed by John Dewey has had a profound impact on educational practices in the United States in the 20th century. Descendants of this movement include the current efforts in philosophy for children, which are part of philosophy education. Carl von Clausewitz's political philosophy of war has had a profound effect on statecraft, international politics, and military strategy in the 20th century, especially in the years around World War II. Logic has become crucially important in mathematics, linguistics, psychology, computer science, and computer engineering.

Other important applications can be found in epistemology, which aid in understanding the requisites for knowledge, sound evidence, and justified belief (important in law, economics, decision theory, and a number of other disciplines). The philosophy of science discusses the underpinnings of the scientific method and has affected the nature of scientific investigation and argumentation.

As such, philosophy has fundamental implications for science as a whole. For example, the strictly empirical approach of Skinner's behaviourism affected for decades the approach of the American psychological establishment. Deep ecology and animal rights examine the moral situation of humans as occupants of a world that has non-human occupants to consider also. Aesthetics can help to interpret discussions of music, literature, the plastic arts, and the whole artistic dimension of life. In general, the various philosophies strive to provide practical activities with a deeper understanding of the theoretical or conceptual underpinnings of their fields.

Often philosophy is seen as an investigation into an area not sufficiently well understood to be its own branch of knowledge. What were once philosophical pursuits have evolved into the modern day fields such as psychology, sociology, linguistics, and economics, for example. But as such areas of intellectual endeavour proliferate and expand, so will the broader philosophical questions that they generate.

Civilization the procession of human societies generally toward more development and use of more complex technology, higher population densities, increasing per capita gross domestic product, and other significant advancements; or 2) any human society associated with any particular geographical location at a particular time, historical or current. (When used in this second sense, the word is often restricted to apply only to societies that have attained a particular level of advancement, especially the founding of cities, with the word "city" defined in various ways.) The level of advancement of a civilization is often measured by its progress in agriculture, long-distance trade, occupational specialization, and urbanism. Aside from these core elements, civilization is often marked by any combination of a number of secondary elements, including a developed transportation system, writing, standards of measurement (currency, etc.), contract and tort-based legal systems, characteristic art styles (which may pertain to specific cultures), monumental architecture, mathematics, sophisticated metallurgy, and astronomy.

Definition

The word *civilization* comes from the Latin *civilis*, meaning *civil*, related to the Latin *civis*, meaning *citizen*, and *civitas*, meaning *city* or *city-state*.

In the sixth century, the Byzantine Emperor Justinian oversaw the consolidation of Roman civil law. The resulting collection is called the Corpus Juris Civilis. In the 11th century, professors at the University of Bologna, Western Europe's first university, rediscovered Corpus Juris Civilis, and its influence began to be felt across Western Europe. In 1388, the word *civil* appeared in English meaning "of or related to citizens." In 1704, *civilization* was used to mean "a law which makes a criminal process into a civil case." *Civilization* was not used in its modern sense to mean "the opposite of barbarism" — as contrasted to *civility*, meaning politeness or civil virtue — until the second half of the 18th century.

According to Emile Benveniste (1954), the earlist written occurrence in English of *civilization* in its modern sense may be found in Adam Ferguson's *An Essay on the History of Civil Society*:

Not only the individual advances from infancy to manhood, but the species itself from rudeness to civilization.

It should be noted that this usage incorporates the concept of superiority and maturity of "civilized" existence, as contrasted to "rudeness", which is used to denote coarseness, as in a lack of refinement or "civility."

Before Benveniste's inquiries, the New English Dictionary quoted James Boswell's conversation with Samuel Johnson concerning the inclusion of *Civilization* in Johnson's dictionary:

On Monday, March 23 (1772), I found him busy, preparing a fourth edition of his folio Dictionary... He would not admit *civilization*, but only *civility*. With great deference to him I thought *civilization*, from *to civilize*, better in the sense opposed to *barbarity* than *civility*, as it is better to have a distinct word for each sense, than one word with two senses, which *civility* is, in his way of using it.

Benveniste demonstrated that previous occurrences could be found, which explained the quick adoption of Johnson's definition. In 1775 the dictionary of Ast defined *civilization* as "the state of being civilized; the act of civilizing", and the term was frequently used by Adam Smith in *An Inquiry into the Nature and Causes of the Wealth of Nations* (1776). Beside Smith and Ferguson, John Millar also used it in 1771 in his *Observations concerning the distinction of ranks in society.*

As the first occurrence of *civilization* in French was found by Benveniste in the Marquis de Mirabeau's *L'Ami des hommes ou traité de la population* (written in 1756 but published in 1757), Benveniste's query was to know if the English word derived from the French, or if both evolved independently — a question which needed more research. According to him, the word *civilization* may in fact have been used by Ferguson as soon as 1759.

Furthermore, Benveniste notes that, contrasted to *civility*, a static term, *civilization* conveys a sense of dynamism. He thus writes that it was not only a historical view of society; it was also an optimist and resolutely non theological interpretation of its evolution which asserted itself, sometimes at the insu of those who proclaimed it, and even if some of them, and first of all Mirabeau, still counted religion as the first factor of 'civilization.In his book *The Philosophy of Civilization*, Albert Schweitzer, one of the main philosophers on the concept of civilization, outlined the idea that there are dual opinions within society: one regarding civilization as purely material and another regarding civilization as both ethical and material. He stated that the current world crisis was, then in 1923, due to a humanity having lost the ethical conception of civilization. In this same work, he defined civilization, saying:

It is the sum total of all progress made by man in every sphere of action and from every point of view in so far as the progress helps towards the spiritual perfecting of individuals as the progress of all progress.

"Civilization" is often used as a synonym for the broader term "culture" in both popular and academic circles. This is understandable, because each distinct civilization tends to have a distinct culture, and generally anyone who is a part of a civilization is also a part of that civilization's culture. However, the words are not always interchangeable. For example, a small nomadic tribe may be judged not to have a civilization, but it would surely be judged to have a culture (defined as "the arts, customs, habits... beliefs, values, behaviour and material habits that constitute a people's way of life".). It could be said that civilization relates more to science and technology, and culture more to the liberal arts, but of course the two are closely related, and usually develop in parallel. Civilizations can generally be identified by a relatively complex agricultural and urban culture.

Civilized cultures, based on a complex of stories, institutions, and artifacts, both lead to and emerge from the urban lifestyle, with people living permanently in one place in densities high enough to require the routine importation of food and other necessities of life.

In an older but still frequently used sense, the term "civilization" can be used in a normative manner as well. In societal contexts where complex and urban cultures are assumed to be superior to other "savage" or "barbarian" cultures, the concept of "civilization" is used to imply the cultural (and often ethical) superiority of certain groups. In a similar sense, civilization can mean "refinement of thought, manners, or taste".

This normative notion of civilization is heavily rooted in the thought that urbanized environments provide a superior living standard, both in material benefits and mental potentialities. Civilization requires advanced knowledge of science, trade, art, government, and farming.

Characteristics

Social scientists such as V. Gordon Childe have named a number of traits that distinguish a civilization from other kinds of society. Civilizations have been distinguished by their means of subsistence, types of livelihood, settlement patterns, forms of government, social stratification, economic systems, literacy, and other cultural traits.

All human civilizations have depended on agriculture for subsistence. Growing food on farms results in a surplus of food, particularly when people use intensive agricultural techniques such as irrigation and crop rotation. Grain surpluses have been especially important because they can be stored for a long time. A surplus of food permits some people to do things besides produce food for a living: early civilizations included artisans, priests and priestesses, and other people with specialized careers. A surplus of food results in a division of labour and a more diverse range of human activity, a defining trait of civilizations.

Civilizations have distinctly different settlement patterns from other societies. The word *civilization* is sometimes simply defined as "'living in cities'". Non-farmers tend to gather in cities to work and to trade.

Compared with other societies, civilizations have a more complex political structure, namely the state. State societies are more stratified than other societies; there is a greater difference among the social classes. The ruling class, normally concentrated in the cities, has control over much of the surplus and exercises its will through the actions of a government or bureaucracy. Morton Fried, a conflict theorist, and Elman Service, an integration theorist, have classified human cultures based on political systems and social inequality. This system of classification contains four categories:

- *Hunter-gatherer bands*, which are generally egalitarian.

- *Horticultural/pastoral societies* in which there are generally two inherited social classes; chief and commoner.
- *Highly stratified structures*, or chiefdoms, with several inherited social classes: king, noble, freemen, serf and slave.
- *Civilizations,* with complex social hierarchies and organized, institutional governments.

Economically, civilizations display more complex patterns of ownership and exchange than less organized societies. Living in one place allows people to accumulate more personal possessions than nomadic people. Some people also acquire landed property, or private ownership of the land. Because a percentage of people in civilizations do not grow their own food, they must trade their goods and services for food in a market system, or receive food through the levy of tribute, redistributive taxation, tariffs or tithes from the food producing segment of the population. Early civilizations developed money as a medium of exchange for these increasingly complex transactions. To oversimplify, in a village the potter makes a pot for the brewer and the brewer compensates the potter by giving him a certain amount of beer. In a city, the potter may need a new roof, the roofer may need new shoes, the cobbler may need new horseshoes, the blacksmith may need a new coat, and the tanner may need a new pot. These people may not be personally acquainted with one another and their needs may not occur all at the same time. A monetary system is a way of organizing these obligations to ensure that they are fulfilled fairly.

These ten Indus glyphs were discovered near the northern gate of Dholavira, India.

Writing, developed first by people in Sumer, is considered a hallmark of civilization and "appears to accompany the rise of complex administrative bureaucracies or the conquest state." Traders and bureaucrats relied on writing to keep accurate records. Like money, writing was necessitated by the size of the population of a city and the complexity of its commerce among people who are not all personally acquainted with each other. Aided by their division of labor and central government planning, civilizations have developed many other diverse cultural traits. These include organized religion, development in the arts, and countless new advances in science and technology.

Through history, successful civilizations have spread, taking over more and more territory, and assimilating more and more previously-uncivilized people. Nevertheless, some tribes or people remain uncivilized even to this day. These cultures are called by some "primitive," a term that is regarded by others as pejorative. "Primitive" implies in some way that a culture is "first" (Latin = primus), that it has not changed since the dawn of mankind, though this has been demonstrated not to be true. Specifically, as all of today's cultures are contemporaries, today's so-called primitive cultures are in no way antecedent to those we consider civilized. Many anthropologists use the term "non-literate" to describe these peoples. In the USA and Canada, where many people of such cultures were displaced by European settlers, the term "First Nations" is used. Generally, the First Nations of North America had hierarchical governments, religion, a barter system, and oral transmission of their traditions, cultures, laws, etc. Respect for the wisdom of elders and for their natural environment (7th Generation decision-making) sustained these cultures for over 10,000 years.

Civilization has been spread by invasion, genocide, religious conversion, the extension of bureaucratic control and trade, and by introducing agriculture and writing to non-literate peoples. Some non-civilized people may willingly adapt to civilized behaviour. But civilization is also spread by force. If a non-civilized group does not wish to use agriculture or to accept a "civilized" religion, it is often forced to do so by the civilized people, who usually succeed due to their more advanced technology and greater numbers. Civilizations often use religion to justify their actions, claiming for example that the uncivilized are "primitive," savages, barbarians or the like, who should be "elevated" by "a civilized religion."

Cultural Identity

"Civilization" can also refer to the culture of a complex society, not just the society itself. Every society, civilization or not, has a specific set of ideas and customs, and a certain set of manufactures and arts that make it unique. Civilizations tend to develop intricate cultures, including literature, professional art, architecture, organized religion, and complex customs associated with the elite.

The intricate culture associated with civilization has a tendency to spread to and influence other cultures, sometimes assimilating them into the civilization (a classic example being Chinese civilization and its influence on Korea, Japan, Vietnam, and other nearby countries). Many civilizations are actually large cultural spheres containing many nations and regions. The civilization in which someone lives is that person's broadest cultural identity.

Many historians have focused on these broad cultural spheres and have treated civilizations as discrete units. One example is early twentieth-century philosopher Oswald Spengler, even though he uses the German word "Kultur," "culture," for what we here call a "civilization." He said that a civilization's coherence is based on a single primary cultural symbol. Civilizations experience cycles of birth, life, decline, and death, often supplanted by a new civilization with a potent new culture, formed around a compelling new cultural symbol.

This "unified culture" concept of civilization also influenced the theories of historian Arnold J. Toynbee in the mid-twentieth century. Toynbee explored civilization processes in his multi-volume *A Study of History,* which traced the rise and, in most cases, the decline of 21 civilizations and five "arrested civilizations." Civilizations generally declined and fell, according to Toynbee, because of the failure of a "creative minority", through moral or religious decline, to meet some important challenge, rather than mere economic or environmental causes.

Samuel P. Huntington similarly defines a civilization as "the highest cultural grouping of people and the broadest level of cultural identity people have short of that which distinguishes humans from other species." Besides giving a definition of a civilization, Huntington has also proposed several theories about civilizations, discussed below.

Complex Systems

Another group of theorists, making use of systems theory, looks at a civilization as a complex system, i.e., a framework by which a group of objects can be analyzed that work in concert to produce some result. Civilizations can be seen as networks of cities that emerge from pre-urban cultures, and are defined by the economic, political, military, diplomatic, social, and cultural interactions among them. Any organization is a complex social system, and a civilization is a large organization. Systems theory helps guard against superficial but misleading analogies in the study and description of civilizations.

For example, urbanist Jane Jacobs defines cities as the economic engines that work to create large networks of people. The main process that creates these city networks, she says, is "import replacement". Import replacement is the process by which peripheral cities begin to replace goods and services that were formerly imported from more advanced cities. Successful import replacement creates economic growth in these peripheral cities, and allows these cities to then export their goods to less developed cities in their own hinterlands, creating new economic networks. So Jacobs explores economic development across wide networks instead of treating each society as an isolated cultural sphere.

Systems theorists look at many types of relations between cities, including economic relations, cultural exchanges, and political/diplomatic/military relations. These spheres often occur on different scales. For example, trade networks were, until the nineteenth century, much larger than either cultural spheres or political spheres. Extensive trade routes, including the Silk Road through Central Asia and Indian Ocean sea routes linking the Roman Empire, Persian Empire, India, and China, were well established 2000 years ago, when these civilizations scarcely shared any political, diplomatic, military, or cultural relations. The first evidence of such long distance trade is in the ancient world. During the Uruk phase Guillermo Algaze has argued that trade relations connected Egypt, Mesopotamia, Iran and Afghanistan. Resin found later in the Royal Tombs of Ur it is suggested was traded northwards from Mozambique.

Many theorists argue that the entire world has already become integrated into a single "world system", a process known as globalization. Different civilizations and societies all over the globe are economically, politically, and even culturally interdependent in many ways. There is debate over when this integration began, and what sort of integration – cultural, technological, economic, political, or military-diplomatic – is the key indicator in determining the extent of a civilization. David Wilkinson has proposed that economic and military-diplomatic integration of the Mesopotamian and Egyptian civilizations resulted in the creation of what he calls the "Central Civilization" around 1500 BC. Central Civilization later expanded to include the entire Middle East and Europe, and then expanded to a global scale with European colonization, integrating the Americas, Australia, China and Japan by the nineteenth century. According to Wilkinson, civilizations can be culturally heterogeneous, like the Central Civilization, or relatively homogeneous, like the Japanese civilization. What Huntington calls the "clash of civilizations" might be characterized by Wilkinson as a clash of cultural spheres within a single global civilization. Others point to the Crusades as the first step in globalization. The more conventional viewpoint is that networks of societies have expanded and shrunk since ancient times, and that the current globalized economy and culture is a product of recent European colonialism.

Future

Political scientist Samuel Huntington has argued that the defining characteristic of the 21st century will be a clash of civilizations. According to Huntington, conflicts between civilizations will supplant the conflicts between nation-states and ideologies that characterized the 19th and 20th centuries. These views have been strongly challenged by others like Edward Said and Muhammed Asadi. Ronald Inglehart and Pippa Norris have argued that the "true clash of civilizations" between the Muslim world and the West is caused by the Muslim rejection of the West's more liberal sexual values, rather than a difference in political ideology.

Currently, world civilization is in a stage that has created what may be characterized as an industrial society, superseding the agrarian society that preceded it. Some futurists believe that civilization is undergoing another transformation, and that world society will become a so-called informational society.

Some environmental scientists see the world entering a Planetary Phase of Civilization, characterized by a shift away from independent, disconnected nation-states to a world of increased global connectivity with worldwide institutions, environmental challenges, economic systems, and consciousness. In an attempt to better understand what a Planetary Phase of Civilization might look like in the current context of declining natural resources and increasing consumption, the Global scenario group used scenario analysis to arrive at three archetypal futures: Barbarization, in which increasing conflicts result in either a fortress world or complete societal breakdown; Conventional Worlds, in which market forces or Policy reform slowly precipitate more sustainable practices; and a Great Transition, in which either the sum of fragmented Eco-Communalism movements add up to a sustainable world or globally coordinated efforts and initiatives result in a new sustainability paradigm.

The Kardashev scale classifies civilizations based on their level of technological advancement, specifically measured by the amount of energy a civilization is able to harness. The Kardashev scale makes provisions for civilizations far more technologically advanced than any currently known to exist.

The Fall of Civilizations

There have been many explanations put forward for the collapse of civilization.

Edward Gibbon's work *"The Decline and Fall of the Roman Empire"* began an interest in the Fall of Civilizations, that had begun with the historical divisions of Petrarch between the Classical period of Ancient Greece and Rome, the succeeding Medieval Ages, and the Renaissance. For Gibbon:-

> *"The decline of Rome was the natural and inevitable effect of immoderate greatness. Prosperity ripened the principle of decay; the cause of the destruction multiplied with the extent of conquest; and, as soon as time or accident had removed the artificial supports, the stupendous fabric yielded to the pressure of its own weight. The story of the ruin is simple and obvious; and instead of inquiring why the Roman Empire was destroyed, we should rather be surprised that it has subsisted for so long."*

Gibbon suggested the final act of the collapse of Rome was the fall of Constantinople to the Ottoman Turks in 1453 AD.

Theodor Mommsen in his *"History of Rome (Mommsen)"*, suggested Rome collapsed with the collapse of the Western Roman Empire in 476 AD and he also tended towards a biological analogy of "genesis," "growth," "senescence," "collapse" and "decay."

Oswald Spengler, in his *"Decline of the West"* rejected Petrarch's chronological division, and suggested that there had been only eight "mature civilizations." Growing cultures, he argued, tend to develop into imperialistic civilizations which expand and ultimately collapse, with democratic forms of government ushering in plutocracy and ultimately imperialism.

Arnold J. Toynbee in his *"A Study of History"* suggested that there had been a much larger number of civilizations, including a small number of arrested civilizations, and that all civilizations tended to go through the cycle identified by Mommsen. The cause of the fall of a civilization occurred when a cultural elite became a parasitic elite, leading to the rise of internal and external proletariats.

Joseph Tainter in *"The Collapse of Complex Societies"* suggested that there were diminishing returns to complexity, due to which, as states achieved a maximum permissible complexity, they would decline when further increases actually produced a negative return. Tainter suggested that Rome achieved this figure in the 2nd Century AD.

Jared Diamond in his 2005 book *"Collapse: How Societies Choose to Fail or Succeed"* suggests five major reasons for the collapse of 41 studied cultures: environmental damage, such as deforestation and soil erosion; climate change; dependence upon long-distance trade for needed resources; increasing levels of internal and external violence, such as war or invasion; and societal responses to internal and environmental problems.

Peter Turchin in his *Historical Dynamics* and Andrey Korotayev *et al.* in their *Introduction to Social Macrodynamics, Secular Cycles, and Millennial Trends* suggest a number of mathematical models describing collapse of agrarian civilizations. For example, the basic logic of Turchin's "fiscal-demographic" model can be outlined as follows: during the initial phase of a sociodemographic cycle we observe relatively high levels of per capita production and consumption, which leads not only to relatively high population growth rates, but also to relatively high rates of surplus production. As a result, during this phase the population can afford to pay taxes without great problems, the taxes are quite easily collectible, and the population growth is accompanied by the growth of state revenues. During the intermediate phase, the increasing overpopulation leads to the decrease of per capita production and consumption levels, it becomes more and more difficult to collect taxes, and state revenues stop growing, whereas the state expenditures grow due to the growth of the population controlled by the state. As a result, during this phase the state starts experiencing considerable fiscal problems. During the final pre-collapse phases the overpopulation leads to further decrease of per capita production, the surplus production further decreases, state revenues shrink, but the state needs more and more resources to control the growing (though with lower and lower rates) population. Eventually this leads to famines, epidemics, state breakdown, and demographic and civilization collapse.

Peter Heather argues in his book *The Fall of the Roman Empire: a New History of Rome and the Barbarians* that this civilization did not end for moral or economic reasons, but because centuries of contact with barbarians across the frontier generated its own nemesis by making them a much more sophisticated and dangerous adversary. The fact that Rome needed to generate ever greater revenues to equip and re-equip armies that were for the first time repeatedly defeated in the field, led to the dismemberment of the Empire. Although this argument is specific to Rome, it can also be applied to the Asiatic Empire of the Egyptians, to the Han and Tang dynasties of China, to the Muslim Abbasid Caliphate, and others.

Bryan Ward-Perkins, in his book *The Fall of Rome and the End of Civilization*, shows the real horrors associated with the collapse of a civilization for the people who suffer its effects, unlike many revisionist historians who downplay this. The collapse of complex society meant that even basic plumbing disappeared from the continent for 1,000 years. Similar Dark Age collapses are seen with the Late Bronze Age collapse in the Eastern Mediterranean, the collapse of the Maya, on Easter Island and elsewhere.

Arthur Demarest argues in *Ancient Maya: The Rise and Fall of a Rainforest Civilization*, using a holistic perspective to the most recent evidence from archaeology, paleoecology, and epigraphy, that no one explanation is sufficient but that a series of erratic, complex events, including loss of soil fertility, drought and rising levels of internal and external violence led to the disintegration of the courts of Mayan kingdoms which began a spiral of decline and decay. He argues that the collapse of the Maya has lessons for civilization today.

Jeffrey A. McNeely has recently suggested that "A review of historical evidence shows that past civilizations have tended to over-exploit their forests, and that such abuse of important resources has been a significant factor in the decline of the over-exploiting society."

Thomas Homer-Dixon in "*The Upside of Down: Catastrophe, Creativity, and the Renewal of Civilization*", considers that the fall in the energy return on investments; the energy expended to energy yield ratio, is central to limiting the survival of civilizations. The degree of social complexity is associated strongly, he suggests, with the amount of disposable energy environmental, economic and technological systems allow. When this amount decreases civilizations either have to access new energy sources or they will collapse...

11

Juvenile Vagrancy

A vagrant is a person in poverty, who wanders from place to place without a home or regular employment or income. Many towns in the Developed World have shelters for vagrants. Common terminology is a tramp or a 'gentleman of the road'.

Vagrancy was a crime in some European countries, but most of these laws have been repealed. Laws against vagrancy in the United States have partly been invalidated as violative of the due process clauses of the U.S. Constitution. However, the FBI report on crime in the United States for 2005 lists 24,359 vagrancy violations. In legal terminology, a person with a source of income is not a vagrant, even if he/she is homeless.

History

In the fairy tales of medieval Europe, beggars cast curses on anyone who was insulting or stingy towards them. Witches would beg door-to-door for "milk, yeast, drink, pottage" in England. In some East Asian countries, vagrants are still revered and feared, believed to possess semi-religious spiritual powers.

In the 16th and 17th century in England, a vagrant was a person who could work, but preferred not to (or could not find employment, so took to the road in order to do so), or one who begs for a living. Vagrancy was illegal, punishable by branding, whipping, conscription into the military, or at times penal transportation to penal colonies. Vagrants were different from impotent poor, who were unable to support themselves because of advanced age or sickness. However, the English laws usually did not distinguish between the impotent poor and the criminals, so both received the same harsh punishments. The Poor Law was the system for the provision of social security in operation in England and Wales from the 16th century until the establishment of the Welfare State in the 20th century.

In colonial America, if a person wandered into a town and did not find work, he/she was told to leave town or be prosecuted. In the U.S., vagrancy laws were vague and covered a wide range of activities and crimes associated with vagrants, such as loitering, prostitution, drunkenness, and associating with known criminals. Under the vagrancy laws, police arrested people who were suspected of crime, but who had not committed a crime. Eventually, punishments were changed to a fine, or several months in jail.

After the U.S. Civil War, the South passed Black Codes, laws that tried to control freed black slaves. Vagrancy laws were included in these codes. Homeless unemployed black Americans were arrested and fined as vagrants. Usually, the person could not afford the fine, and so was sent to county labor or hired out to a private employer.

In the U.S. of the 1960s, vagrancy laws were found to be too broad and vague, and in violation of the due process requirements of the Fourteenth Amendment to the U.S. Constitution, as citizens were not informed of which behaviours were illegal. Police had too much power in deciding whether or not to arrest someone. Vagrancy laws could no longer violate Freedom of Speech, such as when police use them against political demonstrators and unpopular groups. U.S. vagrancy laws became clearer, narrower, and more defined. Since then, the status of being a vagrant is punished by the vagrancy laws, while other actions are punished under other laws.

In *Papachristou v. Jacksonville,* 405 U.S. 156 (1972), the U.S. Supreme Court ruled that a Florida vagrancy law was unconstitutional because it was too vague to be understood.

Nevertheless, new local laws in the U.S. have been passed to criminalize aggressive panhandling activities by vagrants. In recent years, there has been an increase in laws criminalizing vagrancy and related activities in the United States – see 2009 Homes Not Handcuffs – some under the rubric of sit-lie ordinances. In the U.S., some local officials encourage vagrants to move away instead of arresting them. The word *vagrant* has been replaced by *homeless person*. Prosecutions for vagrancy are rare, being replaced by prosecutions for specific offenses such as loitering. England eventually changed its poor laws, and today vagrancy is legal, while crimes are punished separately.

Street Children

Street children is a term used to refer to children who live on the streets of a city. They are basically deprived of family care and protection. Most children on the streets are between the ages of about 5 and 17 years old, and their population between different cities is varied.

Street children live in huge houses, cardboard boxes, parks or on the street itself. A great deal has been written defining street children, but the primary difficulty is that there are no precise categories, but rather a continuum, ranging from children who spend some time in the streets and sleep in a house with ill-prepared adults, to those who live entirely in the streets and have no adult supervision or care.

A widely accepted set of definitions, commonly attributed to UNICEF, divides street children into two main categories:

1. Children on the street are those engaged in some kind of economic activity ranging from begging to vending. Most go home at the end of the day and contribute their earnings to their family. They may be attending school and retain a sense of belonging to a family. Because of the economic fragility of the family, these children may eventually opt for a permanent life on the streets.
2. Children of the street actually live on the street (or outside of a normal family environment). Family ties may exist but are tenuous and are maintained only casually or occasionally.

Street children exist in many major cities, especially in developing countries, and may be subject to abuse, neglect, exploitation, or even, in extreme cases, murder by "cleanup squads" hired by local businesses or police. In Latin America, a common cause is abandonment by poor families unable to feed all their children. In Africa, an increasingly common cause is AIDS.

Definitions

The question of how to define a street child has generated much discussion that is usefully summarized by Sarah Thomas de Benítez in, "The State of the World's Street Children: Violence."

'Street children' is increasingly recognized by sociologists and anthropologists to be a socially constructed category that in reality does not form a clearly defined, homogeneous population or phenomenon. 'Street children' covers children in such a wide variety of circumstances and characteristics that policy-makers and service providers find it difficult to describe and target them. Upon peeling away the 'street children' label, individual girls and boys of all ages are found living and working in public spaces, visible in the great majority of the world's urban centres.

The definition of 'street children' is contested, but many practitioners and policymakers use UNICEF's concept of boys and girls aged under 18 for whom 'the street' (including unoccupied dwellings and wasteland) has become home and/ or their source of livelihood, and who are inadequately protected or supervised.

Names

Street Children is a widely used term in the English language and has analogues in other languages such as French (les enfants des rues), Spanish (niños de la calle), Portuguese (meninos da rua), Hungarian (utcagyerekek), Romanian (copiii strãzii) and German (Straßenkinder). *Street kids* is also commonly employed although it is sometimes considered pejorative. In other languages children who live and/or work in the streets are known by many names. Some examples are listed below:

"Gamín" (from French gamin, kid) and "chinches" (bed bugs) in Colombia, "pivetes" (little criminals/marginals) in Rio de Janeiro, as "pajaro frutero" (fruit bird) and "pirañitas" (little piranhas) in Peru, "polillas" (moths) in Bolivia, "resistoleros" (glue sniffers; Resistol is a major brand) in Honduras, "scugnizzi" (spinning tops) in Naples, (persons without supervised living) in Russia, "Batang Lansangan" or "Pulubi" in the Philippines, (the dust of life) in Vietnam, "saligoman" (nasty kids) in Rwanda, or "poussins" (chicks), "moustiques" (mosquitos) in Cameroon and "balados" (wanderers) in the democratic Republic of the Congo and the Congo Republic.

The term *Street Arab* came to the fore in the mid-19th century, first appearing in 1848, according to the OED. Horatio Alger's book *Tattered Tom ; or, The Story of a Street Arab* (1871) is an early example; it is about a homeless girl lives by her wits on the streets of New York. Charles Dickens likewise propagated its early use in 1855 but in a more clearly derogatory sense when he declared "a wretched, ragged, untaught street Arab boy is ugly." In 1890, Danish-American journalist Jacob Riis described street children in New York in an essay titled "The Street Arab". The Victorian association of street children with Arabs is probably reflected in the nomadic tradition of Arabs who were wanderers; the 19th century notion that non-Europeans from less civilized cultures were like children; of European and American travelers who saw many "street children" in Arab countries during the period; and a xenophobic tendency to scapegoat social problems. The term has fallen out of favor.

Numbers and Distribution

Numbers

Estimates vary but one often cited figure is that the number of children living independently in the streets totals between 100 million and 150 million worldwide.

According to a report from the Consortium for Street Children, a United Kingdom-based consortium of related NGOs:

Estimating numbers of 'street children' is fraught with difficulties. In 1989, UNICEF estimated 100 million children were growing up on urban streets around the world. 14 years later UNICEF reported: 'The latest estimates put the numbers of these children as high as 100 million' (UNICEF, 2002: 37). And even more recently: 'The exact number of street children is impossible to quantify, but the figure almost certainly runs into tens of millions across the world. It is likely that the numbers are increasing' (UNICEF, 2005: 40-41). The 100 million figure is still commonly cited, but has no basis in fact. Similarly, it is debatable whether numbers of street children are growing globally or whether it is the awareness of street children within societies which has grown.

Distribution

Street children may be found on every inhabited continent in a large majority of the world's cities. The following estimates indicate the global extent of street child populations.

- India 11 million
- Egypt 1.5 million
- Pakistan 1.5 million
- U.S. 750,000-1 million
- Kenya 250,000-300,000
- Philippines 250,000
- Congo 250,000
- Morocco 30,000
- Brazil 25,000
- Germany 20,000
- Honduras 20,000
- Jamaica 6,500
- Uruguay 3,000
- Switzerland 1,000

History

Children making their home/livelihoods on the street is not a new or modern phenomenon. In the introduction to his history of abandoned children in Soviet Russia 1918-1930, Alan Ball states:

Orphaned and abandoned children have been a source of misery from earliest times. They apparently accounted for most of the boy prostitutes in Augustan Rome and, a few centuries later, moved a church council of 442 in southern Gaul to declare: "Concerning abandoned children: there is general complaint that they are nowadays exposed more to dogs than to kindness." In tsarist Russia, seventeenth-century sources described destitute youths roaming the streets, and the phenomenon survived every attempt at eradication thereafter. Long before the Russian Revolution, the term *besprizornye* had gained wide currency.

In 1848 Lord Ashley referred to more than 30,000 'naked, filthy, roaming lawless and deserted children', in and around London.

By 1922 there were at least 7 million homeless children in Russia as a result of nearly a decade of devastation from World War I and the Russian Civil War. Abandoned children formed gangs, created their own argot, and engaged in petty theft and prostitution.

Examples from popular fiction include Kipling's "Kim" as a street child in colonial India, and Gavroche in Victor Hugo's *Les Misérables*. Fagin's crew of child pickpockets in "Oliver Twist" as well as Sherlock Holmes's "Baker Street Irregulars" attest to the presence of street children in 19th-century London.

Causes

Children may end up on the streets for several basic reasons: They may have no choice – they are abandoned, orphaned, or disowned by their parents. Secondly, they may choose to live in the streets because of mistreatment or neglect or because their homes do not or cannot provide them with basic necessities. Many children also work in the streets because their earnings are needed by their families. But homes and families are part of the larger society and the underlying reasons for the poverty or breakdown of homes and families may be social, economic, political or environmental or any combination of these.

In a 1993 report, WHO offered the following list of causes for the phenomenon:

- family breakdown
- armed conflict
- poverty
- natural and man-made disasters
- famine
- physical and sexual abuse
- exploitation by adults
- dislocation through migration

- urbanization and overcrowding
- acculturation
- disinheritance or being disowned.

The orphaning of children as a result of HIV/AIDS is another cause that might be added to this list.

By Country

Russia : In Russia, street children usually find a home in underground pipe and cable collectors during the harsh winter. These underground homes offer space, shelter and most importantly of all, heat from hot water and central heating pipes.

Russia has 1 million street children, and one in four crimes involves underage youths. Officially, the number of children without supervision is more than 700,000. However, experts believe the real figure has long been between 2 and 4 million.

India : India is home to the world's largest population of street children, estimated at 18 million. The Republic of India is the seventh largest and second most populous country in the world. With acceleration in economic growth, India has become one of the fastest growing developing countries. This has created a rift between poor and rich; 22 percent of the population lives below the income poverty line. Owing to unemployment, increasing rural-urban migration, attraction of city life and a lack of political will, India now has one of the largest number of child labourers in the world.

Street children are subject to malnutrition, hunger, health problems, substance abuse, theft, commercial sexual exploitation of children, harassment by the city police and railway authorities, as well as physical and sexual abuse, although the Government of India has taken some corrective measures and declared child labor illegal.

Vietnam : According to data by the Street Educators' Club, the number of street children in Vietnam has shrunk from 21,000 in 2003 to 8,000 in 2007. The number dropped from 1,507 to 113 in Hanoi and from 8,507 to 794 in Ho Chi Minh City. In the meantime the number of migrant children is increasing. This number is, however, unconfirmed owing to varying definitions of street children. Some experts mention several different categories of street children in Vietnam: "children who have run away from home or who have no home, and who sleep on the street; children who sleep on the street with their family or guardian; children who have a family or guardian and who usually sleep at home, but work on the streets; economic migrants who rent rooms with other working children; and bonded labourers".

There are almost 400 humanitarian organisations and international non-governmental organizations providing help for about 15,000 children, who live in especially difficult conditions.

Bucharest, Romania : A report of the Council of Europe of year 2000 estimated that there were approximately 1,000 street children in Bucharest, Romania.

Some Romanian street children are preyed on by sex tourists, mainly from Western Europe, and many can be seen inhaling aurolac (an aluminium-based paint traditionally used for painting a type of wood-burning stove) from plastic bags, the substance of choice for those of limited means.

Romania has made much progress, allowing the number of street children drop to low levels, which is lying at or below the European average. Given that socio-economic conditions continue to improve in Romania, the number of street children is expected to diminish.

Brazil : The Federal Government estimates that 31,992 adults live on the streets in major cities. There are no national statistics for minors. An NGO, putting together various local government counts and other estimates, arrived at c. 9578 street-dwellers younger than 18, in state capitals; it estimates they number 25,000 nation-wide. It has also been pointed out that most minors living on the streets are adolescents, rather than children.

The main means of surviving in Brazil's streets include: finding food in garbage bins or on refuse tips; being financially exploited by street sellers as shoe shiners, thieves, prostitutes, drug runners, and street performers.

Street children are known to receive beatings and death from the police or members of the public and also can face imprisonment, malnutrition, disease and AIDS.

The Philippines : According to the 1998 report, entitled "Situation of the Youth in the Philippines," there are about 1.5 million street children in the Philippines.

75% of street children in the Philippines spend the night in the homes of their families, but spend the rest of the day working in the street. Between 25%-30% of street children often create a sort of family among fellow street children, and some of them may maintain an interrupted relationship with their families and the homes of their families. 5%-10% of street children are completely abandoned.

Street Children as young as 10 years old are often imprisoned under the Vagrancy Act, sometimes in cells which include adults, resulting in recurrent physical and sexual abuse, sometimes by guards as well.

Many street children were in danger of summary execution during the Marcos Government. Human rights groups said the killings have become an unwritten government policy to deal with the street children phenomenon, and that they are openly endorsed by local officials, strengthening the long-running suspicion that the death squads were formed by the government.

Government and Non-government Responses

Responses by Governments

Because they have not reached the age of majority, street children have no representation in the governing process. They have no vote themselves nor by proxy through their parents, from whom they likely are alienated. Nor do street children have any economic leverage. Governments, consequently, may pay little attention to them.

The rights of street children are often ignored by governments even though nearly all of the world's governments have ratified the UN Convention on the Rights of the Child. Governments are often embarrassed by street children and may blame parents or neighbouring countries. Non-Governmental Organizations (NGOs) may also be blamed for *encouraging* children to live in the streets by making street life more bearable or attractive through the services they provide.

When governments implement programs to deal with street children these generally involve placing the children in orphanages, juvenile homes or correctional institutes. However, some children are in the streets because they have fled from such institutions and some governments prefer to support or work in partnership with NGO programs. Governments sometimes institute *roundups* when they remove all the children from city streets and deposit them elsewhere or incarcerate them. In the most extreme cases, governments may tacitly accept or participate in *social cleansing* operations that murder street children.

NGO Responses

Non-government organizations employ a wide variety of strategies to address the needs and rights of street children. These may be categorized as follows:

- Advocacy-through media and government contacts agencies may press for the rights of street children to be respected.
- Preventive-programs that work to prevent children from taking to the streets, through family and community support and education.
- Institutional;
    - residential rehabilitation programs-some agencies provide an environment isolated from the streets where activities are focused on assisting children to recover from drug, physical or sexual abuse.
    - full-care residential homes-the final stage in many agencies' programs is when the child is no longer in the streets but lives completely in an environment provided by the agency. Some agencies promote fostering children to individual families. Others set up group homes where a small number of children live together with houseparents employed by the agency. Others set up institutional care centres catering to large numbers of children. Some agencies include a follow-up program that monitors and counsels children and families after the child has left the residential program.
- Street-based programs-these work to alleviate the worst aspects of street life for children by providing services

to them in the streets. These programs tend to be less expensive and serve a larger number of street children than institutional programs since the children still must provide for themselves in the streets.

- o feeding program
- o medical services
- o legal assistance
- o street education
- o financial services (banking and entrepreneur programs)
- o family reunification
- o drop-in centres/night shelters
- o outreach programs designed to bring the children into closer contact with the agency.

- Conscientization-change street children's attitudes to their circumstances-view themselves as an oppressed minority and become protagonists rather than passive recipients of aid.

Many agencies employ several of these strategies and a child will pass through a number of stages before he or she "graduates". First he/she will be contacted by an outreach program, then may become involved in drop-in centre programs, though still living in the streets. Later the child may be accepted into a halfway house and finally into residential care where he or she becomes fully divorced from street life.

Juvenile Truancy in School

Truancy is any intentional unauthorized absence from compulsory schooling. The term typically describes absences caused by students of their own free will, and usually does not refer to legitimate "excused" absences, such as ones related to medical conditions. The term's exact meaning differs from school to school, and is usually explicitly defined in the school's handbook of policies and procedures.

It may also refer to students who attend school but do not go to classes.

In some schools, truancy may result in an ineligibility to graduate or to receive credit for class attended, until the time lost to truancy is made up through a combination of detention, fines, or summer school.

Truancy is a frequent subject of popular culture; perhaps most famously *Ferris Bueller's Day Off*, which is entirely about the titular character's (played by Matthew Broderick) day of truancy in Chicago with his girlfriend and best friend. *Truancy* is also the title of a 2008 novel about a student uprising against a dictatorial educational system.

There are a number of expressions in English which refer to truancy. In South Africa, the slang used is *bunking*, *skipping* or *jippo*. In Jamaica, it is called *skulling*. In Guyana *skulking*. In Antigua and Barbuda, it is called *skudding*. In Australia truancy is called *wagging*, *ditching*, *skipping school*, *jigging*, *dogging* or *bludging*. It is called *bunking off*, *skiving* or *twagging* or also *wagging* in England, *mitching*, *wagging* or *on the knock* in Wales, *sagging* in Liverpool, *bunking* or *cutting class*, *doggin*, *skiving* or *puggin* in Scotland and *on the hop*, *on the bunk*, *mitching*, *scheming* or *dossing* in Ireland. In the United States and Canada expressions include *(playing) hookey*, *ditching*, *jigging*, *sluffing*, *skipping*, or *cutting class*.

Punishments Imposed for Truancy

In the United Kingdom, failure to secure regular school attendance of a registered pupil is a criminal offence for parents. Also, a police officer of or above the rank of superintendent may direct that for a specified time in a specified area a police officer may remove a child believed to be absent from a school without authority to that school or to another designated place. This is commonly known as a "truancy sweep".

In many Canadian provinces, a police officer who suspects a child of the correct age to be deliberately missing school for no legitimate reason has the authority to take that child to the school he or she is supposed to attend.

In the United States, the fine for truancy can range from $250 to as much as $5000. In some cities teenagers found on the streets during school hours are sometimes even handcuffed. About 12,000 students were ticketed for truancy in 2008 in Los Angeles. Many states provide for the appointment of local truancy officers who have the authority to arrest habitually truant youths and bring them to their parents or to the school they are supposed to attend. Many states also have the power to revoke a students driver's license. It is an office which, where it exists, is often held by a person also a constable or sheriff. However, the position of a full-time truancy officer is generally viewed as being a relic from the 19th century when mandatory school attendance was relatively new. Truancy regulations today are generally enforced by school officials under the context of parental responsibility. New automated calling systems allow the automated notification of parents when a child is not marked present in the computer, and truancy records for many states are available for inspection online.

In Australia, schools, in most cases, contact and keep a close relationship with local police to combat 'wagging'. Most schools, who have a nearby police station, have police vehicles monitoring the areas around the school grounds who look for truant students. In most cases the students are returned to the schools. The Australian Government threatened to take action on parents who have truanting students by withdrawing child support payments to any parent whose child is caught multiple times. Recently, schools have started a system whereby if students are not marked as present, the school computers will automatically SMS the parent(s) of the child to notify of their absence. Also, the use of marking present lists at schools has been taken over by that of computers. This way of checking if a student is absent, is a more accurate way to identify if the student is wagging and in what class.

In Germany, the parents of a child absent from school without a legitimate excuse are notified by the school. If the parents refuse to send their child to school or are unable to control their child, local child services or social services officers may request the police to escort the child to school, and in extreme cases can petition a court to partially or completely remove child custody from the parents. Parents may also be fined in cases of refusal.

In Denmark, some welfare benefits can be confiscated for a period if the child does not attend school. However, not all cities use this approach to keep the children in school. Most cities watch for families who have not returned their children to school after the summer vacation because some groups exiled their children to their ethnic home countries for behaviour modification. In the city of Aarhus, 155 children had not turned up one week after the school started. April 2009 a research among 4,000 students showed that more than every third student had been absent during the last 14 days.

In Finland truant pupils usually get detention in comprehensive schools. The police are not involved in truancy controlling but the teachers of the school monitor the school area and sometimes the nearby areas during recess to avoid unauthorized leaving from the school area. If the pupil is absent for a long period of time the parents can be fined. Anyway, fining is the only way to force parents to put their children into school. The child will not be escorted to school or taken from parents.

When students are chronically truant from school, missing long stretches at a time, it seems like a tragically natural progression to — at some point — simply not return. Truancy is a well-established risk factor for school dropout, which is a very serious and all too common problem. Each year, approximately five out of every 100 high school students (five percent) drop out of school.

Over the last decade, between 347,000 and 544,000 tenth- through twelfth-grade students left school each year without successfully completing a high school program. However, a substantially higher proportion of students quit school for some period of time during their educational careers.

For example, one longitudinal study found that 21 percent of students who were in eighth grade in 1988 had dropped out at some point between eighth grade and high school graduation, even though only 12 percent of them had actually failed to graduate by 1994.

It is difficult to draw a clear line between chronic or extended truancy and periodic school dropout. In fact, truants are the young people most likely to drop out of school. According to Guillermo Montes and Christine Lehmann from the Children's Institute in Rochester, N.Y.:

"Dropping out is better conceptualized as an evolving process rather than an event. It is a process that starts prior to the child entering school. Along the way the

process manifests itself in a variety of forms. Truancy, disciplinary problems, and failing grades in high schools are late manifestations of the process and immediate markers of dropping out behaviour, while behaviour problems and low school achievement are midcourse markers that provide additional time for prevention and intervention strategies to work."

School dropouts have significantly fewer job prospects, make lower salaries, and are more often unemployed than youth who stay in school. In 1999, just over 14 percent of workers who had dropped out of school were poverty-stricken as compared with six percent of workers who had completed high school. The following are some powerful measures of the social and financial impact of truancy and the dropouts that result:

- Less educated workforce
- Business loss because of youth who "hang out" and/or shoplift during the day
- Higher daytime crime rates (in some cases)
- Cost of social services for families of children who are habitually truant
- Loss of federal and state education funding for schools.

Juvenile and Adolescent Delinquency

Juvenile delinquency refers to antisocial or illegal behaviour by children or adolescents, for dealing with juveniles, such as juvenile detention centres. There are a multitude of different theories on the causes of crime, most if not all of which can be applied to the causes of youth crime.

A Juvenile Delinquent is one who repeatedly commits crime. These juvenile delinquents sometimes have mental disorders/ behavioural issues such as post traumatic stress disorder or bipolar disorder, and are sometimes diagnosed with conduct disorder partially as a result of their delinquent behaviours.

Juvenile Sex Crimes

Minor who commit sexual crimes refer to individuals adjudicated in a criminal court for a sexual crimes are defined as sexually abusive behaviour committed by a person under the age of 18 that is perpetrated "against the victim's will, without consent, and in an aggressive, exploitative, manipulative, or threatening manner. Examining prevalence data and the characteristics of juvenile sex offenders is a fundamental component to obtain a precise understanding of this heterogeneous group. With mandatory reporting laws in place, it became a necessity for providers to report any incidents of disclosed sexual abuse.

Rational Choice

Classical criminology stresses that causes of crime lie within the individual offender, rather than in their external environment.

Social Disorganization

Current positivist approaches generally focus on the culture. A type of criminological theory attributing variation in crime and delinquency over time and among territories to the absence or breakdown of communal institutions (e.g. family, school, church and social groups.) and communal relationships that traditionally encouraged cooperative relationships among people. Merton's suggests five adaptations to this dilemma:

1. *Innovation*: individuals who accept socially approved goals, but not necessarily the socially approved means.
2. *Retreatism*: those who reject socially approved goals and the means for acquiring them.
3. *Ritualism*: those who buy into a system of socially approved means, but lose sight of the goals. Merton believed that drug users are in this category.
4. *Conformity*: those who conform to the system's means and goals.
5. *Rebellion*: people who negate socially approved goals and means by creating a new system of acceptable goals and means.

A difficulty with strain theory is that it does not explore why children of low-income families would have poor educational attainment in the first place. More importantly is the fact that much youth crime does not have an economic motivation. Strain theory fails to explain violent crime, the type of youth crime which causes most anxiety to the public.

Differential Association

The theory of Differential association also deals with young people in a group context, and looks at how peer pressure and the existence of gangs could lead them into crime. It suggests young people are motivated to commit crimes by delinquent peers, and learn criminal skills from them. The diminished influence of peers after men marry has also been cited as a factor in desisting from offending. There is strong evidence that young people with criminal friends are more likely to commit crimes themselves. However it may be the case that offenders prefer to associate with one another, rather than delinquent peers causing someone to start offending. Furthermore there is the question of how the delinquent peer group became delinquent initially.

Labelling

Labelling theory states that once young people have been labelled as criminal they are more likely to offend. The idea is that once labelled as deviant a young person may accept that role, and be more likely to associate with others who have been similarly labelled. Labelling theorists say that male children from poor families are more likely to be labelled deviant, and that this may partially explain why there are more lower-class young male offenders.

Male Phenomenon

Youth crime is disproportionately male: theorists and others have examined why this is the case. One suggestion is that ideas of masculinity may make young men more likely to offend. Being tough, and reckless may be a way young men attempt to express their masculinity. Acting out these ideals may make young men more likely to engage in antisocial and criminal behaviour. Alternatively, rather than young men acting as they do because of societal pressure to conform to masculine ideals; young men may actually be naturally more aggressive, daring etc. As well as biological or psychological factors, the way young men are treated by their parents may make them more susceptible to offending. According to a study, adolescent males who possess a certain type of variation in a specific gene are more likely to flock to delinquent peers.

Risk Factors

Individual Risk Factors

Individual psychological or behavioural risk factors that may make offending more likely include intelligence, impulsiveness or the inability to delay gratification, aggression, empathy, and restlessness. Children with low intelligence are likely to do worse in school. This may increase the chances of offending because low educational attainment, a low attachment to school, and low educational aspirations are all risk factors for offending in themselves. Children who perform poorly at school are also more likely to truant, which is also linked to offending. If strain theory or subcultural theory are valid poor educational attainment could lead to crime as children were unable to attain wealth and status legally. However it must be born in mind that defining and measuring intelligence is troublesome. Young males are especially likely to be impulsive which could mean they disregard the long-term consequences of their actions, have a lack of self-control, and are unable to postpone immediate gratification.

Mental Disorders

Conduct disorder usually develops during childhood and manifests itself during an adolescence life. Some juvenile behaviour is attributed to the diagnosable disorder known as conduct disorder. Juvenile delinquents who have recurring encounters with the criminal justice system are sometimes diagnosed with conduct disorders because they show a continuous disregard for their own and others safety and property. Once the juvenile continues to exhibit the same behavioural patterns and turns eighteen he is then at risk of being diagnosed with antisocial personality disorder and much more prone to become a serious criminal offender.

One of the main components used in diagnosing an adult with antisocial personality disorder consists of presenting documented history of conduct disorder before the age of 15. These two personality disorders are analogous in their erratic and aggressive behaviour. This is why habitual juvenile offenders diagnosed with conduct disorder are likely to exhibit signs of antisocial personality disorder as they mature. Once the juveniles reach maturation their socially unacceptable behaviour has grown into a life style and they develop into career criminals. "Career criminals begin committing antisocial behaviour before entering grade school and are versatile in that they engage in an array of destructive behaviours, offend at exceedingly high rates, and are less likely to quit committing crime as they age.

Family Environment

Family factors which may have an influence on offending include; the level of parental supervision, the way parents discipline a child, parental conflict or separation, criminal parents or siblings, and the quality of the parent-child relationship Children brought up by lone parents are more likely to start offending than those who live with two natural parents, however once the attachment a child feels towards their parent(s) and the level of parental supervision are taken into account, children in single parent families are no more likely to offend than others. Conflict between a child's parents is also much more closely linked to offending than being raised by a lone parent. If a child has low parental supervision they are much more likely to offend. Many studies have found a strong correlation between a lack of supervision and offending, and it appears to be the most important family influence on offending.When parents commonly do not know where their children are, what their activities are, or who their friends are, children are more likely to truant from school and have delinquent friends, each of which are linked to offending. A lack of supervision is connected to poor relationships between children and parents, as children who are often in conflict with their parents may be less willing to discuss their activities with them. Children with a weak attachment to their parents are more likely to offend.

Prevention

Delinquency Prevention is the broad term for all efforts aimed at preventing youth from becoming involved in criminal, or other antisocial, activity. Increasingly, governments are recognizing the importance of allocating resources for the prevention of delinquency. Because it is often difficult for states to provide the fiscal resources necessary for good prevention, organizations, communities, and governments are working more in collaboration with each other to prevent juvenile delinquency.

With the development of delinquency in youth being influenced by numerous factors, prevention efforts are comprehensive in scope. Prevention services include activities such as substance abuse education and treatment, family counseling, youth mentoring, parenting education, educational support, and youth sheltering.

Reductionism-e.g. over-simplfying complex experiences and circumstances by converting them to simple quantities, relying on a psychosocial focus whilst neglecting potential socio-structural and political influences;

Determinism-e.g. characterising young people as passive victims of risk experiences with no ability to construct, negotiate or resist risk;

Imputation-e.g. assuming that risk factors and definitions of offending are homogenous across countries and cultures, assuming that statistical correlations between risk factors and offending actually represent causal relationships, assuming that risk factors apply to individuals on the basis of aggregated data.

Societal Consequences

Once the juvenile offender reaches maturation he is likely to continue exhibiting maladaptive behaviours and increases his risk of being cycled through the criminal justice system as an adult offender. Due to the small population of habitual adult and juvenile offenders attributing for the large percentage of violent crimes (i.e. murder and aggravated assault) the criminal justice system should supervise the small population of career criminals in an effort to prevent the spawning of serious violent offenders. If mental disorders such as conduct disorder go undiagnosed and untreated the juvenile offender has the increased potential to later develop antisocial personality disorder and continue his life as a career criminal. The majority of violent offenders exhibit characteristics of antisocial personality disorder and exhibit it no later than age 15. Antisocial personality disorder is a common diagnosis for a serial killer. Authors Alvarez and Bachman found that one similarity among serial killers was their prior criminal convictions. In this case conduct disorder can become a probable constituent to serial murder if not diagnosed and treated before it fully develops in adulthood as antisocial personality disorder. Both conduct disorder and antisocial personality disorder are categorized as personality disorders under the DSM-IV-TR and share extremely similar definitions as explained above in 'Mental Disorders'. Some of the common characteristics include consistent violation of societal norms, aggressive behaviour towards people, and a disassociation to the emotion of empathy. These traits are also common amongst serial killers and if the maladaptive behaviours are not treated they have the potential to conceive a person that fantasizes about killing several victims and then fulfills their impulsivity when they are no longer capable of suppressing it.

Women Offenders

While criminologists insist that female offenders represent only a fraction of the crime perpetrated in our society, the numbers of female criminals appear to be growing. Some act out in male-female teams while many initiate crimes on their own. Female killers get more press than offenders in other types of crimes, yet the less violent behaviours still do reveal a lot about women who break the law.

In *Good Girls Gone Bad*, journalist Susan Nadler talked with a variety of women in prison and found that they tended to fit into one of several categories:

- Acting out or defying an image: People think of you in a certain way and you want to do something outrageous to prove that you're not what they think.
- Snapping: While this is a controversial diagnosis, in ordinary language it means that someone was pushed by events to the breaking point.
- Being the outlaw: they pursue crime to develop an image that they perceive as cool or working outside social boundaries. (One woman with whom Nadler talked had grown up privileged, but by the time she was 24, "Rosa" had pulled over 500 burglaries, had three men working for her, and was earning over $200,000 a year.)

- Addiction: 90% of women in prison have substance abuse problems.
- Following a role model: Especially in gangs, girls who see those they respect committing a crime tend to do the same.
- Keeping someone's attention or affection: Many women who team up with men get involved in their criminal activities as a way to keep them romantically involved. They end up in prison for crimes they might not otherwise have done.
- Obsession: Some women develop a fixation that involves crossing legal boundaries.
- Justification by the act of others: they did it and so can I.

What Nadler does not mention is that many women end up in prison because they've retaliated against abuse as a way to protect themselves and their children. The majority of violent crimes committed by women fall into this category. Some women are also duped by boyfriends or spouses to become part of an illegal operation, and they unwittingly participate and get arrested. As a Court TV movie *Guilt by Association* illustrated, sometimes a woman has only to pick up the phone or carry a package, and she'll get a heftier prison sentence than the man—even than many murderers.

Wensley Clarkson interviewed many women in maximum security prison, as documented in *Women Behind Bars*, and found females who had kicked someone to death, slaughtered family members, based a business on drugs, and hired hit men to kill someone. "Female crime is now increasing at an alarming rate," he says, "fueled by a drastic increase in drug use and the cold hard fact that many women are now having to fend for themselves—and some of them, just like their male counterparts, cannot cope."

Yet there's been little research on the nature of female aggression. In *Odd Girl Out*, Rachel Simmons, a trainer for the Ophelia Project, tries to raise the self-esteem of girls, discusses female bullies and the fact that little has been written about what she calls the hidden aggression prevalent in the culture of girls. She went to several grade schools and sent out requests for stories from other women about experiences in their lives with female bullies, and she was amazed at the response. While society at large supports the myth that females are "civilized" and nice, in fact, there are some who simply want to gain power and control over others, and even to harm them. They do it in subtle ways, such as a hurtful glance, passing nasty notes, ganging up, and using innuendo to ruin another girl's reputation. "If girls are whispering," says one, "the teacher thinks it's going to be all right because they're not hitting people."

Such teachers contribute by accepting social stereotypes. The damage these girls do in quieter ways can be just as devastating as a bruise or broken bone and can have residual effects throughout the sufferer's lifetime. It isn't necessarily an outsider with a chip on her shoulder who does this, either; it might be the queen bees in some clique who plan to make the life of a target girl miserable.

"The adults pass through the same rooms and live the same moments," Simmons writes, "yet they are unable to see a whole world of action around them. So, too, in a classroom of covertly aggressing girls, victims are desperately alone even though a teacher is just steps away." And sometimes those victims want to hurt someone back.

It's no wonder then, that given the opportunity, some women will freely do things that harm others. In a culture that protects female bullies and psychopaths through denial and superficial stereotypes, aggression can seep in through many forms.

12

The Changing Pattern of Institutions in Uttar Pradesh

An institution is any structure or mechanism of social order and cooperation governing the behaviour of a set of individuals within a given human community. Institutions are identified with a social purpose and permanence, transcending individual human lives and intentions, and with the making and enforcing of rules governing cooperative human behaviour.

The term "institution" is commonly applied to customs and behaviour patterns important to a society, as well as to particular formal organizations of government and public service. As structures and mechanisms of social order among humans, institutions are one of the principal objects of study in the social sciences, such as political science, anthropology, economics, and sociology (the latter being described by Durkheim as the "science of institutions, their genesis and their functioning"). Institutions are also a central concern for law, the formal mechanism for political rule-making and enforcement.

Types of Institution

- Marriage and Family
- Religion
- Education
- Scientific institutions
- Hospitals
- Legal systems

- Penal systems
- Psychiatric hospitals and Asylums
- Military
- Mass media and News media
- Factories and Corporations
- Organisations.

Also (*in an extended context*):

- Art and Culture
- Language
- The Nation State-Social and political scientists often speak of the state as embodying all institutions such as schools, prisons, and so on. However, these institutions may be considered private or autonomous, whilst organised religion and family life certainly pre-date the advent of the nation state. In the Neo-Marxist thought of Antonio Gramsci, for instance, a distinction may be felt between the institutions of political society (the police, the army, legal system, etc.) which dominates directly and coercively, and civil society (the family, the education system, trade unions, etc.) where leadership is constituted through ideology or by means of consent.

Aspects of Institutions

Although individual, formal organizations, commonly identified as "institutions," may be deliberately and intentionally created by people, the development and functioning of institutions in society in general may be regarded as an instance of emergence; that is, institutions arise, develop and function in a pattern of social self-organization, which goes beyond the conscious intentions of the individual humans involved.

As mechanisms of social cooperation, institutions are manifest in both objectively real, *formal* organizations, such as the U.S. Congress, or the Roman Catholic Church, and, also, in *informal* social order and organization, reflecting human psychology, culture, habits and customs. Most important institutions, considered abstractly, have both objective and subjective aspects: examples include money and marriage. The institution of money encompasses many formal organizations, including banks and government treasury departments and stock exchanges, which may be termed, "institutions," as well as subjective experiences, which guide people in their pursuit of personal well-being. Powerful institutions are able to imbue a paper currency with certain value, and to induce millions into cooperative production and trade in pursuit of economic ends abstractly denominated in that currency's units. The subjective experience of money is so pervasive and persuasive that economists talk of the "money illusion" and try to disabuse their students of it, in preparation for learning economic analysis.

Perspectives of the Social Sciences

While institutions tend to appear to people in society as part of the natural, unchanging landscape of their lives, study of institutions by the social sciences tends to reveal the nature of institutions as social constructions, artifacts of a particular time, culture and society, produced by collective human choice, though not directly by individual intention. Sociology traditionally analyzed social institutions in terms of interlocking social roles and expectations. Social institutions created and were composed of groups of roles, or expected behaviours. The social function of the institution was executed by the fulfillment of roles. Basic biological requirements, for reproduction and care of the young, are served by the institutions of marriage and family, for example, by creating, elaborating and prescribing the behaviours expected for husband/father, wife/mother, child, etc.

The relationship of institutions to human nature is a foundational question for the social sciences. Institutions can be seen as "naturally" arising from, and conforming to, human nature—a fundamentally conservative view—or institutions can be seen as artificial, almost accidental, and in need of architectural redesign, informed by expert social analysis, to better serve human needs—a fundamentally progressive view. Adam Smith anchored his economics in the supposed human "propensity to truck, barter and exchange". Modern feminists have criticized traditional marriage and other institutions as element of an oppressive and obsolete patriarchy. The Marxist view which sees human nature as historically 'evolving' towards voluntary social cooperation, shared by some anarchists, is that supraindividual institutions such as the market and the state are incompatible with the individual liberty which would obtain in a truly free society.

Economics, in recent years, has used game theory to study institutions from two perspectives. Firstly, how do institutions survive and evolve? In this perspective, institutions arise from Nash equilibria of games. For example, whenever people pass each other in a corridor or thoroughfare, there is a need for customs, which avoid collisions. Such a custom might call for each party to keep to their own right (or left—such a choice is arbitrary, it is only necessary that the choice be uniform and consistent). Such customs may be supposed to be the origin of rules, such as the rule, adopted in many countries, which requires driving automobiles on the right side of the road.

Secondly, how do institutions affect behaviour? In this perspective, the focus is on behaviour arising from a given set of institutional rules. In these models, institutions determine the rules (i.e. strategy sets and utility functions) of games, rather than arise as equilibria out of games. For example, the Cournot duopoly model is based on an institution involving an auctioneer who sells all goods at the market-clearing price. While it is always possible to analyse behaviour with the institutions-as-equilibria approach instead, it is much more complicated.

In political science, the effect of institutions on behaviour has also been considered from a meme perspective, like game theory borrowed from biology. A "memetic institutionalism" has been proposed, suggesting that institutions provide selection environments for political action, whereby differentiated retention arises and thereby a Darwinian evolution of institutions over time. Public choice theory, another branch of economics with a close relationship to political science, considers how government policy choices are made, and seeks to determine what the policy outcomes are likely to be, given a particular political decision-making process and context.

In history, a distinction between eras or periods, implies a major and fundamental change in the system of institutions governing a society. Political and military events are judged to be of historical significance to the extent that they are associated with changes in institutions. In European history, particular significance is attached to the long transition from the feudal institutions of the Middle Ages to the modern institutions, which govern contemporary life.

Institutionalisation

The term "institutionalisation" is widely used in social theory to refer to the process of embedding something (for example a concept, a social role, a particular value or mode of behaviour) within an organisation, social system, or society as a whole. The term may also be used to refer to committing a particular individual to an institution, such as a mental institution. To this extent, "institutionalisation" may carry negative connotations regarding the treatment of, and damage caused to, vulnerable human beings by the oppressive or corrupt application of inflexible systems of social, medical, or legal controls by publicly owned, private or not-for-profit organisations.

The term "institutionalisation" may also be used in a political sense to apply to the creation or organisation of governmental institutions or particular bodies responsible for overseeing or implementing policy, for example in welfare or development.

Institutionalisation as a Socio-political Phenomenon

During the period of the industrial revolution in Europe many countries went through a period of "institutionalisation", which saw a large expansion and development of the role of government within society, particularly into areas seen previously as the private sphere. Institutionalisation is also seen as being an important part of process of modernisation in developing countries, involving again the expansion and improved organisation of government structures.

Public and civic organisations acquired great authority and wealth during and in the century following the Industrial Revolution in the UK and other rapidly developing nation states. The growing demands of industry for high volume labour supplies in the nineteenth century also created an ethos in which the needs and rights of the unproductive or vulnerable individual were deemed less important than the needs of society as a whole. Large numbers of beggars and high rates of crime and disease were a consequence of the massive social and economic changes experienced in the period following the battle of Waterloo. Social unrest from the Peterloo riots onwards resulted in a significant Chartist challenge to established authority on the streets of major cities like Sheffield, Manchester, and Glasgow in the 1840s.

During the period from 1850-1930 many types of institutions were created by public subscription, parliament and local authorities to provide housing, healthcare, education, and financial support for individuals in need. At the upper end of the scale, public boarding schools such as Eton and Harrow were founded or greatly extended to meet the growing demand for the education of the children of those in colonial service overseas. These were seen as models of social improvement, and many inferior imitations followed for the lower social orders. Virtually every borough in the UK was required by legislation to make provision for paupers, homeless, released prisoners, convicted criminals, orphans, disabled war veterans, older people with no means of support, deaf and blind schools, schools and colonies for those with learning disabilities or mental health problems.

Distinguishing features of such institutions were frequently, but not exclusively:

- communal dormitories
- communal kitchens and dining facilities
- rural, isolated locations
- restrictions on personal liberty and possessions
- uniforms
- oppressive, authoritarian regimes
- strict systems of rules and codes of conduct
- boards of visitors or trustees, usually drawn from the ranks of the upper middle classes, the so-called "great and good"
- hierarchical systems of management
- compulsory religious attendance
- involvement of inmates as unpaid or poorly rewarded labour in return for small privileges

- widespread abuse of human rights, dignity
- rigid separation of the sexes
- excessive reliance on medication and physical restraints.

Many of these organisations, whilst originally expressing idealistic aspirations and aims, became "total" institutions within a generation or two of their foundation, providing in some cases cradle to grave housing, occupation and social control. Founding charters usually proclaimed beneficial outcomes of "reform" (or rehabilitation) of character through moral and occupation education and discipline, but in practice inmates were often trapped in a system that provided no obvious route of escape or promotion. As late as the 1950s, in Britain, several hundred thousand people lived in Victorian asylums and "colonies".

Jean-Jacques Rousseau wrote in his opus *The Social Contract* that "Slaves lose everything in their chains, even the desire of escaping from them: they love their servitude". Institutionalisation is a similar process.

Deconstruction of Major Social Institutions

The dangers of institutions were chronicled and criticised by reformers almost since their foundation. Charles Dickens was an outspoken and high profile early critic, and several of his novels, in particular *Oliver Twist* and *Hard Times* demonstrate his insight into the damage that institutions can do to human beings.

Enoch Powell, when Minister for Health in the early 1960s, was a later opponent who was appalled by what he witnessed on his visits to the asylums, and his famous "water tower" speech in 1961 called for the closure of all NHS asylums and their replacement by wards in general hospitals:

> *"There they stand, isolated, majestic, imperious, brooded over by the gigantic water-tower and chimney combined, rising unmistakable and daunting out of the countryside- the asylums which our forefathers built with such immense solidity to express the notions of their day. Do not for a moment underestimate their powers of resistance to our assault. Let me describe some of the defences which we have to storm."*

Scandal after scandal followed, with many high profile public inquiries. These involved the exposure of abuses such as unscientific surgical techniques such as lobotomy and the widespread neglect and abuse of vulnerable patients in the USA and Europe. The growing anti-psychiatry movement in the 1960s and 1970s led in Italy to the first successful legislative challenge to the authority of the mental institutions, culminating in their closure.

During the 1980 s and 1990s the hospital population started to fall rapidly, mainly because of the deaths of long-term inmates. Significant efforts were made to re-house large numbers of former residents in a variety of suitable or otherwise alternative accommodation. The first 1,000+ bed hospital to close was Darenth Park in Kent, swiftly followed by many more across the UK. The haste of these closures, driven by the Conservative governments led by Margaret Thatcher and John Major, led to considerable criticism in the press, as some individuals slipped through the net into homelessness or were discharged to poor quality private sector mini-institutions. The resistance of many institutions to change, predicted by Enoch Powell, has continued into the 21st century, and there are still several thousand people permanently resident in the dwindling asylums and long stay hospital replacement campuses scattered across the UK.

Disciplined Minds by Jeff Schmidt details how professional training programs and other induction procedures to institutions socialize new recruits to respect group norms whilst selecting those newcomers not only technically capable to function within the institution but also responsive to its socialization process.

Bibliography

Abraham, Francis : *Contemporary Sociology : An Introduction to Concepts and Theories*, Oxford University Press, New York, 2006.

Anderson, Elijah: *Streetwise: Race, Class, and Change in an Urban Community*. Chicago, IL: University of Chicago Press, 1990.

Arnold, Matthew: *Culture and Anarchy*, Macmillan and Co., New York, 1882.

Behera, M C : *Marriage in Tribal Societies: Cultural Dynamics and Social Realities*, Bookwell, Delhi, 2007.

Boris Erasov and Singh, Yogendra : *The Sociology of Culture*, Rawat, Delhi, 2006.

Chand, Khem : *Social and Cultural Development of Indian Dalits*, ABD Pub, Delhi, 2007.

Choudhury, Jamil : *Cultural Cooperation in South Asia : The Search for Community*, The University Press, Delhi, 1999.

Das, Veena : *Handbook of Indian Sociology*, Oxford University Press, Delhi, 2004.

Deva, Indra : *Society and Culture in India : Their Dynamics through the Ages*, Rawat, Delhi, 1999.

Diwan, Jagmohan : *Fundamentals of Rural Sociology*, Cyber Tech Pub, Delhi, 2009.

Geertz, Clifford: *The Interpretation of Cultures: Selected Essays*. New York, 1973.

Griswold, Wendy: *Cultures and Societies in a Changing World*. Thousand Oaks, CA: Pine Forge Press, 2004.

Hanson, Royce: *Civic culture and urban change : Governing dallas*. Detroit: Wayne State University Press, 2003.

Hass, Jeff : *Economic Sociology: An Introduction*, Manohar, Delhi, 2008.

Jayapalan, N. : *Rural Sociology*, Atlantic Pub, Delhi, 2002.

Khan, Ali : *Cultural Sociology of India*, Arise Pub, Delhi, 2006.

Khan, Yasmin : *Cultural Reorientation in Society*, Mittal, Delhi, 2001.

Kukreja, Sunil : *Case Studies in Political Sociology*, Serials Pub, Delhi, 2006.

Madan, T N : *Images of the World : Essays on Religion, Secularism and Culture*, Oxford University Press, Delhi, 2006.

Mohanty, P.K. : *Cultural Heritage of Indian Tribals*, Rajat, Delhi, 1999.

Mukherji, D.P. : *Social and Cultural Diversities*, Rawat, Delhi, 1997.

Pandey, S.P. and Awadhesh Kumar Singh: *Folk Culture in India*, Serials, Delhi, 2005.

Pathak, Avijit : *Indian Modernity : Contradictions, Paradoxes and Possibilities*, Gyan, Delhi. 1998.

Rathod, P B : *Fundamentals of Political Sociology*, ABD, Delhi, 2005.

Reddy, K. Viswanadha : *Cultural Ecology of Indian Tribes*, Raj, Delhi, 2002.

Ruhela, S.P. : *Research Tools in Sociology of Education*, Indian, Delhi, 2001.

Sharma, Karan Raj: *Sarup Dictionary of Sociology*, Sarup, Delhi, 2002.

Sharma, Ramesh: *Philosophy of Indian Sociology*, Global Vision, Delhi, 2005.

Singh, Yogendra : *Culture Change in India : Identity and Globalization*, Rawat, Delhi, 2000.

Somayaji, Sakarama and Somayaji, Ganesha : *Sociology of Globalisation : Perspectives from India*, Rawat, Delhi, 2006.

Sujatha, V. : *Health by the People : Sociology of Medical Lore*, Rawat, Delhi, 2003.

Tripathy, Byomakesh : *Cultural Heritage of Arunachal Pradesh*, Indus Pub, Delhi, 2006.

Wald, Kenneth D.: *Religion and Politics in the United States*. New york: Rowman & Littlefield Publishers, Inc, 2003.

Index

L

M

N

O

P

R

S

T

U

V

W

□□□